ABOUT ISLAND PRESS

Island Press, a nonprofit organization, publishes, markets, and distributes the most advanced thinking on the conservation of our natural resources—books about soil, land, water, forests, wildlife, and hazardous and toxic wastes. These books are practical tools used by public officials, business and industry leaders, natural resource managers, and concerned citizens working to solve both local and global resource problems.

Founded in 1978, Island Press reorganized in 1984 to meet the increasing demand for substantive books on all resource-related issues. Island Press publishes and distributes under its own imprint and offers these services to other nonprofit organizations.

Support for Island Press is provided by Apple Computer, Inc., Mary Reynolds Babcock Foundation, Geraldine R. Dodge Foundation, The Charles Engelhard Foundation, The Ford Foundation, Glen Eagles Foundation, The George Gund Foundation, William and Flora Hewlett Foundation, The Joyce Foundation, The John D. and Catherine T. MacArthur Foundation, The Andrew W. Mellon Foundation, The Joyce Mertz-Gilmore Foundation, The New-Land Foundation, The J. N. Pew, Jr. Charitable Trust, Alida Rockefeller, The Rockefeller Brothers Fund, The Florence and John Schumann Foundation, The Tides Foundation, and individual donors.

The Snake River

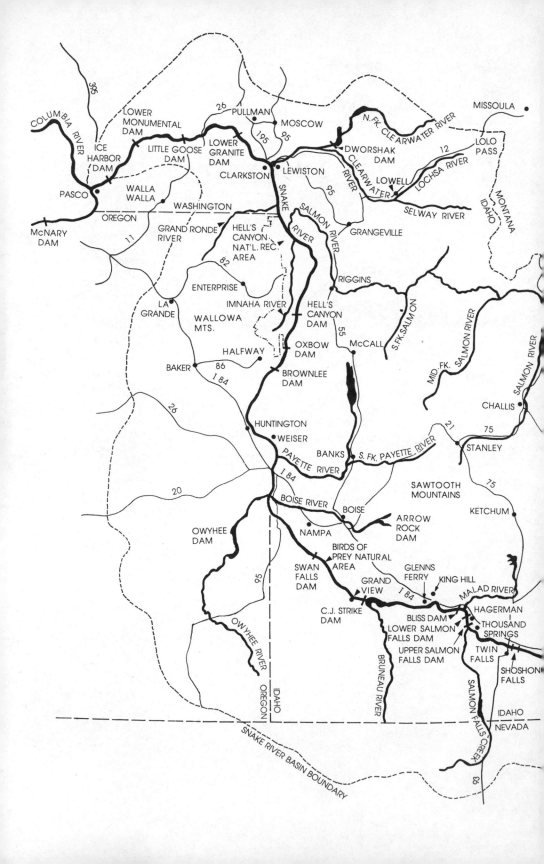

SNAKE RIVER BASIN

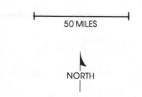

50 MILES

NORTH

SALMON

89

191

287

212

YELLOWSTONE
NAT'L. PARK

HENRY'S
LAKE

YELLOWSTONE
LAKE

15

ISLAND PARK
DAM

89

28

ASHTON

20

SNAKE

RIVER

93

ST. ANTHONY

TETON

COLTER BAY

JACKSON
DAM

ROBERTS

RIVER

DRIGGS

GRAND TETON
NAT'L. PARK

RATERS
F THE MOON
AT'L. MON.

INEL

20

SWAN
VALLEY

JACKSON

93

26

IDAHO
FALLS

189

SHELLEY

PALISADES
DAM

ALPINE

HOBACK
RIVER

BLACKFOOT

GREY'S RIVER

AMERICAN FALLS
DAM

FORT HALL
INDIAN RES.

POCATELLO

89

MINIDOKA
DAM

I 86

AMERICAN
FALLS

I 15

BURLEY

MILNER
DAM

I 84

IDAHO

WYOMING

UTAH

The Snake River

Window to the West

Tim Palmer

ISLAND PRESS

Washington, D.C. □ *Covelo, California*

For my mother, Jane Palmer May

Photographs by Tim Palmer

Cover photograph: The Snake River in Grand Teton National Park.

Library of Congress Cataloging-in-Publication Data

Palmer, Tim.
    The Snake River : Window to the West / by Tim Palmer.
        p.   cm.
    Includes bibliographical references and index.
    ISBN 0-933280-59-9 (alk. paper) : $34.95. — ISBN 0-933280-60-2 (pbk. : alk. paper) : $17.95
    1. Stream ecology—Snake River (Wyo.-Wash.) 2. Stream conservation—Snake River (Wyo.-Wash.) 3. Water-supply—Snake River (Wyo.-Wash.)—Management. I. Title.
QH104.5.S55P35 1991
333.91'62'097961—dc20   91-8585
                                                       CIP

Printed on recycled, acid-free paper

Manufactured in the United States of America
10 9 8 7 6 5 4 3 2

Contents

Preface xi

INTRODUCTION: WATER, LAND, AND PEOPLE 3

1 ROCKY MOUNTAIN RIVERWAY 9

2 THE SNAKE RIVER PLAIN 33

3 IDAHO'S UPSTREAM WATER PROJECTS 53

4 IRRIGATION, PART I 83

5 IRRIGATION, PART II 113

6 MILNER DAM TO SWAN FALLS 141

7 THE MIDDLE RIVER AND HYDROPOWER 183

8 HELLS CANYON 199

9 TO THE COLUMBIA 217

10 THE TETONS AND THE MOUNTAIN RIVER 231

11 JACKSON HOLE 249

12 TO THE SOURCE 269

Notes, Other Sources, and Interviews 283

Acknowledgments 311

Index 313

Preface

I set off with a sense of curiosity and adventure, with an urge to see all of the Snake River, a lifeline of the Rockies, of Idaho, and of the Pacific Northwest. I launched my journey with open eyes and an open mind, with a light heart and a lot of time. I wanted to know the river, to discover what was happening to it, and to understand why.

Eventually I realized that the years ahead will see new and widespread involvement in the care and management of the river from beginning to end, and I wanted this book to be useful in those efforts. Because precise descriptions are needed to go beyond the philosophic and esoteric points of view and into the economic, ecologic, and hydrologic realities of the river, some chapters hold a great deal of data. This can be easily skimmed by readers less concerned about the figures.

Agencies collect different sets of data for the Snake River basin (all the lands that drain into the river), for the Snake River plain, for the upper basin, and for Idaho, Wyoming, Oregon, and Washington. Notes on the sources of data at the end of the book are provided where questions might arise. While the information I unearthed led at times to a scathing report on some uses of the river, I also presented opposite points of view and included the arguments of people who disagreed with my analysis. My information was drawn from several years of traveling and living along the river, hundreds of interviews, and toppling stacks of written material, much of it difficult for researchers to find. The notes and sources can lead the curious reader further.

I've kept most technical terms and acronyms to a minimum, but one essential technical term used throughout the book is cubic feet per second (cfs), a measure of volume of flow. Seven and a half gallons fit into one cubic foot. As a gross translation of this odd but necessary term, a flow of 100 cfs could be considered a creek. Three hundred cfs in a small channel will float a canoe and might be as wide as a four-lane highway. A thousand cfs would be a small river. Two thousand cfs can float large rafts even in a wide riverbed and might be seen in summer flows at Grand Teton National Park in Wyoming. Five thousand cfs and more form a large river. The Snake often carries 13,000 cfs in Hells Canyon in August.

In the interest of economy, I've cut many pages about watershed management, logging, grazing, towns, tributaries, people, and politics. In its tightened form, the book describes the Snake River and addresses the core issues of its management.

The Snake River

Introduction

Water, Land, and People

A NEW GENERATION

Decades ago a first generation of conservation causes swept the nation. Grand Teton National Park along the Snake River in Wyoming was created and expanded. Congress designated the Sawtooth National Recreation Area and the Frank Church River of No Return Wilderness in central Idaho. Conservationists fought and defeated unnecessary dams; the spotlight of this movement shone on the Snake River when Congress banned hydroelectric projects in lower Hells Canyon in 1975.

Now a new generation of issues, representative of river conservation in the late twentieth century, is sweeping across the country, and the wide territory of the Snake River basin is embroiled in controversies that are both complex and subtle when compared with the old debates. Some wilderness and dam fights remain, but the new issues include instream flows for fish and wildlife, groundwater management and quality, water conservation and efficiency, pollution of streams from agriculture and logging, small hydroelectric development, reclamation of riparian habitat, maintenance of entire bottomlands through hydrologic science, and restoration of the salmon and steelhead that once blessed the Pacific Northwest.

Fables rather than facts often surround the discussion of these topics, and the government acts on some problems and anachronistically ignores others, but that doesn't change the fact that a new time has come. Like the urge for personal freedom or the curiosity of scientific thought, momentum builds to learn what's at stake, to avoid the tragedy of other lost landscapes, and to invest in a future

3

of hope, equity, and quality. These issues that affect the Snake River involve nothing less than the future of the American West.

The threats and the qualities, the lost dreams and the new possibilities seen here can be seen in rivers across America. Unlike most other large rivers, the Snake presents a fine opportunity to do things differently. The river carries enough water to provide for everyone's needs if management becomes innovative. Qualities that have been hopelessly lost elsewhere still survive here or could feasibly be restored. The problems of the Snake River are typical of those on other western rivers, but, here, the opportunities for solving those problems are greater.

Preconceptions are inevitably misleading on a 1,056-mile-long river, dropping from 9,840 feet above sea level in Yellowstone National Park in Wyoming to 340 feet where it meets the Columbia River in Washington.[1] The Snake is a mountain river, an agricultural river, a canyon river, a desert river. It's the home of colorful cutthroat trout, 9-foot sturgeon, and teeming crowds of suckers, catfish, and carp. Tributaries and lower reaches are critical to one of the most vital salmon and steelhead fisheries in the nation. Pacific Creek—a headwaters tributary—links with Atlantic Creek, creating a nonstop waterway from one ocean to the other. The Snake River thus forms the closest thing to the fabled Northwest Passage, though it is too rugged to be navigable.

No sooner did I realize that the Snake River offered a soul-soaring Eden than I found it was being served up totally to irrigation. Diversions result in a flow of nearly zero and a desiccated riverbed in several places. The stream recovers through springs, then is dammed many times for hydropower, but reappears in frothy turbulence in Hells Canyon. A wet phoenix of sorts, the Snake may be our foremost example of a river that is repeatedly killed off but repeatedly returns to life. Finally, the lower river ebbs into reservoirs for barges hauling grain to foreign markets. The Snake is a river of the Rockies and of the Pacific Northwest, a shaper of people's lives, a giver of natural wealth and livelihood, a home of interwoven myth and fact.

THE BIG PICTURE

The Snake is the largest river in Wyoming, the Mississippi of Idaho, the principal tributary to the Columbia. On the West Coast south of Canada, only the Columbia carries more water. The Snake is the tenth longest river in the United States.[2] Carrying 37 million acre feet a year, it exceeds by two and a half times the volume of the Colorado River (1 acre foot covers an acre with 1 foot of water). The Snake receives 30 percent of the runoff from the eight mountain states and drains much of the northwestern Rockies, or 109,000 square miles, an area larger than Colorado.[3] The basin is roughly 450 miles in length and width.

The headwaters of the Snake flow from our first national park, Yellowstone. Eighty miles down from the source, riverfront views of the Tetons are perhaps the most classic mountain scene in North America, photographed by millions. The river through Jackson Hole, Wyoming, may be the richest high elevation riparian habitat in the nation. In the Rocky Mountain foothills, the river provides for Idaho's greatest population of bald eagles and its largest cottonwood forest—one of the largest in the West. Shoshone Falls on the middle river in Idaho is higher than Niagara Falls in New York state. The volcanic plain of southern Idaho contains one of the greatest groundwater aquifers in the world. The Birds of Prey Refuge houses the continent's densest population of raptors. Hells Canyon has carved the second deepest canyon in the United States and offers a premier rafting run. The lower river provides the critical flow to some of the most important yet threatened stocks of salmon and steelhead.

The river flows through two of our most visited national parks—Yellowstone and Grand Teton—and the basin drains eleven national forests. The federal Bureau of Land Management is responsible for hundreds of riverfront tracts, the Deer Flat National Wildlife Refuge includes eighty-six islands, and the Hells Canyon National Recreation Area incorporates the Snake as a national wild and scenic river.

The Snake's tributaries are a who's who of American wild rivers. The Salmon runs longer than any other free-flowing stream in forty-nine states. Prodigious runs of steelhead spawn in the Clearwater. The Selway, Lochsa, Middle Fork Clearwater, and Middle Fork Salmon were among our first national wild and scenic rivers. The Owyhee and Bruneau carve quintessential desert canyons. The Wood River riffles through the town of Ketchum in Idaho; nearby, Silver Creek meanders as one of the country's superior trout streams. The Buffalo, Gros Ventre, and Hoback spill from Rocky

Mountain vastness to the upper Snake River. The Henry's Fork in eastern Idaho is spoken of in mythic tones by dry fly fishermen. The South Fork Payette glimmers as one of the most exquisite un-dammed yet unprotected rivers in the West. The Boise River serves up a recreational playground for Idahoans. The Grande Ronde winds gracefully from northeast Oregon, and the Imnaha erupts from the Wallowa Mountains in secretive beauty. The Snake is nurtured by fifty-six rivers and seventy-four large creeks.

Many people in Idaho call the Snake a "working river." Exploita-tion began when the Hudson's Bay Company trapped all the bea-vers it could from 1818 to 1827—a scorched-earth policy to discourage Americans' westward movement.[4] Twenty-five dams now block the main stem's flow. Basinwide, the river irrigates 3.8 million acres, accounting for much of Idaho's agriculture. The flow is diverted into canals and ditches, killing most of the river's life in several sections. An economic and political reality has created a hydrologic and ecologic reality. As the Idaho State Water Plan states, "The Snake River is intensively managed."

I knew that diversions were needed to grow crops, but I didn't know if it was really necessary to dry up the river. Hydroelectric dams have also altered the flow with unexpected consequences and blocked the migration of 30 percent of the basin's salmon and steelhead. From Idaho, State Senator Gail Bray said, "What has been done to the Snake River is both a blessing and a curse. We've taken that great river and we've minimized it in order to maximize material goods." The Snake River shows everything, from the fin-est mountain landscapes to the most pathetic abuses imaginable.

This twisted fate is a source of embarrassment to some and pride to others. It is both a reason for hopelessness and a basis for wealth. To some, the river's plight justifies more of the same. Some people who dismiss the Snake as a "working river" do not see the richness of life that remains and are blind to the potential of restoration.

The Snake River basin is a homeland, a vacationland, a white-water dream, an irrigated field, a clearcut, an electric power plant, an Indian reservation, a Mormon stronghold, a border between states, a colossal provider of water, a pipeline, a bombing range, a toxic waste dump, a paradisiac wonderland, a habitat extraordi-naire, and a wilderness exceeding anything in forty-nine states. In other words, it is the American West. It is not, however, known or understood.

In 1876 James Brisbin, an early visitor to the area, wrote, "That a river in the interior of the west should have remained unexplored so long is remarkable."[5] The same could be said in the 1990s regarding a complete view of this river. Little has been written about it. Published materials include a picture book, river-running guidebooks for two sections, and local histories. Writers with a nationwide or western perspective have typically ignored the Snake River and investigated debates over the Colorado River and the California waterworks with their high political drama and large readership. Scores of agency reports on the Snake River can be unearthed, yet the thousands of pages are best described as technical reading and fail to look at the river as a living entity. Much remains unexplained and unconsidered. No book has looked at what's happening to this waterway today.

What about the attitudes of the people who live there? What do they consider the possibilities and the limits of river use? Many people share in their need for this river, but do they share in its wealth? If not, is that legal? Is that fair, intelligent, or workable? Whose investment made the wealth possible in the first place?

Among major watersheds in North America, this is one of the more lightly populated; about a million people live in a basin the size of New York, Pennsylvania, Maryland, and Massachusetts. A density of nine people per square mile compares with 192 in California and sixty-three for the nation. Yet this is not an empty region. People live in most of the places where it makes any sense to live, and most points of view are represented. Without understanding one another or what one another does, some individuals cling to stereotypes that perpetuate misunderstandings. It's easy to blame "those" people. The stereotypers say that anglers care more about fish than people, that environmentalists are meddlesome easterners who don't understand the way things work, that irrigators have closed minds because they've already answered the really big questions in life, that the farmer wastes water even if it's the last drop in the river. Portraits have also been painted of the tourist, the bureaucrat, and the politician, and just about everybody is a victim to freakish distortions.

Stereotypes hold enough truth to make them cunningly dangerous, but all hold much that is false. They fail to come to grip with reality and with vital questions about the future. This book looks at the people and searches for who they seem to be, but mainly it looks at what people *do* with the water and at their aspirations for the river's future.

The northwestern region of our country clearly depends on the Snake River, but why, I wondered, would Americans beyond the Northern Rockies and Pacific Northwest be interested in a river 600 air miles from San Francisco and 2,100 from Washington, D.C. World-class qualities are one reason. Looking further, the Snake River basin represents the West, and a good portion of it is owned by us all. In these eleven states, 47 percent of the land is publicly owned; 64 percent of Idaho is owned by federal taxpayers. Agriculture, mining, and logging were economic mainstays in the Snake River basin and throughout the West, but those markets have faltered, and recreation has gained ascending prominence. As in other mountain states, resource protection, upon which recreation and other values depend, lags because agriculture and extractive industries dominate in clubs of political power. Yet the times are inevitably changing. What happens on the Snake illuminates the issues of resource management elsewhere. The river is both a window and a mirror to the rest of the West.

Much of this book is based on field work done from April to November 1988 as I traveled along the river. Chapters follow mostly in sequence from the top of the river to the bottom, but not entirely. I began at Palisades Dam in Idaho and traveled from there to the Columbia River in Washington, then returned to the headwaters in Wyoming in August. The uppermost reach in Yellowstone and the Bridger–Teton Wilderness comes last—the final chapter describes a hike to the source.

1

Rocky Mountain Riverway

BEGINNING AT PALISADES DAM

The equinox was long past on May 1, but for me, it was the first day of spring—a rebirth of life and the start of my first voyage on the Snake River. The blustery rigors of the early spring had proven to be excessive for outdoor living in Jackson Hole, Wyoming, where I had started my explorations near the headwaters of the Snake, so I skipped over the highest 154 miles of waterway and drove down to Palisades Dam, just across the state boundary in Idaho.

I unloaded my canoe from the roof of my van, and guarding against an upset, I lashed waterproof bags into the boat. My first Snake River voyage will take me 106 miles from Palisades to Idaho Falls. All but the final 10 miles run without dams—the third longest free-flowing reach of the river.

Palisades Dam stills the water upstream for 29 miles. The second dam down from the headwaters, it forms the third largest reservoir on the Snake (almost the size of Brownlee Reservoir, above Hells Canyon). Palisades was built by the Bureau of Reclamation in 1958 for supplemental irrigation water on 670,000 acres—lands that had already been irrigated but were now assured deliveries in dry years.[1]

I had arrived thirty years too late to see Grand Valley, which is now beneath the reservoir. Bernard DeVoto, the great western historian, wrote about this reach in 1947: "The Snake is a noble and various river, nowhere lovelier than in the stretch from the lower end of its first great canyon till it comes entirely out of the mountains."[2] On my way to the river, at a local cafe, I met Jerry Hansen, who grew up in Grand Valley.

It was wide, with farms, cottonwoods, and willows, a lot like Swan Valley today. There were about thirty farms, and the hot springs at Indian Creek were flooded too. The local people didn't want the dam but felt powerless. The government was going to take it; you just tried to get a good price for your farm. It was good fishing, but fishermen didn't fight it much. There was a feeling that you could always go someplace else. Me, I have no bitterness about the dam. I have a new way of life. I have a motorboat now. It's part of the change that goes on. I didn't like farming anyway.

A superb river flows for 69 miles from the dam to the Henry's Fork of the Snake, which most Idahoans used to call the North Fork. To many it was the dominant river of eastern Idaho. Even though the Snake River carries three times the volume of the North Fork, Idahoans call the main stem the "South Fork." Above Palisades Dam, however, everyone simply calls it the Snake River. Thus, the main stem perversely empties into a "fork" of much greater size, like a river dumping into a creek. Unaffected by the Idaho tradition, the U.S. Geological Survey—the official carrier of geographic names—calls this the Snake River from source to mouth.

The 50 miles from Palisades to Heise are a nationally known trout fishery where thousands of people embark on float trips each year, though in May I stood alone in the brittle wind, looking up-river at the dam's rock pile and downriver at the alluring landscape of mountain and valley. In a boat, two fishermen arrived and eyed my gear. "How far you going?" one asked.

"Idaho Falls."

"Today?"

"No. Five or six days."

"A long trip."

To me, it didn't seem far on a river that, if straightened, would reach from its source to Mexico. Six free-flowing sections are long enough for overnight trips by canoe or raft, yet people rarely speak of multiday outings except in Hells Canyon.

Downriver—an eagle? Yes. Light glinted from white head, white tail. From Yellowstone to the Henry's Fork, the Snake River is prime eagle habitat. This endangered species has survived until now along the upper river because of clean water, plentiful fish, and sparse development. A great blue heron stalked through the shallows, a winter wren fluttered among willows, sandpipers bobbed on beaches, mergansers dove into pools, and swallows darted from insect to insect. In sheer numbers, the swallow is the bird of the Snake River.

Swan Valley, amid snowy peaks of the Snake River Range to the northeast and the Caribou Range to the southwest, is a graben or sink created by faults lowering the valley on both sides. I entered a complex of sloughs that split and resplit to form wetlands, sandbars, and swampy cottonwood coves.

The Bureau of Land Management (BLM) is responsible for 15,000 acres on this section of the river. The BLM manages as much land in the West as the Forest Service and Park Service combined, most of it drylands unclaimed by homesteaders. The agency manages three major reaches of the Snake, plus several major tributaries. On this reach, thirty-nine islands are eligible for wilderness status.[3] A hundred pages of BLM paperwork fail to explain why the islands are not recommended for protection, though the environmental statement repeatedly mentions Lynn Crandall Dam, a dusty old proposal of the Bureau of Reclamation—a dominant bureau within the Department of the Interior. Banning the dam is the only major effect that wilderness status would have.

At the mouth of Fall Creek, I paddled to the base of the tributary's waterfall, which drops directly into the river; the crash and spray were loud and soaking. Below the Swan Valley bridge, the road sliced away from the valley, and I entered the river's third canyon (the uppermost is in Yellowstone; the second is below Jackson Hole). The Big Hole Range rose to my right, the Caribou foothills to my left. With tiny hooves but effective, long legs, a deer swam across the river as fast as I could paddle. Pools alternated with riffles that had formed where bedrock crossed the channel and where rocks had washed down from tributaries. Additional shoals resulted from the physics of the current; hydrologists have found that a pool and riffle sequence occurs at intervals equal to five to seven widths of river. Flood flows erode pools deeper and deposit gravel at the riffles, accentuating each. At low flows, riffles gradually erode and pools are filled, subduing each. The cycles maintain a balance to which life of the river is well adapted. With-

out occasional floods, the river becomes a "glide" of nearly uni-
form gradient without the pools needed for fish cover, without the
riffles needed for spawning. Ducks, otters, eagles, and other creatures suffer.

I camped at a sandy beach where the music of riffles lightened
the air. The yellow-green grass of springtime had broken through
moist soil, and the robins sang a mating song. Cottonwoods had
released constellations of newborn leaves. The cottonwood—the
tree of the Snake River—is the maker of fruitful forest edges and
the keeper of many lives. The shells of its buds lay pungent on the
ground and stuck to my shoes like honey. Volcanic cliffs jutted up
to dark slopes. Grouse drummed in the woods, muskrats surfaced
in the eddy. Moose and coyote tracks decorated the ground. Here, I
thought, is the Snake River as it always was.

A RIPARIAN KINGDOM

While frost still slicked the morning grass, I paddled on my second
day to Dry Canyon and its rich tangle of vegetation in the river-
dependent zone called riparian. I picture the river in halves of blue
and green equipoise: first, the water, then the green river of plant
life on either side. For wildlife, this zone is the most important part
of the earth. Three-quarters of all endangered species need riparian
habitat. Biologists in the Blue Mountains, bordering the Snake River in Oregon, found that 285 of 378 terrestrial species depend on
riparian zones.[4]

Through much of the Snake River's course, the average precipitation is 15 inches or less, the sun shines a lot, humidity is low, and
the wind blows hard. All of this means aridity, and along the desert river, only the riparian zone supports more than sagebrush, bit-
terbrush, hardy grasses and forbs, and noxious weeds, many of
them introduced from Eurasia. On searing days, the riparian plantlife becomes nature's air conditioner, a shaded refuge. During
floods, the riparian areas dissipate high flows and reduce the over-
flow downstream. Riverfront wetlands improve water quality by
filtering sediment, wastes, and nutrients and buffer pollution coming from cropland, excavated soil, and overgrazed range.[5]

Though lowland areas are undisputedly the richest for wildlife and provide winter range that is scarce habitat for many species, few bottomlands of large streams are protected. Many national park and wilderness areas, for example, are in higher country and were set aside only after proven to have no economic value. "Rock and ice" conservation was often the main concern of early conservationists lobbying for preservation of spectacular high country. The wilderness system represents only eighty-one of 233 ecosystem types in America; fifty are not even found on federal lands.[6]

William Platts, a Boise-based national authority on riparian habitat, believes that interest in this area is growing. "The name 'riparian' just came into use in the seventies," he noted. A veteran of the Forest Service, Platts recalled, "For awhile you couldn't use the word 'riparian' in the Forest Service or the BLM. There was anxiety over what would happen to grazing and logging. In the Southwest the government clearcut cottonwoods and willows because they were 'water users.' Those streams fell apart, and then the agencies recognized that the vegetation had been a water retainer. Now the pendulum has swung back, and we've done plans and plans for riparian protection, but action is still hard to come by."

Eighty percent of the riverfront habitat along the Snake River has been lost, according to the U.S. Fish and Wildlife Service. Rich sections such as in Grand Teton National Park and here above the Henry's Fork are not only rare but unrepeated in Wyoming and Idaho. Most riparian habitat has been leveled, cleared, farmed, developed, riprapped, leveed, dammed, or ditched.

The story of the Snake River is also the story of the West and the United States. In California, where land use in the Central Valley is far more similar to the Snake River plain than Idahoans want to admit, 90 percent of the riparian habitat has been lost. Along the Missouri River, dams flooded most riparian acreage, and on the little that remains, reduced floods led to a 67 percent reduction of wetlands.[7] Along the Colorado River, 90 percent of the riparian values are gone.[8] The Ohio River is comparable in length to the Snake, but every inch is dammed, flooded, and lined with railroad tracks, highways, industries, or towns. The Mississippi River flows through a constant chain of dams from Minneapolis to St. Louis and then a levee straitjacket to the Gulf of Mexico. The Army Corps of Engineers dammed the one remaining section of the Savannah River in South Carolina, with deadly impacts on wildlife

and water quality. The corps channelized the Tennessee and Tom-
bigbee rivers for 232 miles, burying a biological utopia at a cost of
$4 billion, all to duplicate an existing barge route.

Dependent on wetlands that include riverfronts, North American
duck populations plummeted from 46 million in 1971 to 30 million
in 1985. Mallards, a duck of the Snake River, declined from 14
million on the continent in 1957 to 8 million in 1987.[9] Nationwide,
we lose 450,000 acres of wetlands each year; farming and logging
cause 80 percent of the losses. Urban and agricultural uses preempt 70 percent of the floodplains along rivers. Once covering 6
percent of North America, riparian ecosystems remain intact on 1.5
percent.[10]

Valuable riparian areas survive along the Snake River at Jackson
Hole, Wyoming; from Palisades to Idaho Falls; from the town of
Blackfoot to American Falls Reservoir; and at shorter reaches
downriver. Riparian forests in Idaho total 327,347 acres or 0.6 percent of the land, down from a million acres, and within the remaining forests, the quality of habitat is reduced.[11] "The frustrating
thing about habitat is that there's only one direction you can go,"
said Al Van Vooren, head of resident fisheries (fishes that do not
migrate to the ocean) for the Idaho Department of Fish and Game.
"At our best we only decrease the rate of decline."

On the flood plain at Dry Canyon, red osier dogwood grew in a
barrier impenetrable by me but prized by evening grosbeaks, purple finches, robins, hermit thrushes, mule deer, and elk. Though
the flowering dogwood is better known, red osier is the most widespread dogwood on the continent. Water birch, box elder, and
white alder also rank high in importance along the river. Alders fix
350 pounds of nitrogen in the soil per acre each year—comparable
to an alfalfa field.[12] The Pacific and other willows flourish as a
favorite food of spruce grouse, moose, elk, deer, beaver, and snow-
shoe hares.

The cottonwood crowns the riparian ecosystem. I found the narrowleaf species, *Populus angustifolia*, along the upper river and the
black cottonwood, *Populus trichocarpus*, mostly below American
Falls and especially along tributary streams. The narrowleaf grows
to a 1.5-foot diameter and a 60-foot height; the black cottonwood—king of the deciduous forest—can grow to 4 feet in diameter, 125 feet high. Both species and hybrids of the two are used by

a host of birds and animals for shelter, nesting, and food. Also called poplars, the cottonwood family includes aspens and about fifteen species in the United States. Half of a beaver's diet comes from this family. Grouse eat the buds and catkins. Elk, deer, and rabbits savor the bark, twigs, and leaves. A moose's diet may be one-fourth cottonwood and aspen. The endangered bald eagle nests in cottonwoods.

The Fish and Wildlife Service called the riparian zone "extremely important" and credited this section of the Snake River as "one of the largest such ecosystems in the western intermountain region," "the most important fish and wildlife habitat site in Idaho," and "one of the most important areas for wildlife in the northwest." This reach of the Snake is to the Rockies what the Everglades are to the Southeast.

Like everything else in the riparian zone, the cottonwoods depend on the river. Roots probe sandy soils for water. Some cottonwoods, including the black, can reproduce from root sprouts, though sprouted trees frequently lack vigor. Others germinate from seeds, dependent on precise conditions. They require deposits of river-borne silt delivered by large floods. When the timing is right, the receding floodwaters carry the seeds to the fertile new silt. In this and other ways, riparian life depends on seasonal variations in flow, the erosion and deposition of silt, and other factors, all of them upset when dams arrest floods and trap silt in reservoirs.

Because of upstream dams, researchers found little new germination of the plains cottonwood on Montana's Milk River. Cheryl Bradley, a research botanist, wrote that without revised management there will be a "slow elimination of cottonwood forests. With most of the North American prairie rivers regulated by dams, we predict that most of the floodplain cottonwood forests will be eliminated by the end of the next century."[13] Botanists found similar effects on the Missouri River, the South Platte in Colorado, the Salt in Arizona, the Bighorn in Wyoming, and the St. Mary and Waterton in Alberta.[14] There are no studies of cottonwood regeneration on the Snake River, though the Fish and Wildlife Service is initiating a "trend analysis" for the corridor above Heise, Idaho. Biologist Platts said, "Any species dependent on fluctuating water levels is going to be drastically reduced unless the Bureau [of Reclamation] emulates natural floods when releasing water from the dams."

For now, I walked as if released from all cares through one splendid cottonwood grove after another. They lay in slender bands parallel to the shore—a river of cottonwoods above the river of water. The trees within each grove appeared to be the same age, probably germinating after the same receding flood. The river had deposited silt on the inside of the bend because the current was slower there, and while the trees grew, the bank increased in height around them. Unlike other trees, cottonwoods are not "suffocated" by the silt; in fact, silt protects the trunks from high water, from bombardment by rocks, and from claws of driftwood. The river is a life-support system for the trees. Inevitably the current changes course and begins cutting into the banks it had formed a century before. It undermines mature cottonwoods, which only live about a hundred years anyway, and they plunge into the river and form cover for fish or wash down to shoals where they cause the formation of islands. They may drift to established islands and act as further traps for driftwood. Eventually those piles of trunks and branches become soil-covered, but underneath are hollow places, homes for beaver, muskrat, and otter.

Three-foot-tall sandhill cranes thrive at the side channels, the wetlands, and the benches of the river; I heard their growling ratchet call. For feeding, the cranes need wet meadows fed by high water tables. For protection, they need swaths of river channel with sand and gravel bars lacking shrubs where predators might lurk. Both conditions demand healthy river flows to supply groundwater and to prevent shrub growth on sandbars.[15]

Leaving the understories and overstories of stacked-up plantlife on the floodplain, I climbed the slope to a rim of cliffs. Douglas fir darkened hillsides. A bald eagle soared over the river; an osprey lighted on its nest of sticks woven into a broken cottonwood crown.

The Fish and Wildlife Service called this reach "essential" habitat for bald eagles. Cottonwood trees here host 35 percent of Idaho's nesting population and half its eagle production. About fifty birds winter along the river, which is "essential for the restoration and maintenance of the greater Yellowstone bald eagle population." The service's "Species of Special Emphasis" include the Canada goose, snow goose, trumpeter swan, tundra swan, wood duck, redhead, canvasback, osprey, goldeneye, bald eagle, peregrine falcon, sandhill crane, mourning dove, cutthroat trout, and rainbow trout. About 15,000 ducks and 1,300 geese winter along the Snake and use the 220 islands between Palisades and the Henry's Fork. Over 800 elk, 2,000 mule deer, and 60 moose winter in riparian zones or along canyon walls. Forty elk summer in the canyon, and others require the riparian belt for calving. The white-tailed deer, mountain goat, otter, and cougar live at the river's edge or nearby.

"There are few areas in Idaho or in the West where the critical habitat needs for so many big game species are provided in such a small area," the Fish and Wildlife Service stated. "Over 260 wildlife species live here—a good portion of all species in Idaho." An Idaho Fish and Game biologist said that the lack of roads is "one of the most vital qualities of the area. This allows undisturbed winter foraging at lower elevations."

GOLF COURSE OR EAGLES

Idaho's Antelope Flat, now farmed, forms a bench above the south shore of this canyon but would see sixty-six recreational homes if the Hays Ranch subdivision is approved. A road would be built to the river, a clubhouse erected 500 feet from the water, and a pitch-and-putt golf course would be mowed on the floodplain. Regarding its adjacent islands, the Bureau of Land Management (BLM) stated that subdivisions of property could create impacts that would "degrade considerably" the natural setting and that eagles may abandon the nesting area and relocate. Even though less than 20 percent of the land in the canyon is privately owned, the Fish and Wildlife Service reported, "The single major threat . . . is residential development of privately owned lands adjacent to the river," and cautioned that year-round access would disturb wildlife because their isolation needs are greatest in winter and spring.

The subdivision, on land zoned agricultural, was denied by the Bonneville County Planning Commission, but the Board of Commissioners overturned the action. The South Fork Coalition sued, arguing that the development conflicted with the county's comprehensive plan. In 1985 a judge ruled that the rezoning had "granted a discriminatory benefit to Hays without public advantage or justification." Further appeals have been swatted back and forth; the outcome is anyone's guess.

The planning staff in this county of 75,000 people consists of only two people, which is typical; Teton County has no planning staff. In Idaho Falls, the planning director, Steve Serr, assured that the Hays homesites would not be seen from the river. "What they're doing is better than what could have been done with conventional development."

As an alternative to development on this section of the river, agencies and environmental groups have united to support open space protection by federal acquisition under the Land and Water Conservation Fund. Earmarked for conservation, the moneys were largely impounded during the Reagan years. County officials, fearing losses in the tax base, oppose additional acquisition, though many private lands are assessed for dry ranching at 35 cents an acre and others as wasteland having no value, while the Forest Service pays 61 cents an acre to counties "in lieu of taxes."

Land trades offer another solution. The Forest Service arranged to trade 250 acres slated for condominiums at the nearby Targhee ski area for 600 acres having a comparable market value along this section of the river. Ironically, the Targhee owner faced opposition to the scale of his development, and the trade may be off. In Arizona, the BLM acquired 157,000 acres of riparian land through exchanges—a program that could be applied throughout the West.[16] To protect Lake Tahoe in Nevada and California where real estate is far more expensive than in the Snake River canyon, the Burton–Santini Act allows receipts from sale of BLM lands near Las Vegas to buy environmentally critical acreage at Tahoe.

Conservationists have launched nationwide movements for protection of parks, wilderness, seashores, and old-growth timber. Fortunately, a new initiative is unnecessary to save riparian lands because one already exists for wetlands, enjoying high-level policy directives. Most riverfront areas are in fact wetlands, officially defined by hydric (water-influenced) soils. "Riparian areas can be protected under the wetlands umbrella," Bill Platts said, "though it will take a broadened view." Measures such as a Burton–Santini Act for wetlands and riparian zones could save vast acreage at little expense to the taxpayer.

Back on the water, I edged my canoe into a slough where the flow instantly dropped from 10,000 to 200 cfs. Here I saw even more wildlife. A kingfisher rattled as it fled from its perch on a cottonwood limb. Downy woodpeckers hammered on a dead cottonwood. A flicker called to its foraging mate, who returned with food to the nest in a cavity in the tree. Eyeing rodents, a rough-legged hawk circled above the floodplain. Gleaming white in a blue sky, gulls cried from high above.

Casual paddling took me past deep pools, graveled riffles, isolated islands, and shaded forests. At Black Canyon, a road had been scratched into the north bank. A slough lured me to an island where I camped surrounded by yellow warblers singing and feeding in the alders.

Near this site the Bureau of Reclamation proposed the Lynn Crandall Dam to back up 1.5 million acre feet of water burying 20 miles of river to the Swan Valley bridge. Four eagle nests would be lost, accounting for 70 percent of the canyon's births, and 75 percent of the eagles' winter habitat would be flooded. Irrigators flocked out in support of the dam at hearings in 1961, but in 1988 the bureau's John Keys said, "I don't want to build that dam. We would study it only if the local people and the state of Idaho request it." The Bureau of Reclamation, however, has not relinquished its hold on twenty-five BLM islands reserved for the reservoir—an administrative action that would lend credence to Keys' view.

A BEAUTIFUL FISH

During my second evening on the river, fish feeding on a hatch of mayflies rippled the water like a rain of pebbles. *Idaho Wildlife* reported that this river is one of the nation's finest cutthroat trout fisheries. Idaho's record brown trout of over 32 pounds was taken here; the Idaho Department of Fish and Game estimated that the river supports 3,500 adult cutthroat and a mob of 30,000 whitefish per mile.[17] After regulations in 1984 required barbless hooks and a slot limit, which allowed anglers to keep only two cutthroat under 10 inches or over 16 inches, the size of fish increased. *Fly Fisherman* editor John Randolph said, "I know of no other river that combines these species of wild trout in such numbers and sizes of fish. . . . The South Fork is a continental crown jewel." The Forest Service reported that 120,000 recreation days a year are spent here, mostly by fishermen. Their contribution to the local economy was conservatively estimated at $4 million. The survival of the fish depends on adequate flows released from Palisades Dam.

The river level is raised or lowered on "ten minutes notice," according to Bureau of Reclamation operators. Sometimes beneficial to fish, releases prevent summer flows from dropping too low. In the nonirrigation seasons, however, artificially low flows have caused sloughs and back channels to dry up. These are the primary spawning areas because of a gentle current, many riffles, and shaded banks. Below 1,700 cfs, an estimated 95 percent of the channels are affected. At 900 cfs, 85 percent of the channels are severed from the main channel by gravel bars. At 750 cfs a lot of fish die, and at 500, much of the water disappears into the gravel. Low winter flows kill young fish by stranding them in shallow pools that dry up or freeze and by forcing them into the main channel with larger predator fish.

In the fall of 1987, 2,200 cfs flowed into Palisades Dam, but to fill the reservoir, a puny 850 was released. The low flow killed about 600,000 cutthroat and brown trout along with much of the aquatic food chain. The Fish and Wildlife Service had recommended a minimum flow of 1,000 cfs. A gentleman's agreement among the Department of Fish and Game, the Fish and Wildlife Service, and the Bureau of Reclamation settled on a release of 1,000 cfs from Palisades, though the agreement that actually counts is between the bureau and the Idaho irrigators' Committee of Nine, which calls for a 550 cfs minimum. That level was hit in 1977, and it took the river's food chain years to recover.

Do the irrigators support a healthy fishery? "Yes, so long as you don't disturb any licensed water rights," said Bob Burks, past president of the Idaho Water Users Association. About the 550 cfs he said, "We've given them a pretty good flow." Because the irrigators have been given rights to most of the water in the river and have reserved most of the storage space in the federal dams, they assume that the Bureau of Reclamation will cater entirely to their needs when managing the reservoirs. They argue that irrigators paid for the dams.

The water, in fact, is available even in dry years. It takes only 75,000 acre feet to increase flows from 750 to 1,000 cfs all winter long, and at the end of a very dry 1988, 300,000 acre feet remained in federal reservoirs of the upper Snake. Another 170,000 acre feet sits in Palisades as an "inactive pool" for hydroelectric power. There are two problems: Irrigators will not voluntarily release their water even if the storage is not likely to be used, and the inactive pool is needed for hydroelectricity, necessary in the economic formula that makes water essentially free for the irrigators—they pay 25 cents an acre foot to the government, which is 13,000 gallons per penny.

Minimum stream flow is the critical issue on this section of the river and the most pervasive from Jackson Hole to the Columbia River. Idaho's 1976 draft water plan stated, "The most significant environmental need not met is instream flows in the Snake River."[18] Minimum flows are a crucial issue throughout the West, though the U.S. Water Resources Council showed the Snake to be unique in having artificially diminished streamflow problems in a basin that's incredibly water-rich relative to the rest of the West.[19]

To determine what the minimum flows should be, fisheries biologists use an Instream Flow Incremental Methodology (IFIM) to address such problems as dried-up rearing channels, the level at which summertime flows become too warm for trout, and the winter level needed to prevent anchor ice on the bottom of the riverbed—concerns of immediate life-and-death import to fish. Unconsidered are additional riparian values such as flows needed to protect island-nesting birds from predators, to sustain a healthy streambed by both erosion and deposition of silt, to scour pools and build riffles in floods, and to nourish groundwater. Despite a loathsome heritage of equating floods with plagues and tornadoes, high runoff is essential to the health of the river by cleansing gravel beds, depositing beaches, fertilizing the flood plain, and recharging groundwater, yet studies below twenty-nine western dams found average peak flows to be 40 percent of predam values.[20] "It was once a balanced system. Now we've upset the balance of everything," said Gene Gray, chair of the Idaho Water Resource Board.

"There's resistance even in the fisheries community to looking beyond IFIM," said Mark Hill, a consulting fisheries biologist. "It's not something we learned in school. Only by looking at the whole system will we be able to maintain a healthy river. Without providing water for the streambed and the whole riparian corridor, we're not going to protect the fishery in the long run." The minimum flows for fish, in fact, are something like a bread-and-water diet, not for prisoners but for one of the choice attractions of the Rocky Mountain West.

Little thought was given to fisheries flows, let alone other ecological consequences, when the Bureau of Reclamation reduced river volumes in the past, though in 1975 the agency's *Westwide* study specified the need for minimum-flow requirements.[21]

Some people assume that the bureau fulfills its responsibility to the public by serving the owners of the water rights. The irrigators, however, do not own the water or the dams. They hold "usufructuary rights"—permission to use water held in trust by the state (see Chapter 4)—and they reserve space in the federal reservoirs. That doesn't guarantee their space will be filled. Nonetheless, by everybody's standards the bureau has managed the dams for the irrigators.

The Committee of Nine, founded in 1919 to make peace among quarreling farmers, is an ad hoc group elected by irrigators to advise the bureau. An organization of enormous outward confidence but deep and abiding fear that their control will be eroded. the committee is widely regarded as the official mouthpiece of irrigators in the upper basin above King Hill. Political journalist Randy Stapilus wrote, "No sane Southern Idaho politician intentionally would get on their wrong side." Regarding releases from Palisades Dam, Dale Rockwood and Claude Storer represented the committee and insisted, "Irrigators *own* the space in federal reservoirs and are entitled to divert all water available to fill their water rights." They referred to the state constitution—"The right to divert and appropriate the unappropriated waters of any natural stream to beneficial uses, shall never be denied. . . . " While the two issues of storage rights in federal reservoirs and water rights from natural streamflow are different, they are packaged by the irrigators into one argument—the irrigators "own" the water and are entitled to take or store it whenever they want. Critics regard these points not as water law but as "folk water law."

Minimum flow supporters clarify that they are not talking about "optimum" flows, which allow fish populations to be healthy, nor are they talking about essential riparian maintenance as described by biologist Hill, but simply the prevention of wholesale and immediate losses of fish. Without taking issue with irrigators' water rights, the improved flow people say that the management of a federal dam is the issue.

"It's a myth that the federal reclamation projects are owned by the irrigators and that no one else has an interest in them," said Dick Schwarz, president of the South Fork Coalition. "People who have purchased space in the reservoirs have a legal entitlement to that water, but on the other side, there are values that existed before the dams, and those values should be protected."

An unlikely environmentalist, Schwarz found his preferred career in military combat cut short by injuries in Korea. As a captain in the Army Corps of Engineers, he worked on McNary Dam, which partially blocked salmon passage on the Columbia River. "We didn't look at what we were doing in those days." After an assignment with the Atomic Energy Commission, he was hired as a civilian to direct construction at the Idaho National Engineering Laboratory. An abiding interest in fish led him to the presidency of the Idaho Wildlife Federation in 1974, to a governor's appointment on the Fish and Game Commission and its chairmanship in 1979, and to an appointment on the Pacific Fisheries Management Council. Schwarz contends that the federal projects were funded to a significant degree by the taxpayers. "I'm not taking issue with what's been done," he said; "however, we as citizens should get a reasonable minimum streamflow in return for what we've paid."

The South Fork Coalition maintained that a minimum flow of 1,688 cfs—the historic low before Palisades Dam—should be available as an instream flow. Reminding the state that it is "the trustee for fish and wildlife," Schwarz pressed for the Department of Fish and Game to take action for a guaranteed flow. To no avail. "Let's get our priorities straight. The department took legal action over a wrecked truck that polluted the Little Salmon River in 1987 and accidentally killed 180,000 trout and steelhead, but meanwhile the Bureau of Reclamation deliberately allowed 600,000 fish to die through their narrow-sighted operation of a federal dam." Schwarz questioned why the Committee of Nine—with no legal authority at all—should overrule the Department of Fish and Game with its myriad legal obligations. "We're not trying to put the irrigators out of business," he asserted. "The question is, how much water that's needed for a decent streamflow is not needed by the irrigators?"

Questions have been raised about the effects of the dams, payment for the dams, water rights, efficient use of water, responsibilities of the Bureau of Reclamation, and the political power of the irrigators. So far, there are no answers.

THE PUBLIC TRUST DOCTRINE

The low-flow problem could be solved, according to Schwarz, if the Bureau of Reclamation recognized its broader responsibilities. As another option, water rights could conceivably be rented or bought from the irrigators and returned to the fish, but Schwarz sees no reason why the public should pay for something he feels it already owns—the right to a healthy environment and to the minimum flows that existed before Palisades Dam.

The public trust doctrine may help to open the sticky door of reform. This legal principle states that even though individuals secured rights to water, they are not entitled to destroy a public resource, a notion that sounds reasonable to some, but to others it is antithetical to civilization in the West. The Idaho Supreme Court recognized the doctrine at Lake Coeur d'Alene and Billingsley Creek near the Snake River. "The public trust doctrine takes precedence even over vested water rights," the court stated.[22] The strength of the court's language made Idaho a leader in recognition of the public trust.[23] Those rulings allow decisions of the past— some of them a hundred years ago—to be questioned in light of modern times. Though the irrigators hold that their rights and authority over the Bureau of Reclamation are untouchable, society has reconsidered century-old decisions in other respects. Women would otherwise not be voting and slavery would be legal.

The doctrine has been confirmed in other states, most notably where Los Angeles diverts water that flows into the biologically vital Mono Lake. Just like Idaho irrigators, North America's third largest city claimed that because it owned rights to water, it could do as it pleased. The city lost in the California Supreme Court— instructively the same court that had given birth to the prior appropriation doctrine on which the Idaho irrigators are so adamant.[24]

Lawyer Joseph Sax wrote that of all the concepts in American law, the public trust doctrine is the best legal tool for protection of water, fish, and wildlife.[25] The courts found that water diversions that destroy resources can constitute "waste" or "unreasonable diversion." The more unique and valuable the resource, the more likely the courts will enforce the doctrine. "If the irrigators continue to ignore other legitimate uses of the river," wrote Marv Hoyt of Trout Unlimited, a fishermen's group in Idaho Falls, "this is a way the people of Idaho can seek to impose their will on the use of water."

"The public trust doctrine is very frightening to us," said Sherl Chapman, director of the Idaho Water Users Association. "If people talk about it enough, they'll begin to believe in it. We'll do anything we can to frustrate it. It's a taking of property rights without compensation." In a conference attended by dozens of people, water master Ron Carlson stated that he looked at the public trust doctrine the way he looks at AIDS—anathema to life in southern Idaho.

Though it may be the only solution, public trust's polarity elicits the siege mentality of the irrigation establishment. "But so does everything else aimed at reconsidering the one-sided formula for using Snake River water for irrigation," said Scott Reed, a lawyer who served on Idaho's State Water Board for twelve years.

In a practical sense, the doctrine remains a last resort for maintaining minimum flows in the river. If all groups were concerned about all uses of water, which include not only irrigation and fish but wildlife, recreation, hydroelectric power, water supply, a tourist economy, and more, use of the doctrine would be unnecessary. Through negotiation, reform, restraint, science, economics, and the effective administration of state law that theoretically limits diversions to amounts actually used for beneficial purposes, other possibilities exist for restoring health to the river.

THE GREAT FEEDER

By the third day on the river I had canoed out of the high mountains and through the foothills. Cliffs rose to Lookout Mountain, and beyond it, near Heise, the mouth of the canyon marked the end of the Rocky Mountains.

Now 206 miles below its source, the river carried an average of 4.9 million acre feet a year, and the withdrawals for irrigation were about to begin. I had been warned that a diversion structure for a canal called the Great Feeder was a death trap to boaters, but, first, I had to survive the preliminaries. As if to symbolize my leaving the mountains, the first diversion bulwark rose on the left shore. Typical of dozens to come, it was a cement wall about 8 feet high and 20 feet wide with a hole for a canal that leads to ditches. Thousands of fish get sucked into the unscreened canals and die in fields or in the canals when drained in winter. A man hired as a "ditch rider" adjusts a gate according to irrigators' water rights and amounts requested. To assure that water is shunted into the canal during low flows, rocks had been bulldozed into the river as a weir, though at this high level the water flowed over the top, curling and turbulent. I passed another diversion and the Poplar boat ramp, where many people disembark from the river a few miles above the Heise bridge.

Following advice given to me, I clung to the far right, though just ahead, some percentage of the river disappeared over an odd dam, not crossing the main stem of the river but crossing the inlet to a slough; at lower levels the dam blocks a channel from spilling to the right of an island. After beaching and walking downstream to look at the channel dam, I paddled past it, then spotted another canal headgate and a second channel dam of angular rock dumped by canal companies. A third headgate rose on my left, and beyond it, a cement wall appeared to block the river's flow entirely. It was the Great Feeder. Half the Snake at medium flows and most of the water at low levels are diverted at this single site into a canal that can carry 4,500 cfs—twice as much as the river often carries in Grand Teton National Park.

A number of people have been sucked into the wall and jammed into its holes and metal grates, drowned or battered to death before washing out the other side. The Feeder Board, elected by the ditch companies, offered no clue of warning. A single sign, "Keep right," could save people's lives. The water master said that the reason for no warning was a fear of increased liability if the irrigators openly recognized the danger of their facility.

A massive, channelized flow charged straight toward the bull's-eye of the concrete wall where much of the river disappeared. Just in front of the Feeder's wall, the river bent in an unlikely dogleg to the right, where I zipped through, avoiding a whirlpool below the bend. The Feeder's jaws were finally behind me, and I relaxed, though the river was considerably smaller than it had been.

Once again, the Snake braided through a cottonwood forest. High water covered a rock diversion dam, and pumps and canals drew water from the river. Quarried rocks had been dumped over the banks to keep the river in its place. The piles grew and became levees; below the Highway 20 bridge, 18 miles of levees were built by the Army Corps of Engineers to segregate the river from farmland, incidentally blocking the flow from spaghettilike sloughs, oxbows, and wetlands and creating a biological desert out of a riparian forest. The corps built 250 levee or channelization projects throughout the basin. On the main stem, the corps erected 60 miles of levees; others were built by the Soil Conservation Service, counties, and farmers.

The river had faded from green to brownish-green and then the dirt-brown Henry's Fork entered from the north, carrying an average of 2,088 cfs. At a bend below the confluence, I beached and camped.

THE HENRY'S FORK AND THE TRUMPETER SWAN

Fly Fisherman editor John Randolph called the Henry's Fork "the premier dry fly fishing stream in the entire world."[26] Anglers have caught 18-pound trout here, though fishing these waters is "like climbing Mount Everest," according to M. R. "Mick" Mickelson, president of the Henry's Fork Foundation. "The clean water with its glassy surface makes it more difficult than a riffling stream such as the Madison. The fish look up at you through a window. Nowhere else do we have the combination of spring-fed flows, water quality, low gradient with still water, and insect life."

The upper Henry's Fork crosses the Island Park caldera, a 25-mile-diameter basin remaining after an eruption and the land's subsidence. This and Yellowstone are among the world's largest calderas.[27] Geologically and in other ways, the upper Henry's Fork is the closest thing the world knows to another Yellowstone. The spacious riverine meadows of the Henry's Fork could be carbon-copied from Yellowstone's famed Hayden Valley, and the wooded reaches of the Henry's Fork resemble Yellowstone's Bechler River. Wildlife here does not rate with Yellowstone, though the potential is perhaps greater because Island Park is 1,431 feet lower than Yellowstone Lake. Management, not landscape, defines the major difference between the two areas. Here in the Targhee National Forest, clearcutting has been rampant, and 70 percent of the land is open to oil and gas leasing. Perhaps, when the nation needs another Yellowstone, it will turn to the upper Henry's Fork.

Just as the Bureau of Reclamation manages Jackson and Palisades dams, it also manages Island Park Dam for irrigation, though a healthy flow below the dam is vital to the rare trumpeter swan, the largest bird in North America. Needing slow-moving, unfrozen water in which to eat tubers and stems of aquatic plants, swans had congregated at Island Park because of its hot springs. The reservoir flooded those, but the Bureau of Reclamation coincidentally replaced the warm water with temperate winter releases from the bottom of the reservoir. Hundreds of swans winter here, with another 100 on the Snake River near Jackson and up to 200 on the Teton River.

Winter inflow to Island Park is 450 cfs, but in a dry year the bureau holds most of the water for irrigation. "If there isn't an adequate flow below the dam, we could lose one-third of the resident Rocky Mountain trumpeter population at once," explained Ruth Gale, an Idaho Fish and Game biologist, "and we came very close to that in the winter of 1987." Five hundred trumpeters wintered at Harriman State Park below the dam while the bureau released pulses of water to break ice. The surplus supply available to swans was nearly gone and the birds would have died, but then the temperature rose and melted some ice. In 1989 the swans would not be as lucky, and in spite of irrigators' contributing 8,000 acre feet and the Henry's Fork Foundation and Idaho Nature Conservancy buying another 8,000 from farmers, about 100 swans died. The reservoir still filled, leaving the irrigators with full supplies. "I don't think the public would stand for it if people really knew what a grip the irrigators have on that water," Gale said, "but people don't know. Regardless of releases from the dam, there is excellent habitat along the Snake River at the Fort Hall

Bottoms on the Shoshone and Bannock Indian Reservation. We'll move young swans down there and hope they stay."

THE TETON DAM DEBACLE

Tributary to the Henry's Fork, the Teton River drops from an oval basin at the western foot of the Teton peaks. After opposition by fishermen, hunters, and canoeists and after an economic analysis that exposed a benefit-cost ratio of 50 cents on the dollar, Teton Dam was built with unanimous support from Idaho politicians. The $103 million dam would have held 288,250 acre feet for irrigation of lands already receiving water, some of them flooded by an average of 11 acre feet per year—five times the rainfall of farmland in Iowa.

Construction had just been completed in 1976 when the right abutment ruptured. From within the dam itself, a hole grew and vomited a fury of mud. Destroyed from the inside out, the dam burst and the reservoir descended with the horror of a 20-foot wave bearing down on the Teton River valley. The dam failure killed eleven people, scoured 100,000 acres of farmland, obliterated thousands of buildings, drowned 16,000 head of livestock, flushed away toxic chemicals stored on the floodplain, and forced 25,000 people from their homes.[28] Seventeen percent of the dam's justification had been for flood control; the man-made flood made mud-splattered carnage out of Sugar City, battered nearby Rexburg and Roberts along the Snake River, then inundated parts of Idaho Falls and Blackfoot. Teton waters were contained at American Falls Dam, though there was great concern that the ailing structure, overdue for reconstruction, would fail with cataclysmic potential as far as the Pacific Ocean.

Bureau of Reclamation officials had not heeded warnings from their own geologists or those of the U.S. Geological Survey; the inability of the bureau to fill the fatal voids with concrete was even the topic of lunchroom conversations casually overheard in the federal building in Boise. In 1976 the Congressional Committee on Government Operations stated that the bureau had been "deficient in the geologic examination of the site" and "in resolving satisfactorily the warning of safety hazards." The disaster had seismic impact on the federal water bureaucracy (see Chapter 3) and cracked what had been an impervious shell of hype in Idaho for water development. The fourth-graders' Idaho history book, which ventures to say nothing on costs or side effects from any other dam, now features a full-page photo of Teton collapsing.[29]

A portion of the 305-foot-high rock pile remains a monument of wreckage, though much of the 9.5 million cubic yards of earth-fill washed downriver. Bullet holes made by vandals riddle a Bureau of Reclamation sign, and the Teton River riffles peacefully at its old elevation through the breach.

A MANIPULATED FATE

On my fourth morning on the Snake River, I broke camp below the Henry's Fork confluence, paddled to the north shore, and landed where cliffs mark the advance of lava that pushed the river southward. The Menan Buttes—800-foot volcanic cones half a million years old—lured me to the top. From the summit I saw the Snake River exiting the Rocky Mountains and entering the plain of southern Idaho with its lava and its soil called loess, brought by the wind from the West. For hundreds of miles the Snake River will wind through fields or cut desert canyons. Farms crowded the water's edge, but a border of willows buffered denuded pastures. Though the cottonwoods and sloughs were gone—victims of levees—the riparian corridor advanced as an attenuated battlefront of life into the desert.

Six miles below the Menan bridge I beached for lunch and then tracked a deer into a willow thicket. With my fingers, I felt the uneroded edges of the fresh tracks. A twig snapped, and I saw the khaki flank of a doe. But behind her, a massive form arose in the brush. A moose! Like the beaver and eagle, the moose signified the wealth of the riparian world.

Interrupted only by Jackson and Palisades reservoirs, the hospitable belt of cottonwood, willows, alder, and dogwood survives from the headwaters to here. A muskrat or beaver could travel the distance without leaving home. But below here, the belt is broken, and riparian life is scarce.

From a sky blotchy with clouds, an afternoon wind gained force as it does from Palisades to the Columbia; only constant paddling pulled me down river. The gale, nearly shrieking, buffeted my boat. A 6-inch chop coalesced into waves a foot high and broke as whitecaps, somewhat menacing. On a beach gifted at every step with cow manure, I scrounged for shelter in the lee of some willows and pitched my tent.

In a sunrise calm I launched my canoe for my fifth and final day to Idaho Falls. In slow water I watched new birds with my binoculars: the cormorant, pintail, cinnamon teal, Franklin's gull, and western grebe, all living on the water. Land birds were absent on the overgrazed banks. Car bodies had been dumped onto eroding shorelines of pasture, but some of the trashed vehicles rusted in the river; its current had chewed and swallowed the bank behind them. For the first time, levees crowded not one but both shores. I drifted under the Roberts bridge and began to acclimatize to pipes, pumps, poles, powerlines, dams, ditches, and canals of the Snake River plain.

The Grand Teton pierced the eastern horizon; this was the first I could see the mountain since Jackson Hole. Pumps sucked water at frequent intervals. Rich wetlands once saturated this Rigby fan and Roberts area—all of it a deltalike flat where the river empties onto the plain. This section had once represented not an end of riparian values as the levees at Roberts now do, but a grand embodiment of marshes and sloughs for a multitude of ducks and wildlife. The state protects a remnant as the Market Lake Wildlife Management Area, but most of the flats are marginal farmland and thistled pasture, problematic in its double demands to be drained and irrigated. For restoration of lost wetland habitat, the Roberts area has more potential than any other along the entire Snake River because here the historic wetlands are not flooded by reservoirs.

Ten miles farther, the Idaho and Great Western Canal Dam seems to be eroding in the current but still requires portage of a canoe. I carried it to the right of the upper Idaho Falls hydroelectric dam, 20 feet high, enjoyed a brief riffle, and entered the pool above the Porter Canal Dam, 8 feet high. I sneaked down the canal to circumvent the dam, then carried the canoe over a gravel bar to the river.

Immediately I dropped into the backwater of the fourth dam in as many hours. Grain elevators rose on the right, an office building on the left. Kids sat at an age-old swimming hole beneath the Highway 20 bridge. Here in the flatwater of Idaho Falls' second hydroelectric dam lay the thinnest width of the Snake since the Narrows above Palisades Reservoir. The city of Idaho Falls, 260 miles from the river's source, rose from the riverbanks. A Mormon tabernacle in typical block-and-cube design towered over the left shore. Without towns until now, the Snake River had already run longer than many major rivers in America.

There was no doubt that my passage through the Rocky Mountains had ended above the Henry's Fork, and no question that the riparian ecosystem came to a halt—I hoped temporarily—above the Roberts bridge. After the Great Feeder, a dozen canals, a score of pumps, and four dams nearly back-to-back, little doubt remained that the Snake River was headed toward a harshly manipulated fate. Through the irrigated empire of Idaho, a different kind of waterway flowed ahead of me.

2

The Snake River Plain

Idaho's Snake River plain stretches west to the Owyhee Mountains near the Oregon border, north to the end-grain of central Idaho's ranges, east to the foothills of the Rocky Mountain flanks, and south to the Great Basin uplift in southern Idaho. The Geological Survey identified the eastern Snake River plain as a valley roughly 50 miles wide flanking the river from the community of Heise to the town of King Hill, and a shorter western plain running to the town of Weiser, altogether 15,600 square miles, 400 miles in length.[1] On a relief map of the western states, only the Central Valley of California and the plateau of eastern Washington show a greater mass of flat land rimmed by mountains. The plain is part of the Columbia Plateau province of Idaho, Oregon, and Washington—one of the world's largest expanses of lava.[2]

The Snake River plain was awash in molten rock, graphically exposed at Craters of the Moon National Monument, textbook lava that erupted 2,100 years ago, a geologic blink of the eye. Geophysicist Robert Smith at the University of Utah studied the continent's westward drift over a "hot spot" within the earth that caused the volcanism and that now lies beneath Yellowstone. He pointed to a progression of volcanic areas running from older to younger from the southwest end of the plain to Island Park in eastern Idaho and on eastward to Yellowstone, which he predicted will someday be a flat basaltic floor.[3] Conversely, today's plain was once a land of hot springs and mountains. The hot spot is caused by radiation, detected in high amounts in the basements of some homes. The Idaho Department of Health and Welfare wrote that "further study is needed" of radiation on the plain.[4]

Much of the plain receives less than 10 inches of rain a year compared with New York's 42 and a U.S. average of 30. Shoshone

Indians called the Snake the "river of the sagebrush plain."[5] The idea that this sparsely watered landscape represents a worthless wasteland is a myth that is only recently unraveling as people are beginning to appreciate the life of deserts. In Congress, for example, a bill would protect the Mojave Desert, and national parks in deserts receive unprecedented use.

Millions of acres of the Snake River plain once nurtured an abundance of dryland wildlife. Early accounts describe "a relatively lush plain of bunch grasses waving in the wind like an ocean."[6] The Raft River ran year-round through a sea of grass but is now an intermittent stream through a land of sage. Enormous herds of deer, migrating from the Lost River Range in Idaho to Utah, used to cross the Snake River where Minidoka Dam later formed a reservoir. A person only needs to visit the world's largest concentration of raptors at the Snake River Birds of Prey area or the herds of pronghorn antelope, deer, and bison on the sagebrush plains at Grand Teton National Park in Wyoming to see what existed before cattle saturated the range and irrigation rendered horizon-scale expanses into a monoculture. The conversion included sixteen dams on the Snake River plain, diversion of most water, and the demise of riparian areas. The plain's free-flowing sections of river are mostly short in length and short on water.

"Spudland," say Idahoans and Wyomingites of Idaho's plain.

"The agricultural heartland of Idaho," residents say.

"God's plan," say the Mormons.

"Home—it's where we've always been," said a Shoshone Indian.

"A bastion of conservatism."

"A society that exists because of the Snake River."

"A place to take stock of the future of the West."

The Snake River plain is in fact hot, dry, flat, intensively farmed, dependent on the river, conservative, Mormon. The crime rate is low, families are large, and people are friendly. Irrigators converted 3 million acres from grasslands and high desert to irrigated farmland.[7] Cattle graze on most of the rest. Dams and water rights are held in the esteem of the flag, or the church, or the right to bear arms.

The plain includes 19 percent of the state's land and represents much of the essence of Idaho, which, like Wyoming, achieved

statehood in 1890. That was the same year the frontier was officially proclaimed to exist no more, though aspects of that concept have
survived to a greater extent in Idaho than in perhaps any other
state but Alaska. This often enchanting, sometimes confounding,
occasionally enraging, and always enigmatic state is far-flung culturally and geographically. The south, north, and central reaches of
Idaho are said to recognize three capitals: Salt Lake City, Spokane,
and Boise. One million people inhabit 83,600 square miles—twelve
people per square mile. For all its wilderness and potatoes, Idaho
has a predominantly urban population; seven small cities account
for half the people (the West is the most urban region in North
America based on the percentage of residents in developed areas).[8]

About 85 percent of the state's people live in the Snake River
basin, which constitutes 87 percent of the land.[9] Idaho's five largest
cities sprawl along the Snake River or lower reaches of tributaries.
Eighty percent of the river's flow at its mouth originates in Idaho.

While most of Idaho's people live along the Snake River and at
low elevations, the nation knows the state for its Rocky Mountains,
its wilderness, its hunting and fishing. For wild rivers, Idaho is
revered more than any other state except Alaska. About 40,000
miles of waterways offer some of the nation's finest for fishing and
whitewater boating.

Business and government capitalize on the mountain image for
tourism—the third largest industry and growing fast, though the
political power remains squarely with agriculture and resource extraction. A constant reminder of biculturalism is the state's two
license plates. The standard plate says "Famous Potatoes." The
"centennial" plate, ordered for an extra fee, has the numbers surrounded by a scene of mountains and forests. Its popularity took
state officials completely by surprise. The state responded by con-
tinuing the pictorial motif but adding once again the old slogan.
The tenacity of potato-pride is nothing new; in 1941 the license
slogan was "Scenic Idaho," but in 1947 it was switched back to
"World-Famous Potatoes."

Though it's the state's primary artery, the Snake River has rarely
been regarded as a member in the club of natural wonders pro-
moted by Idaho. Nationwide, people know of the Salmon River,
but few are aware of the much larger Snake, perhaps because most

reaches were degraded generations ago, and perhaps because the river's qualities and potential have been squelched and hidden.

"In this basin," explained Bob Riley, chief of the Bureau of Reclamation's reports branch in Boise, "you really have two Snake Rivers. One ends at Milner Dam. The other begins below there and runs to the Columbia." (Milner Dam is 157 miles below Idaho Falls.) Even the "upper" and "lower" Colorado River, divided at Glen Canyon Dam because of an interstate water compact, does not rival in thoroughness the Snake River's truncation at Milner. "There's also the river of surface flow and a significant river of groundwater," Riley added.

Behind all this lies the river of life, the river that since time immemorial nourished fish, wildlife, clean water for many uses, and the riparian edge. A river is more than water. Yet the living river is only a remnant of what was.

There appear to be several Snake Rivers. Of course it is all one, but does the attitude of fragmentation affect what people *do* to the river? Does acceptance of a broken-up river form a mold for the river's fate?

IDAHO FALLS TO BLACKFOOT

The Snake River is clearly the landmark in the town of Idaho Falls, elevation 4,730, population 39,600. The "falls," more like a radically steep rapid, was converted to a dam early in this century by cementing shut the spaces between the rocks. Water still pours over the top, billed by the chamber of commerce as "Scenic Falls on the Snake River" and as the foremost attraction for sightseers. The Mormon (Church of Jesus Christ of Latter-Day Saints, or as Mormons say, LDS) temple is listed second among tourist attractions in this town only 220 miles north of Salt Lake City, closer than the southern end of Utah itself. A cool relief of parkland borders a short section of the dammed-up river, and recreational paths lead to a pair of hydroelectric plants funded by disaster relief money after Teton Dam failed and its 75,000-cfs flood obliterated older generators. Three city dams generate 8 megawatts (mw) each and the new "Gem State" plant downriver supplies 23 mw. Residential electricity costs 3.5 cents a kilowatt-hour—quite cheap. Idaho Falls is planning a new dam to flood 3 miles of the Snake at Shelley, 12 miles downriver.

Only one-quarter of the distance from the headwaters to the Columbia River, the Snake River had already received a utilitarian share of dams, diversions, farming, and development. Yet it still flowed respectably, watered crops, produced power, supported fish, nurtured wildlife, and accommodated recreation. The natural river had been compromised, yet it remained integrated for many purposes, not yet facing the scourge of single-use development.

Below Idaho Falls, I looked at the current near the Woodville bridge that will be impounded if Idaho Falls builds the Shelley hydroelectric dam. To hear the local view of this, I called a city councilmember, who said the main complaint about the proposed dam was that the town council of Shelley wanted to build the dam itself. "You've also got those environmentalist and protest groups. Some people just don't like to see change. Some of their homes would be affected. Sometimes you change anyway. There're farms in the bottom of Palisades Reservoir."

Railroad tracks occupy one side of Shelley's main street; shops line the other side. I counted nineteen pickups and twenty-three cars going by—about as high as the pickup ratio gets on any main street anywhere. What the pickups carried were children—four or more in the backs of many trucks. A movie, rated G and costing $1, was due to start that Friday evening, and kids crowded the sidewalk. At the other end of the spectrum, all three county commissioner candidates with posters in a store window appeared to be well over seventy.

I drove downriver and stopped at a rock diversion dam bulldozed into place by a canal company. On toward Blackfoot, population 9,000, the Snake River plain stretched westward with its ever-present powerlines, fences, ditches, sprinklers, small homes, metal barns, and fields of astroturf green.

Looking for a place to park and sleep at a community with the promising name of Riverside, I settled below a meat packing plant and across from a cement plant. The river was low, maybe one-twentieth its flow above the Great Feeder. Many dozens of canals, ditches, and pumps had taken the water elsewhere. Chunks of suds bobbed like brown grapefruits, and the essence of burning garbage hung heavy in the stinking night sky. The combined effects produced an appalling assault on the senses. The West has a mythic reputation for pride in open space, but what I saw was trashed and trampled in ways that made streams as far east as Philadelphia sparkle in comparison. Water is said to be the West's most precious wealth, yet the river was treated as though it had no intrinsic value at all.

A BRIEF RENEWAL

As I readied my canoe at the Blackfoot bridge the next morning, I talked to a man supervising two grandchildren. "It's low now because this is when the irrigators need all the water."

The tabescent river was enough to float my canoe but not by much. I paddled past the cement plant and encountered a diversion dam of fractured concrete, hazardous to run. To the far right, water flowed undammed behind an island—a path of least resistance. I entered that channel, drifted awhile, then suddenly felt trapped. The flow of the water was not natural. No headgate had blocked the entrance, yet it seemed that I was being sucked into a canal. Up ahead I saw gravel bulldozed against the left bank, a signature of diversion to the right. Like salmon trying to migrate to sea, would I flop up gasping in an alfalfa field? Go back! I spun the canoe and stroked hard and fast back to the dam. I stepped out of the boat and coaxed it over the jagged concrete rubble.

Paddling on down the river, I was prepared for the worst but smelled no evidence at a sewage treatment plant. Indeed, Blackfoot won an operations award from the Department of Health and Welfare. Upriver views showed snow gleaming on the Rockies, but at my side, the current had exhumed a rusting dump on the floodplain.

Unlike the Snake's low-flow problem below Palisades Dam, which occurs in winter when the Bureau of Reclamation depletes the river in preparation for the irrigation season, the low-flow problem below Blackfoot occurs in summer when farmers deplete the river *during* the irrigation season. Above Milner Dam, over 300 canals and pumps divert Snake River water, cutting flows from sloughs, destroying fish habitat. Studies by a consulting firm indicated that the smaller channels had the greatest spawning habitat per acre; the main and medium channels contained 10 percent or less of the usable habitat.[10] Before diversions, the river through the Fort Hall Bottoms—downstream from Blackfoot—contained 28 miles of small channels. Now it has 16 miles, and the impacts would be even greater here closer to Blackfoot because spring flows do not recharge the sloughs until farther downstream.

As I paddled toward the Bottoms, fresh water seeped in from springs. With many of the banks owned by the Bureau of Land Management (BLM), the riparian forest rose with a green vigor that I had not seen since the Henry's Fork. Heron waded at riffles, sandpipers pecked on mud flats, egrets speared fish in shallows.

I heard a combined hiss, gurgle, and splash—the sound of fish, a lot of them. Then I saw the ridged backbone of one, then another, and another. The first fish fled with a wake like the spread of a zipper opening rapidly. A second fish darted from the boat, but because I constantly drifted downstream, I crept upon more fish and saw perhaps fifty at once. About 18 inches long, one fish positioned herself facing upstream in the riffle. One or two others swam to her side. They all then worked the current with switching tails, splashing the surface, dancing, it seemed, in their ultimate act. They were mating, spawning.

I wish I could say these were salmon, but salmon never lived in this section of the river. I wish I could say they were trout, but they were not. These were suckers, a pigeon of the rivers. Admirably adapted to poor conditions, the sucker has an underslung mouth for scooping mollusks, larvae, and water plants from the bottom, which is where most of the food settles in a nutrient-rich waterway. This fish survives low levels of oxygen, common with the decay of organic matter, and tolerates pollution, concentrated by depleted flows and compounded by a lack of aerating riffles that results from the chronic incarceration of floods in reservoirs. Suckers, catfish, and carp adjust to high water temperatures, which peak with low flows, tepid water returned from ditches, and the loss of shade where cottonwoods have been cut for levees. The lowly sucker, big-lipped and boney, indicates poor habitat, and is a creature of disgust to many people. The inescapable humiliation is that suckers are what we deserve, exactly what should be expected from what we've done to the river.

Heron hunted the suckers. The waist-high birds waded by picking up each foot carefully, reaching over the water, and stepping forward without a sound. If I drifted too close, they flew with fabulously slow wingbeats and squawked, "Awakk!" When the larger birds fled, gulls pecked at the white-bellied carcasses. At one mudflat cafeteria, four heron and forty gulls fed on a dozen fish.

Canada geese cruised over, and when their shadows streaked the water, the suckers fled for deep cover. Geese don't fish but eagles do, and a shadow is a shadow. Forster's terns called "click-click," dove underwater for minnows, and flew off shaking drops from their feathers. At a bend where the current licked against the bank, a furry muskrat clung to a cottonwood, then scurried down the trunk and plopped into the water.

At a low elevation, this section of the river potentially fit many needs of wildlife. It is a myth that adequate wildlife areas exist at higher elevations and on wastelands. By association with photos and films, I had grown up thinking of wild animals in the mountains—bighorn sheep grazing at timberline, for example. To see riverfront wildlife or even to fish, people go to Grand Teton National Park or the upper river. Yet consider the potential here at elevation 4,400 feet and the increasing suitability as the river drops into the climate of mild winters. Bass might thrive here with decent flows. Trumpeter swans could reestablish colonies in ice-free water. Herds of elk could winter on pastures nourished by good soils rather than on the depleted ground that is typically left for wildlife.

"We've had a love affair with the high country," said the riparian spokesman, Bill Platts. "The lower elevations were largely ignored. Once the wilderness issues are settled, we'll see great interest in the low country because it's critical to so much wildlife. The public is going to want more out of low-elevation recreational lands."

A boy with rolled-up trousers and a bow and arrow had mastered the stalk of the great blue heron. "No suckers yet. The carp are easier to hit." I saw no one else during my 12-mile trip on this easy reach that begins in the town of Blackfoot and ends at a paved road.

Ferry Butte lay ahead, a volcanic cone marking the end of my canoe trip. Beyond it, the riparian belt improves for a short while. The Shoshone and Bannock Indians prohibit trespassing on the Fort Hall Bottoms, a 15-mile-long, 13,000-acre expanse of wetlands—the third largest riparian area on the river and the second most important zone of underground aquifer discharge. Through springs, 1,200 cfs seep into creeks to recharge the suffering river.[11]

In 1866 Governor David Ballard encouraged the establishment of the Fort Hall Reservation, writing that the Bottoms would help the Indians to be self-sustaining. "All of the streams abound in fish of the finest quality, and I saw great numbers of antelope and deer, sage hens, grouse, ducks and geese."[12] The Indians are now engaged in a land-planning process that is more thorough than that of many counties in the basin. Tribal planner Kenneth Timbanna said, "We propose to set aside the Bottoms as a fish and wildlife refuge. Some grazing will continue, but we want to protect the area as it is." The Indians' plan includes reintroduction of beavers and trumpeter swans and improvement of water quality.

American Falls Reservoir flooded 28,000 acres of the reservation's Bottoms, 17 miles of the Indian's Snake River, and uncounted springs. The Indians were paid $700,000, $100,000 of it going to an irrigation project that replaced one-fourth of the water lost by flooding the springs. Most of the irrigation on the reservation is by non-Indians.

I had brought along my bicycle in my canoe, and from the takeout I pedaled back to my van in Blackfoot. The river had been nearly destroyed by irrigation withdrawals, but my ride showed another side of the use of this water. Sprinklers swished in the warm evening air. Homes were neat, and the lawns smelled of fresh mowing. Farmers had parked their equipment for Sunday, and in some backyards, hamburgers were being grilled. Children ran and chased one another, laughing with happiness, and I remembered my own childhood in the country. Horses grazed where a ditch brought them water. I bicycled through the American Dream, God's Way, and the Old West, all rolled into one. I could see in those homes that the dream had substance, and that irrigation made this way of life possible. But I wondered: Is it necessary to pay such a high price? Can we have all of this and also a healthy river?

"The river would have certainly been outstanding without the diversions," said Jack Griffith, a fisheries biologist at Idaho State University. "Unfortunately, people have forgotten what it was like." That life-filled river of eighty years ago has disappeared from the collective memory. With no vision of what once was, is there a healthful vision of what could be? "No," Griffith said. "Not many people think about that." But the Indians have thought about it, and what they hope to do is a fascinating study in the science and political art of western water in the closing years of the twentieth century.

THE INDIANS' VIEW

"We must stop dividing up this river as private property and start treating it as a living system," said Howard Funke. "We want to guarantee life to the river, and that means to all the resources in it. The river should not be treated like a piece of junk. The earth is the mother of all things; treat it like your mother. That's the tribal view." Funke, a member of the Lake Superior Band of Chippewas, is the lawyer for the Shoshone and Bannock tribes on the Fort Hall Reservation.

"There's a reverence for the river and a willingness to maintain it as a natural system," said Sue Broderick, a biologist working for the tribes. "The economic tradeoffs of development are not considered worth it."

Shoshone and Bannock councilmember Arnold Appenay said,

The tribes have looked at the river as a system, a life-giving entity that provided for our needs. My grandfather was a medicine man. One day he showed me a spring out here. He talked to the water and said, "Your soul and that water's soul can communicate." The water had religious as well as life-giving properties. Now there are no more medicine men. Up on the Salmon River, my grandfather walked on the backs of salmon. That's something that was once ours. I wish we had it today. A lot of things have been lost. How you pray has pretty much been lost. Now we hire engineers and identify and quantify our "needs" for water. Mankind invented dams and pipes and sprinklers and all these wonderful things and spent a lot of money screwing up the river. Now, no one will spend the money to correct the problems. Now we dam the river and hold the water hostage.

You're asking what *I* think? I see the river and streams as one thing, one system. It works. Or it used to work. We need minimum flows to sustain the river, but the farmer, he couldn't care less. Somebody needs to care about this. This tribe is the strongest entity in the region to do conservation work.

Fish are central to the Indian's heritage, a point evident even in the naming of the river. It was probably not named the Snake because it curves a lot. The most common explanation is that the Shoshone identified themselves in sign language by a curving motion of the hand moving outward from the chest, probably signifying a swimming fish, perhaps meaning "people of the fish." Explorers including Lewis and Clark misread the sign and called the Indians the Snakes.[13] ("Today," an Indian leader told me, "we just call ourselves 'Indians.' You hear 'Native Americans,' but not on the reservation. That's a term I use only when speaking to white, academic groups.")

Howard Funke said, "We are an unsophisticated people living on a large landmass and trying to integrate old ways and new ways." Of course, they used to occupy much more than this roughly 30-by-30-mile piece of ground. The Shoshone had lived throughout the southern half of Idaho, up the Snake River into the future Wyoming and down to Hells Canyon. The Bannock roamed as nomads within the Shoshone territory. The original reservation encompassed 1.8 million acres, much of it ceded back to the government as Caribou National Forest. The tribes now own about 15 miles of Snake River frontage and 544,000 acres. In return for half of Idaho and healthy chunks of Wyoming, Utah, and Nevada, the Shoshone and Bannock were "given" a piece of ground smaller than the Idaho National Engineering Laboratory, where atomic energy and weapons work is done near Idaho Falls.

In the "first in time, first in right" gospel of water law, the Indians were undisputedly here first, but they failed to do the paperwork and to divert water, which was essential, according to the dominant culture, to gaining rights to the water. Now they are depending on their treaty, which granted more than the Fort Hall acreage. They also received the rights to the water flowing past the reservation and the rights to the fish and wildlife of the tribes' entire native territory. This opened unexpected avenues of possibility.

Resulting from a court challenge by the Fort Belknap Indians in

Montana, the Winters Doctrine in 1908 recognized that Indians were given land for a livelihood through farming, and therefore they have rights to the necessary water as well as waters "which arise upon, border, traverse, or underlie a reservation." Indian water rights grew in importance throughout the western states, where 172 reservations comprise 12 percent of the private land. In Wyoming, for example, the Shoshone and Arapahoe received rights to 477,000 acre feet, but with strict limits on their use of the water. Based on soils analysis, the Shoshone and Bannock claimed that 227,000 of their acres are farmable, and they are negotiating for 580,000 acre feet—a lot of water. Because the reservation dates to 1867, Indian rights precede the rights of every non-Indian in the basin. Do Indians farm?

"No," Funke answered. "We want the water so we can put it back in the river. The Indians are concerned not only about the Snake River on the reservation but also about the fishery to which we have treaty rights. Because dams have totally blocked the salmon migration in Hells Canyon, the fish are available to the Shoshone and Bannock only in the Salmon River basin, 120 miles to the north." Migrating from the rivers to the ocean and back up the Columbia and lower Snake, the fish must pass eight dams, and up to 15 percent of the young fish going out to sea die at each dam. If more water were flowing over the dams, survival rates would improve. Fisheries agencies devised a water budget of recommended flow levels during migration, but water stored in all but two dams is unavailable for the budget because storage rights are owned by irrigators, or because the dams belong to the Idaho Power Company, or because the state of Idaho opposes the use of stored water for salmon recovery (see Chapter 9).

To solve the problem of low flows, the tribes want to sell water to agencies responsible for restoring the salmon runs and thus augment lower Snake River flows needed by migrating fish. The Indians hope to see a return of healthy populations of wild salmon in the Salmon River headwaters where tribal members go to fish— not for commercial gain but for religious purposes and for food. The Indians' water could breathe new life into this beleaguered resource and accomplish much to replenish the salmon and steelhead. In addition, the Indians have contracted with fisheries biologist Don Chapman, a private consultant, to determine what flows

are required for maintenance of a healthy riparian ecosystem—
studies transcending the bare-bones objective of minimum flows
for fish. The Indians are thus pushing innovative frontiers of river
science and applying them to the politics and economics of the
modern world.

The Shoshone and Bannock case may be the largest ever for protection of a river and fishery through instream flows. "Presentation
of Claims to Instream Flows and Water Quality for the Fort Hall
Indian Reservation" is a tribal document with all the potential of
every other arid legal brief, but instead, it is the finest piece that
has been written about the need to properly care for the Snake
River and its ecosystem. "We meet today in the center of the remaining Fort Hall Indian Reservation to discuss again the grave
matter of water, the source of all life bestowed by the Creator. We
welcome you all in friendship. We are mindful of our children and
yours, and of the children yet unborn."[14]

With concise recognition of the riparian system, the Indians
claim the right to flows through the Fort Hall Bottoms for "preservation and enhancement of reservation fisheries, wildlife and other
water-dependent natural resources, which comprise, along with
the water systems that sustain them, a unique and unitary ecosystem." The tribes asserted their entitlement to the quantity and
quality of water necessary for a healthy river. "These living resources are central to the cultural, aesthetic, and religious values
and practices of Tribal members." They pressed for a holistic view:
"Additional losses in environmental quality will continue unless
this system is managed in an integrated fashion, for multiple uses."
The tribes called for a "flexible, adaptive and coordinated management approach to conflict resolution." This would be accomplished
"by recognizing that change and adaptation are inevitable and by
working together to meet challenges and resolve conflicts."[15]

Irrigators argued that Indian water rights should be limited to
irrigation supplies, though the tribes maintain that other uses are
eligible, including instream flows.[16] The Winters Doctrine of 1908
contemplated water being reserved not only for farming but for the
"arts of civilization" as well.[17] To re-create a living river indeed
appears to be an "art" in modern civilization. Indians point to
United States v. *Adair* in 1983: "The right to hunt, fish, and gather
. . . [can also be] a primary purpose behind creation of an Indian

reservation." As early as 1866 Idaho Governor David Ballard had touted the fish and wildlife of the Fort Hall Bottoms as vital to the Indians.

One might think that the largest industry in Idaho, the agricultural industry—having done much to destroy the fisheries by damming the rivers, eliminating floods that made a healthy ecosystem possible, diverting flows, causing spawning grounds to dry up, raising water temperatures through flatwater pools and ditches, and polluting the river with sediment and pesticides—would welcome someone else putting water back in the river to compensate for a small part of the loss that agriculture has wreaked.

But in 1988 Sherl Chapman of the Idaho Water Users Association said, "Whatever amount the Indians are awarded, it should be used on the reservation only." He added, "We think the water is better left for multiple use—when the water is used for irrigation, it runs off and is used again, then it percolates into the groundwater and is used even another time by another farmer." Along with a curious description of multiple use as irrigation by multiple farmers, Chapman claimed there will be "impacts" if water is added to the starving river. "If they use that water for instream flows, I think we'll see declining water levels in the groundwater, and some people will not be able to irrigate. The treaty was designed to convert the Sho-Bans from a nomadic life to an agrarian life; to use that water for other than irrigation will disrupt the economy of the Snake River basin."

Sparing no disdain, an irrigation spokesman said, "The Indians don't want to farm; they want the money. They think they can get money to float fish back to the ocean." Straight-faced, another irrigation leader stated, "The Indians *were* here first, but they were subdued. Now they're unhappy. The big problem is that we didn't integrate them into our society. Now they want to send all that water down the river."

After listening to these remarks, one might think that the Indians—retaining 1 percent of Idaho and claiming 2.3 percent of the water that's been withdrawn by irrigators in the basin—are running roughshod over the irrigators. As though the irrigators had considered any other values but agriculture during the last hundred years, Chapman said, "If the Indians got their way, they could transfer water to fishery flows without consideration of other values."

"Those who control water control agriculture and so they control Idaho," Funke said. "No one will admit this, but even though we're the most economically and socially disadvantaged group in the state, there's concern about Indians having economic power— several million dollars a year could be involved."

Irrigators know that virtually all the reservation's irrigation water is used by non-Indians, and nobody expects the Shoshone and Bannock to begin farming on a large scale. By restricting the Indians' use of water to irrigation, the real effect is one of two things: to see *no* new use of water or to see more white people moving onto the reservation and farming on Indian property.

If the Indians overcome the first hurdle of gaining use of their water, some irrigators fear that the Indians' water will be dipped out of farmers' current supplies. This concern is based on the fact that irrigators now monopolize rights to nearly all the water in the system, so *any* water for *anybody* will elicit a fear of loss. The irrigators know that they have more water rights than they need for application on the land (see Chapter 4), though this doesn't mean they're willing to relinquish one bucketful.

If all went well for the Indians, they would sell their new water to the Bonneville Power Administration (BPA), which is obligated to restore salmon and steelhead. One-third of the tribes' income is now from phosphate mining, which will expire in fifteen years, and water sales could fill the financial gap.

Many barriers have stood in the way of the Shoshone and Bannock's goals, but Funke and other Indians are breaking them down.

The way the river's being managed today, there's not enough water. What was good 100 years ago is not necessarily good today. We need flexibility to look at new needs or newly realized needs. There's an economic benefit, not only in taking water out of the river, but also in putting water back in. It was the federal government's responsibility to protect the Indians' rights. By ignoring them, water development was put on a fast track. An old institutionalized system has served up all the water in this river to irrigation projects. Now we want to resolve this problem. We want to use our water as we see fit.

Some people are used to holding all the power. They don't know what will happen when we get our water and send it down the river, so they're opposed. There's a tremendous resistance to change. Instead of setting the system in concrete and bouncing everything off of it, you can allow the system to adapt to people's needs. The system of resource use is not concrete just because you got there first.

The Indian's heritage certainly proves Funke's final statement.

Where *would* the Indians get their water? The tribes seek rights to 48,000 acre feet in American Falls reservoir, 84,000 in Palisades, and rights to flows in several creeks, the Blackfoot River, and the Snake River. They hope to get rights to another 125,000 unallocated acre feet in federal dams. Some water will come from irrigators, who will have to buy replacement water from farmers who don't need their water rights anymore. In negotiations in 1989, the tribes agreed to use only the American Falls water for the salmon's water budget. As if the irrigators were doing the Indians a favor instead of vice versa, the irrigators agreed to let the Indians use their Palisades water for instream flows, but only above American Falls Dam.

Throughout the history of the West there has been a bias—explicit and implicit—for using water for irrigation. Changes are occurring slowly, and to hasten them, the Shoshone and Bannock advocate a system whereby water can be more readily sold for nonirrigation uses (see Chapter 4). Funke said,

We're talking about a water marketing system that can benefit everybody. Today there is no economic reward for keeping water in the river. In dry years, when the market would operate, a farmer could grow crops or sell his water to the BPA for the salmon. If that kind of flexibility is not brought to the system, fights over water use will go on far past our lifetime. This river will become a war zone.

The old rules created an economic system that preempted the living system. The question is, how can we keep the older, living system alive, teeming with fish and wildlife? This is the best economic system as well. The Columbia and its tributaries are an ecosystem, unique because of the anadromous fish and the Indian tribes. I don't think there's ever been a time in water rights history when so many interests have been brought together to deal with instream flow.

The Colorado River has been litigated and studied more than any other river in the West, but according to Funke,

Management there is focused on commercial uses. It's just a commodity, so even the Indians try to get their last share. The focus is on water law. It became a model for other rivers, but it's a bad example to follow—all adversarial, with nobody looking at the common ground.

We're all chained to this river. We have to work it out. The Indians bring a tremendous environmental voice to the process. You hear all kinds of things, but when it comes to the crunch, the tribes go with the environmental point of view every time. And the tribes are growing in power because the American people want them to have that power.

Will this river be managed for short-term or long-term profit? Some people call this the "working river" as if it's just some kind of conveyance system and not a living thing. The real value of the Snake River is in an economy that includes the life of the river. The real value is in keeping the rivers as wild and free as possible, not in using more water than is needed for crops that can't even be sold without subsidies. The real issue is whether we can collectively set aside our fears and our greed and devise workable allocation systems.

The Snake River means more than a job to Howard Funke. "It's my life's work. I once went 30 weeks without pay." He paused.

You see, here is what we're talking about—the last stronghold of indigenous wild salmon. Not hatchery salmon, but *wild* salmon. Here's a fish that begins its life at 7,000 feet above sea level, drops down hundreds of miles, escapes the dams and untold numbers of irrigation ditches, enters the ocean, swims to the Gulf of Alaska, evades the commercial harvest, comes back to the Columbia, climbs over eight dams on the Columbia and lower Snake, evades the sport fishermen and the Indian fishermen, swims up the Salmon River and spawns where it was born. No other creature but the wild salmon can survive all of that. This is a unique creature, and it depends on the water from the Snake River.

AMERICAN FALLS

A concrete wall and array of powerlines, bridge works, riprap, and riverbank fortifications rise below American Falls Dam where the original American Falls had churned thunderously over volcanic rock. Flatwater—58,076 acres inundate 52 river miles—disappears like the ocean beyond the curvature of the earth.

Idaho's Department of Health and Welfare has warned against eating fish from the reservoir because it is contaminated with mercury. The Idaho Water Resources Research Institute reported on high levels of cadmium (a byproduct of phosphate processing, which is done for fertilizer production near Pocatello) and chlorinated hydrocarbons found in pesticides.[18]

Displaced by the reservoir, the town of American Falls was relocated above the southern bank and now has shaded streets and a livable ease found in few other towns carved out of the desert. Landscaped stairs drop to river frontage below the dam where carp and suckers rise and feed in semisolid masses.

The wastes carried by returned irrigation water settle in the reservoir—a big septic tank—and the river is clear below the dam. Running at 8,000 cfs with releases for irrigation, the river chews on cliffs and drops over ledges hundreds of yards wide. "It's a great whitewater run," said Ron Watters, director of Idaho State University's outdoor program in nearby Pocatello.

Biologist Jack Griffith said, "Fishermen take great trout below American Falls, but the river's not well known. Reaches below the Henry's Fork are ignored." An exception was when a dam proposed at Eagle Rock would have slackened water for 5 miles below American Falls, cut flows to 200 cfs, and caused low oxygen, high temperatures, and a wasteland of dried riverbed. Fishermen, kayakers, canoeists, jet boaters, and drift boaters joined in opposition.

Referring to so much of the Snake River that had already been dammed, bumper stickers announced, "They can't have it all." The Federal Energy Regulatory Commission did not approve the application.

The river enters Lake Walcott, a 34-mile-long reservoir that flooded 1,185 acres of riparian forest behind Minidoka Dam. At the outlet, a remnant of flowing water opened a window to the past: I saw thirty western grebes diving for fish, forty cormorants, night heron, great blue heron, gulls, and terns. Downriver, the town of Burley was built where a thicket of willow had been so healthy that even Indian trails skirted around it. The edge of town is now lapped by flatwaters of yet another 34-mile-long reservoir.

MILNER DAM

Any notions of the Snake River as a perdurable natural feature come to a dismal end at Milner Dam. I drove to the site, then walked. The afternoon's heat had accumulated in the rock that stretched as an inhospitable bed across the channel of the river, not flowing with 8,000 cfs as it was above Milner Dam at that very moment, but flowing at about zero. The Snake River was nearly bone dry. A trickle of 6 cfs leaked from cracks between boards of the antiquated structure owned by canal companies since 1905.

The life of the river had ended, utterly and completely. A carp had not yet succumbed to the summer temperatures and flopped in a tepid algal pool. Dried mud caked the rock underfoot. I imagined not only the wealth of water that had been the Snake River, but also the tributaries: the Buffalo, Gros Ventre, Hoback, Greys, Salt, Henry's Fork, Blackfoot, and others. All of the water from all of the rivers was now gone.

Regarding Milner Dam and the area it served, Irvin Rockwell in 1947 wrote of "the singularly constructive achievement in transforming . . . an uninhabited, treeless, windblown, arid desert . . . into a bountiful fruitland."[19]

Regarding Milner Dam in 1988, Howard Funke said, "I don't think people have considered the Snake River dying in its channel." In fact, I found that few Idahoans and virtually no one elsewhere knew that the Snake River flows into the reservoir behind

Milner Dam as a full-bodied river and that nothing flows out. Here
is the largest waterway in America that is stopped all at once and
abandoned as a parched riverbed.

I climbed to the breast of the dam and walked on creaking
boards to the other side. The reservoir lapped brim full and fat at
Milner's upstream face. The Twin Falls Main Canal diverted up to
3,600 cfs, 1 million acre feet a year; the North Side Canal likewise
diverted a large amount, each an artificial river.

Regarding better instream flows on other reaches of the Snake,
Max Van Den Berg, head of the Bureau of Reclamation's Minidoka
office, said, "It would be a good deal if we could work something
out, but in no event are we talking about water flowing past Milner
Dam." Another bureau employee simply said, "For us, the uni-
verse ends at Milner Dam."

Reed Oldham of the Committee of Nine referred to water being
"wasted" if it flows over Milner. Acting like border guards, the
irrigators aimed to allow nothing to escape this rickety old
checkpoint.

In the eyes of the irrigators and the agencies that represent them,
I had come to the end of the upper Snake River. Another Snake
River is said to begin somewhere down below, divorced from the
life of the upper river, absolutely severed by the arid downriver
face of Milner Dam. Walking in the parched riverbed, I saw the
cumulative effects of many upstream water projects.

3

Idaho's Upstream Water Projects

STORING THE WATER

Twenty-three dams impound about half of the river's length—508 miles in reservoirs.[1] Three great water lords have divided the river: above Milner the Snake is dammed by the Bureau of Reclamation along with canal company projects; the middle river is the domain of the Idaho Power Company; and below Hells Canyon, the Army Corps of Engineers built back-to-back impoundments.

In addition to the large dams whose reservoirs bulge like swallowed mice in the belly of a serpent, two low dams required that I carry my canoe. At least four rock weirs reach most of the way across the river and act as dams at low flows, and several weirs divert the flow from one side or the other. Stacked on top of one another, the faces of all the dams would reach 2,140 feet into the sky, nearly four times the height of the Washington Monument. The Tennessee River is also dammed twenty-five times and is renowned as a paragon of despotic engineering. The Snake is no less manipulated, but with its abundance of mileage, half of the river remains free-flowing.

The dams in the upper basin were built mainly for irrigation and brought wealth and the opportunity for 200,000 people to settle on the Snake River plain. Virtually every history book on Idaho speaks of dams and irrigation in glowing terms. Few texts even whisper that associated problems or losses occurred. Still in use, the 1956 textbook *Idaho in the Pacific Northwest* is typical: "Water, and its wide and abundant use in irrigation, has provided the magic touch."[2] The dams made possible a wealth that is as fabulous as the river is impoverished.

What exactly has been gained? What has been lost? Who has paid the price? Why are most of the storage dams the responsibility of the federal government in a region so proud of its antifederal attitudes? What *is* the federal responsibility? How are the dams managed, and for whom? How have times changed since the last constructed project? How does Snake River development compare with development elsewhere? What's planned for the future?

Storage above Milner (the upper basin) totals 5.7 million acre feet.[3] Counting tributaries, the Northwest Power Planning Council listed 13.5 million acre feet of storage in the entire Snake basin. Farmers began with small diversions; the Boise was dammed as early as 1843. Many acres on the eastern plain were settled by Mormon farmers moving from the East or from Utah where they had settled after persecution in New York, Ohio, Missouri, and Illinois. To encourage people to move west, Congress passed the Homestead Act in 1862, the Desert Lands Entry Act in 1877, and the Carey Act in 1894 to give federal lands to farmers and the states for free or for a nominal price.

Stanley Milner, a Salt Lake City businessman, invested $30,000 for irrigation in the Twin Falls area in 1900. Because more money was needed, Frank H. Buhl, a steel industry tycoon from Sharon, Pennsylvania, secured funds, and in 1905 Milner Dam was built. The Kuhn family of Pittsburgh financed much of the distribution system north of the river.[4] Diversions at Milner eventually served 331,000 acres, which is one of the larger contiguous irrigated areas in the United States.[5] Hydropower developers built a dam at American Falls in 1902, private canal companies dammed Henry's Lake, and tentacles of ditches penetrated distant flats of sagebrush across the Snake River plain.

Private irrigation projects succeeded more in Idaho than in other states; two-thirds of all Carey Act claims occurred here, and the Twin Falls project was considered a showcase.[6] But throughout the West, private irrigation largely failed because farmers couldn't pay for the facilities. Wallace Stegner based his 1971 Pulitzer Prize–winning novel *Angle of Repose* on the frustrated attempts to dam the Boise River, later impounded by the federal Arrowrock Dam.

The irrigated West's proverbial lifeblood is water, but much of it remained unavailable without an intravenous stream of federal dollars. Idaho Senator James Pope argued for a federal irrigation program that "could not fail to pave the way for an expected and almost inevitable population movement to the West."[7] The Reclamation Act of 1902 allowed the federal government to plan, construct, and pay for irrigation in seventeen states.

The federal role on the Snake River began in 1906 with the construction of the Minidoka Dam near Burley, the river's first storage project, followed by Jackson Dam, one of the classic bailouts of fumbled private development. Irrigators had built a log dam in 1905 that was washed out by high water, rebuilt by the Bureau of Reclamation in 1907, washed out in 1910, and rebuilt in 1911. In 1916 the bureau raised the concrete dam to 65.5 feet, a move that Idaho historian F. Ross Peterson credited to Ira B. Perrine from Indiana, the orchestrater of land deals for the Twin Falls irrigation projects. Costing $1.1 million, Jackson was the fifth largest dam in the world. At that time few people thought about earthquakes, even though the dam lay in the seismic zone that threw up the Tetons and continued to do so. When geologic analysis seventy years later discovered the north embankment of the dam sitting on a 635-foot depth of sedimentary muck with the load-bearing strength of Jell-O, the dam was rebuilt one more time.

Together, the bureau's facilities on the upper river are called the Minidoka Project. Even though the water users fell $560,000 delinquent in accounts—a substantial debt in the 1920s—they lobbied aggressively for more federal construction, and in 1927 American Falls Dam formed the largest reservoir on the river. In the 1960s the Bureau of Reclamation discovered that the concrete had deteriorated because of a reaction between alkali in the cement and its aggregate. After dropping storage to 66 percent of capacity, a new dam was built in 1977.

The Minidoka Project includes Island Park Dam, 91 feet high on the Henry's Fork; Cross Cut Diversion Dam, 10 feet high on the same river; and Grassy Lake Dam, 118 feet high on Grassy Creek, perched in an otherwise wilderness between Yellowstone and Grand Teton parks. Additional bureau projects in the upper basin are Palisades Dam, 270 feet high; Ririe Dam, 253 feet high on Willow Creek; and Little Wood River Dam, 129 feet high near Carey (Ririe and Palisades are accounted with the Minidoka Project).

Bureau projects in the middle and lower basins are the Boise, Payette, Owyhee, Mann Creek, and Vale.

The Minidoka Project serves a 300-mile-long plain from Ashton to Bliss and can deliver up to 4.5 million acre feet a year by supplying full irrigation on 216,796 acres and supplemental water (added to preexisting supplies) on 947,696 acres. Minidoka director Max Van Den Berg called this the "largest project of the bureau nationwide in acreage of land served." In gross crop value, it is third, behind California's Central Valley and Imperial Valley projects.

For 19,000 farm "units" (many are not entire farms) receiving Minidoka water, the Bureau of Reclamation listed a gross crop value of $383 million, though much of the water was supplemental. The bureau stated that farmers raised $9 billion worth of crops from 1909 to 1987—thirty-six times the federal investment. Three million recreation days a year are spent at the reservoirs, two-thirds at Jackson, where the chief draw is Grand Teton National Park. Flatwater acreage on six reservoirs totals 100,000 acres. The Army Corps of Engineers reported that Minidoka Project flood control saved $237 million in flood damage between 1950 and 1987. The dams generate 900 million kilowatt-hours of electricity worth $2 million a year. The bureau claimed fish and wildlife "enhancement" as a project benefit: "The reservoirs are operated to regulate downstream flows for the maintenance and enhancement of river fisheries."

SWITCHING THE RIVER ON AND OFF

Operation of the labyrinth of dams, diversions, and power plants follows a fundamental irrigator's principle. "The way we operate the river," said Max Van Den Berg, "is that we keep the water as high in the system as we can, for as long as we can." Theoretically, Jackson Reservoir fills first; in actuality, it doesn't work that way because a lot of water enters the river through tributaries farther down. American Falls often fills first. In the irrigation season, all else being equal, water would be drawn out of Minidoka, then American Falls, Palisades, and finally Jackson, where Van Den Berg cited only four years involving major drawdowns of water in the reservoirs during the last thirty years since Palisades was built.

The Bureau of Reclamation releases large amounts of water throughout the irrigation season, which lasts 200 days from April to November; demands peak in late July or early August. During the nonirrigation season, water is held back in preparation for next year's crops.

A basic irrigator's principle is that you can never have too much water in storage. Each new dam allows for greater security against a dry year, and vast reductions in water application have led to even increased security (see Chapter 4). Yet there could always be a drought to exceed that of the 1930s or anything ever imagined. It's possible. "In 1988 we had had two years of drought and were scared silly," said farmer and legislator Reed Hansen from Idaho Falls. "If we had another year of drought, we would have lost production."

A difficult question here is how much security is the federal government obligated to provide at the expense of other public values? As Howard Funke inquired, "Should the river system be dominated by one user group for ninety-nine years to make sure there's no crop loss on the one hundredth year?"

In the management of the reservoirs, irrigation clearly takes priority. About 97 percent of the storage is allocated to this one use. As water master Ron Carlson said, "The first thing is to fill water rights under state law." Flood control is the next priority, then hydropower. Van Den Berg agreed, "The schedule to release water for irrigation is set entirely by the water master." Farmers initiate this process when they tell their ditch rider how much water they want. Irrigation officials notify the water master, who calculates amounts needed in the canals and tells the Bureau of Reclamation how much to release from the dams. Carlson, elected and paid by the irrigators, is also employed as the eastern regional manager of the Idaho Department of Water Resources. Working for the state and working for the irrigators is not regarded by the state as a conflict of interest.

Regarding the other end of the operations spectrum—floods—the Bureau of Reclamation releases water on a "rule curve" to maintain enough reservoir space to catch high water. John Keys, regional director of the bureau, said that the curve for the Snake River projects is "one of the most conservative anywhere." Some adjustment may be possible to accommodate other uses. Additional

needs are met when "feasible"; for example, water might be released for rafting below Jackson Dam. This water does not escape
the irrigation net; it is simply caught behind the next dam. "We try
to bring the water down in a manner that meets those other
needs," Van Den Berg said, "but irrigation definitely comes first."

WHO PAYS?

The Bureau of Reclamation has cited the benefits of the projects,
but what are the costs, financial and otherwise, and who pays? The
systems are not set up to be cost-accountable, partly because the
operations of federal dams and water supplies are complex, partly
because officials care little about the answers, and partly by design
by those who would rather have the inner workings of western
water remain obfuscated behind moats of rhetoric. Bureau officials,
for example, could not tell me how much irrigators pay the government for the storage that the irrigators reserve.

Nationwide, the bureau claims that 85 percent of the capital
costs of irrigation dams are returned to the treasury by direct beneficiaries through water repayment contracts and power sales. With
the righteousness of those who pay the bills, the irrigators demand
their water without interference. "The irrigators took the bull by
the horns and *built* those projects," said Reed Oldham of the Committee of Nine. "The irrigators paid in full for Henry's Lake [a private dam], Island Park, Grassy Lake, Jackson Lake, and American
Falls." In an often repeated argument, Governor Richard Lamm of
Colorado wrote in 1982, "The damming of the West was not an act
of federal charity, and westerners bristle at those who say it was.
The Reclamation Act of 1902 requires repayment of all construction and operation costs by those who benefit from the projects."[8]

The water is free. It is owned by the state. Irrigation districts pay
the federal government for the right to store the water in federal
reservoirs, which presumably covers the irrigators' share of construction and operation costs. Irrigators pay $1.50 per acre for Pali-
sades water, about 30 cents an acre foot, which is enough to supply
a family of five for a year. According to Jack Deakin, manager of
the Twin Falls Canal Company—the largest—irrigators pay the
federal government 12 cents per acre foot for storage in Jackson

Dam. In 1990, to cover their "share" of the $82 million that had already been spent for reconstruction of that dam, the irrigators' rates rose to 41 cents an acre foot—325,000 gallons for one-half the price of one gallon of bottled water at the local grocery store.

In the entire Northwest, the Bureau of Reclamation's operations and maintenance costs averaged $21.56 per acre served in 1986— fourteen times the amount that irrigators pay for Palisades sup- plies.[9] As direct beneficiaries, irrigators and electricity users are to pay only "reimbursable" costs. These exclude costs that can be as- signed to the taxpayers for flood control, recreation, and fish and wildlife.

Taking Palisades Dam as an example because it's the most recent project and should represent the most modern accounting, I found that nonreimbursable costs accounted for $31.8 million of the $76.5 million project,[10] which in all ways but cost accounting is considered an irrigators' project—built because of their political support and unabashedly operated at their behest.

So the taxpayers paid for the first 42 percent outright, and with only 58 percent to go, the Bureau of Reclamation determined that irrigators lacked the "ability to pay" their share. This meant that they were required to repay only $10.3 million. The other irrigation costs of $11.4 million were reassigned as hydroelectric costs. Ac- complishing further reductions, the bureau issued a revised state- ment in 1985 projecting total payments for irrigation and power portions of the project at $42.4 million, of which only $8.5 million was required from the irrigators. The bottom line, so far, is that irrigators will pay for only 11 percent of the project.

As a miscellaneous hidden subsidy to irrigators, the Army Corps of Engineers built 18 miles of levees below the dam to protect farmland with no reimbursement from the farmers. The taxpayer also bears annual maintenance costs of the levees—enormously destructive of river and riparian values.[11]

Furthermore, the Palisades reauthorization in 1950 included a reservation of 55,000 acre feet to exchange storage in nearby Grays Lake. This would help "replace" wildlife habitat lost at Palisades, but it never happened, and the bureau sold the storage space for other uses. As a result, there has been no mitigation of wildlife lost at Palisades where 2,570 riparian acres were inundated. These costs were not considered "costs," meaning they are borne by society.

Though the 11 percent figure is lower than the percentage normally claimed by the bureau and far below the 100 percent implied by the irrigators, it is not the bottom line. Nobody even knows where the bottom line is. For example, unlike municipal and industrial water users, irrigators pay no interest on government loans from the taxpayers. Anyone who has bought a home knows that even low interest payments exceed the principal. At a minimalist rate of 2.5 percent interest, conceivable in the 1950s, a $20 million share of the project would have required interest payments of $12 million over a forty-year period. The interest cost—60 percent of the capital in this very conservative scenario—was paid not by the irrigators but by the taxpayers. And likewise for every bureau project in the United States, including those that were financed when borrowing rates soared to 18 percent and more.

I do not report these figures to argue that Palisades should not have been built. Nor do I argue against subsidizing farmers in reasonable ways. My personal bias is that family farmers deserve help from the taxpayer more than logging conglomerates and more than a plethora of defense contractors. My point with this analysis is simply to clarify who paid for these projects that are now managed so one-sidedly for irrigators at devastating costs to ecosystems and to the future.

The economic figures constitute invisibly fine print when the irrigators say they paid for the dam and when the Bureau of Reclamation refused to yield as little as a few hundred cfs in winter to keep entire fisheries intact. As Bob Burks of the Idaho Water Users Association said, "If the fisheries people and environmentalists want minimum flows, let them build dams just as the farmers did."

The irrigators' view was further expressed by Reed Oldham. "They say we're subsidized because we don't pay interest. It's true, the projects are subsidized, but we subsidize housing in cities. To get the railroads built, we subsidized them. Part of my gasoline tax goes to build subways. Who *isn't* subsidized?"

Reed Hansen said, "The government built a subway in Washington, D.C., that cost more than the whole reclamation program. The farmers are paying back *their* projects. And farmers are taxpayers too."

Most agricultural spokesmen I talked to, from the Commissioner of Reclamation on down, compared their program with the Washington, D.C., subway—it shows up in their literature—but none of them knew how much irrigators in fact pay for Palisades Dam. Awareness ends with the rhetorical, "We paid for it."

For the entire Minidoka Project, the Bureau of Reclamation stated that 70 percent of the $206 million will be repaid by "direct beneficiaries," a vague term used as though synonymous with "irrigators." For Palisades, 80 percent of this share is paid by hydroelectric users, which is to say, by virtually everybody in the Northwest.

Critics of bureau accounting claim that too small a share of capital costs is credited to irrigation in the first place. Teton Dam is another example where the bureau assigned some costs to flatwater recreation though facilities exist nearby at Island Park, Palisades, Jackson, American Falls, and so forth, and even though an excellent recreation resource in the free-flowing river was destroyed without compensation.

As early as 1973 the National Water Commission disclosed that water users of some reclamation projects "repay no more than 10 percent of the construction costs attributable to irrigation, the remaining costs being borne by the federal government." A study by the bureau's own Department of the Interior reported that water from the Columbia River Project was subsidized 96.7 percent.[12]

Further discrepancies between fact and rhetoric come with the reconstruction of the dams. Of the four dams "paid off" by the irrigators, three have undergone reconstruction, not considered a "cost." In 1977, the rebuilding of American Falls, a dam that originally cost $3 million, required $51 million, $19 million of it paid by the Idaho Power Company in return for rights to hydropower.[13] The irrigators paid for a share of the new dam to avoid a reauthorization that would have forced the government to address the delinquent question of the Shoshone and Bannock's water rights. The bureau reconstructed Island Park Dam in 1985 and Jackson Dam in 1988. These dams have, in effect, been built not once, but twice.

Under a 1978 law, Congress required irrigators to pay nothing for safety improvements or reconstruction of bureau dams even if irrigators are sole beneficiaries. The rationale of this $100 million gift was that the safety of U.S. citizens was at stake below the dams and the irrigators were not to blame even though the dams existed for them. *The irrigators demand full control of operations of the reservoirs but accept no responsibility for safety.* The government funded 100 percent of Island Park's reconstruction. When a Committee of Nine representative told me, "We paid back the full cost of Island Park Dam over forty years," he spoke of some portion of the first Island Park Dam, which cost $0.6 million.[14] The second dam cost $6.2 million, is used for irrigation as predominantly as the first, and was funded completely by taxpayers. It is from this reconstructed project that biologist Ruth Gale pleaded with minimal success for small winter releases to keep rare swans alive.

When the $100 million for safety improvements was spent, getting more public money was no problem under the banner of "safety," a cause of crisis importance that ironically has been a boon to bureau reconstructions ever since the Teton Dam disaster in 1976. In 1984 Congress passed a $650 million appropriation, only 15 percent to be paid back by direct beneficiaries. Idaho irrigators paid for some portion of Jackson Dam, costing $1.1 million in 1916, and got taxpayers to fund 85 percent of the new dam costing $82 million, 75 times the amount that irrigators and the bureau boast as being "paid back." Additional multimillions will be paid by taxpayers as interest on the investments. Fully appropriated for irrigation, Jackson included no mitigation for wildlife habitat beneath the reservoir.

Even larger costs come when things go wrong. Teton Dam's construction was a result of lobbying by irrigators, who would have paid 83 cents per acre foot for storage, enough to sustain the illusion of payback only to the most casual observer.[15] The dam resulted in what was probably the most costly man-made flood in American history, with government relief totaling about $400 million. In a matter of hours, the accumulated gains of flood control by all the dams in the Minidoka Project from 1950 to 1987 were dwarfed by flood damage caused by Teton Dam. Restitution came from the taxpayers. As with the Island Park and Jackson Dam reconstructions, the irrigators' claim of proprietary ownership does not extend to these kinds of hard times.

The expense of Teton may be viewed as an isolated thing, but that's not true. The Bureau of Reclamation faces hopeless expenses to correct slower burning disasters such as polluted agricultural runoff in the Central Valley of California and salinization of the Colorado River. And the cases of Teton, Island Park, and Jackson raised questions of safety elsewhere. The Federal Emergency Management Agency coordinates federal efforts for dam safety, the Army Corps of Engineers inspects high hazard dams, and the states regulate nonfederal dams. Few of these costs are paid by direct beneficiaries. Of sixty dams that the Idaho Department of Water Resources investigated, 70 percent were unsafe. The situations were considered "nonemergency," all but one involving inadequate spillway capacities. Nationwide, the Army Corps of Engineers inspected 8,000 dams and found 3,000 to be unsafe, with hazards that are yet another hidden cost of the dams.[16]

Another inevitable but unaccounted cost comes with the silting of the reservoirs. The upper Snake River basin has some of the highest rates of erosion in the nation (see Chapter 4); the accumulation of mud is never-ending. A large part of the bureau's budget may someday be required to dredge fertile soil from drawn-down reservoirs and transport it to wastelands ruined by erosion.

SUBSIDIZED SUBSIDIES

Regarding only the more identifiable forms of subsidies, including interest, the Bureau of Reclamation calculated its 1986 subsidy to western irrigators at $534 million, about $54 per acre on 10 million acres and 150,300 farms (I've seen no calculations by anyone outside the bureau). From 1902 to 1986, an irrigation subsidy of $9.8 billion had been paid by the taxpayers, figured in 1986 dollars.[17]

The western irrigation system is perhaps our finest example of social welfare for a class of people who are not homeless, not jobless, and not handicapped. The bureau reported that, nationwide, 38 percent of the land it irrigated from 1976 to 1986 was used to grow crops receiving subsidies as surplus commodities, making taxpayers' concerns doubly appropriate. For 1981, the Soil Conservation Service showed that 45 percent of the acreage served by bureau water was used to grow "surplus crops," defined as crops for which farmers could receive government payments to curtail production. The government paid this money because supply exceeded demand; the farm economy was gagging on its own surpluses. In some years, such as 1988, the amount is less, but overall the situation hadn't changed much since 1969, when 37 percent of bureau-watered acreage qualified for price supports. Irrigation subsidies alone for the surplus crops alone came to $203 million a year. In contrast, water revenues paid to the bureau by farmers averaged $19 million a year for 1983 through 1985.

The government subsidizes water to irrigators at a rate often exceeding 90 percent, and 38 percent of this water nationwide goes to crops that the government pays farmers to not grow. It is for this economy that the Snake River is dammed, diverted, and subject to low flows. Everyone in our society is subsidized in one way or another, but few people are subsidized to produce a product while at the same time being subsidized to not produce it. The irrigation industry routinely unfurls the threadbare flag of essential crop production.

How much of the Snake River's storage goes to surplus crops that are already subsidized? Details provided by the Bureau of Reclamation's Washington office to California Congressman George Miller showed that 35 percent of the 1 million acres served by the Minidoka Project were used for crops qualifying as surplus. The figure climbed to 56 percent when alfalfa was counted. *Of the 3.7 million acre feet of Snake River water delivered by the bureau, 1.3 million acre feet went to water crops classified as surplus.* This is 2.2 times the storage available from Jackson Dam.

Congressman Miller sponsored legislation, not to reasonably ban federally funded water from crops the federal government pays farmers to not grow, but simply to charge irrigators the government's full cost of federal water used for those crops. Deputy Assistant Secretary of the Interior Wayne Marchant argued for the double subsidy and wrote, "The irrigation subsidy reported here is responsible for much of the current character of the western United States."[18]

Not only is the water subsidized to a high percentage and in repeated ways, but the land itself was a subsidy—hundreds of thousands of acres were given to farmers under the 1894 Carey Act and the 1877 Desert Lands Entry Act programs (nationwide, an estimated 95 percent of the Desert Lands Entry claims were fraudulent, though the figure is probably much lower for Idaho).[19] Energy, too, is subsidized by residential users through preferential rates to farmers and through hydropower's hidden costs such as the elimination of salmon. This beneficent triangle of subsidies—water, land, and power—has created the oasis in the desert of southern Idaho.

Reed Hansen said, "When people have plenty to eat, it's easy to moan about subsidies. Think about the alternative. Imagine a disaster similar to the Irish potato famine."

Reed Oldham said, "I think the federal government made a good deal. The income from agriculture comes back as taxes."

So does the income from agriculture in other regions, and the subsidies to western agriculture have put farmers elsewhere out of business, depleting their countrysides and communities. Most of the irrigation water in the West goes for cattle feed, grain, and fiber crops, all of which can be grown elsewhere. Throughout the West, Bureau of Reclamation records show that only 17 percent of its water goes to vegetables, fruits, and nuts in some western states where their climate—not including Idaho—offers a distinct advantage over other regions where farmers are also trying to earn a livelihood.[20] Researchers Charles Howe and William Easter, professors who had worked for Resources for the Future and the Bureau of the Budget, respectively, reported that "increased reclamation irrigation over the period 1944–64 has displaced 5 to 18 million acres of farmland in nonreclamation areas." In 1978, Thomas Power reported for the bureau, "Subsidized increases in supply can only be at the expense of farmers elsewhere and the taxpayer who supports farm incomes."[21]

Arvin Budge of the U.S. Department of Agriculture reported that when Ore–Ida closed a potato processing plant in Michigan, the company acquired a plant in Idaho. Agricultural census tables show that potato production from 1900 to 1988 increased from 0.7 to 100 million hundredweight in Idaho, 2 to 63 million in Washington, and 2 to 21 million in Colorado. Meanwhile, production fell from 22 to 6 million in New York, 18 to 9 million in Michigan, and 8 to 0.3 million in Iowa. All federally irrigated states growing potatoes showed dramatically higher production in 1988; all but three eastern and midwestern states showed drastically reduced production. "Irrigation is probably the biggest reason for the shift," Budge said.

The irrigators, of course, are not personally to blame for the woes of other farmers. It was federal policy to develop the West even if enormous subsidies were required. But the purpose of developing the West has been achieved. Facing growing criticism about the subsidies that fuel growth in booming western regions while draining tax dollars from the economically troubled Northeast and Midwest, the Bureau of Reclamation recognized the situation: "It is clear that the West can no longer be considered an undeveloped area."[22]

In some circles, much complaining is voiced about the West as a resource colony greedily consumed by the rest of the nation against the protests of westerners. But western insiders are the people who have not only benefited but carried the banner for extraction of resources and for the inordinate federal subsidies. This is true in regard to the four great traditional sources of wealth: irrigation, mining, logging, and grazing.

The gross value of the crops grown in the Minidoka Project since 1916 is thirty-nine times the expenditure for the dams, according to the Bureau of Reclamation. Any economist or taxpayer taking a hard look would increase the bureau's costs and consider net instead of gross value, but for now I'll accept the figure that excludes interest, excludes fish and wildlife losses, excludes replacement of unsafe dams and siltation, excludes relief from dam-caused disasters, excludes piggy-back subsidies for surplus crops, and excludes the unitemized ecological catastrophy. Assuming that the bureau's ratio is accurate, what better argument can be made for irrigators' paying more of their share of the costs and lightening the taxpayers' burden of this highly subsidized, regionally beneficial industry? The response to the continued subsidies is that "agreements were made." Even at the highest office of the bureau, Commissioner Robert Broadbent told me, "Someone's got to keep their word."

THE COST TO THE EARTH

Lands flooded by dams include hundreds of thousands of acres in the Snake River basin, 56,055 by American Falls Dam alone. Some was prime farmland not needing expensive irrigation systems. Much was "free" public land. Nearly all of it was outstanding wildlife habitat. Jackson Dam flooded what may have been the most magnificent meadow and cottonwood forest in the Rocky Mountains, home to elk, eagles, grizzly bear, and otter by the hundreds. Island Park flooded uplands and hot springs carbon-copied from Yellowstone. American Falls flooded the aquifer gardens of the Fort Hall Bottoms and a vital winter range for deer and swans. The Minidoka National Wildlife Refuge was established behind Minidoka Dam, but a riparian belt of wetlands, forests, and river channels was traded for a reservoir whose windswept waters lap eroding hillsides of sagebrush and block the path of wildlife.

The U.S. Fish and Wildlife Service estimated that 50,000 acres of riparian vegetation and 1,000 miles of Snake River shoreline were lost to reservoirs, not counting hundreds of islands and hundreds of sloughs that account for additional hundreds of miles. Reservoirs buried another 13,000 acres and 756 shoreline miles of tributaries. The largest riparian losses were 28,000 acres at American Falls and 12,750 at Jackson—one-third again the size of sprawling Boise. Over 70 percent of the Snake River's riparian habitat and wildlife values are gone because of dams and diversions—80 percent if grazing is counted. Mitigation varied from none at all to fish hatcheries built with Palisades Dam.[23]

Under the Northwest Power Act, agencies are writing "loss statements" about the predam ecosystem in order to plan for replacement of losses from Columbia basin hydropower. Using historical writings, photographs, interviews, and biological studies, scientists calculated enormous losses. The only species showing any recovery at five reservoirs in Montana was the osprey, but this was attributable to a ban on DDT. The first mitigation proposal for the Snake River was for Palisades. The dam had eliminated 38 miles of river habitat including 7,300 acres for big game, 2,550 for waterfowl breeding, 1,300 for Canada geese, 3,000 for grouse and upland game, and prime breeding and wintering grounds for bald eagles. Considerable losses for 260 species were noted. Mitigation would cost $16 million for the first ten years. This is yet another figure, absent in the tabulations of the costs of the dam but exceeding by about two times the amount irrigators will pay.

Aldo Leopold said that the first rule of intelligent tinkering is to keep all the parts, but along much of the Snake River the parts have been thrown away. How is an acre of land "replaced?" As

Will Rogers said, no one makes land anymore. If other habitat exists, it's already filled with wildlife.

Half of the Snake River is dammed, but it's a realist, not a pessimist, who sees a cup half empty. This is because many sections that are not dammed are depleted of water, with impacts on the ecosystem that I've seen below Palisades, Island Park, and Blackfoot. Bureau officials and irrigators say they are not obligated to *any* minimum flows below the dams. (A 1981 water right below Palisades and a 1986 right below Island Park specify minimum flows, but they are subordinate to earlier rights, which leave nothing in dry years.) "We could cut the flows to zero," Max Van Den Berg said, "but we'd never do that. The bureau is committed to not drying up that river."

At American Falls, 350 cfs is the informal minimum—a pittance where the river normally flows hundreds of yards wide. At Owyhee Dam, no minimum is released, though the Oregon Department of Fish and Wildlife has asked for one. Idaho Fish and Game desires additional flows below many dams, but the department's legal staff shunned the issue because most water rights are taken. It is not only fish, but also hydropower, municipal discharge, recreation, wildlife, tourism—nearly all uses except irrigation—that benefit from water being left in the river. John Keys, regional director of the bureau, said, "Instream flow is the most critical issue we'll have to face in the 1990s." The problem is greater than that of the bureau and involves the intricacies of water rights and appropriation (see Chapter 4).

Irrigation spokesmen argue that fish and wildlife have benefited from the projects. They refer to a predammed Snake River that "dried up in its channel in the summer." But nobody remembers the river that predated Jackson Dam. Geological Survey records begin in 1903 at Moran, below the dam where the lowest flow was 0.3 cfs in 1969. At Heise, gauged since 1910, the minimum flow was 460 in 1956. Below American Falls, levels have been measured since 1906, and the 50 cfs minimum occurred in 1941, 1961, and 1970, well after the dams were built. Below Minidoka Dam, the 1895 gauge's minimum was 37 cfs in 1962. At King Hill, flows have been monitored since 1909 and bottomed out at 1,250 in 1950. At Weiser, the minimum since 1910 was 4,570, not before dams but after all of them were built, in 1977.

With irrigation, an undammed river would certainly be dry by late summer, but what of the Snake before irrigation? Look at the Salmon River, the longest tributary. It has no reservoirs but flows year-round with an excellent fishery. Irrigators divert far less water from the Salmon, so it lacks the baked riverbed of the summertime Snake at Blackfoot and Milner. Damless, the Salmon is also spared the Snake's anemic winter flows below Jackson, Palisades, and American Falls.

"We claim we haven't destroyed that resource," Reed Oldham of the Committee of Nine maintained. "The Snake River runs at 2,000 second feet below Palisades in September, and half of that flow is from storage." High flows for three months in late summer and early fall indeed result from the dams, but for six months in winter, flows are decreased. Furthermore, the late-summer blessing below Palisades lasts only until the Great Feeder. Below there, flows are depressed in winter, spring, summer, and fall.

"Those people," Oldham continued, "will get further if they recognize what they're getting from us, such as the fisheries in the reservoirs." He referred to the trophy trout of Henry's Lake, a body of water that has existed since the ice ages and was raised 16 feet by seven canal companies. The old glacial lake had been "teeming with waterfowl and fish," according to historian Richard Bartlett.[24] "The mistake we made," Oldham added, "was we didn't throw a fence around that lake. By using it, the public now has a right to fish there, but we have no quarrel with that." Jackson Reservoir has likewise been noted for its fishery, though it buried a natural lake filled with abundant life.

Oldham said, "We gave a lot of money for the study of swans and eagles below the dams." I was impressed that the Committee of Nine would do this, but then I found that the money was from the Bureau of Reclamation's general appropriations from Congress. Everybody knows that the irrigators and the bureau have operated in concert since the bureau was born, but the quality of this bond took me by surprise. A Committee of Nine representative simply referred to the Bureau of Reclamation as "we."

Nobody knows the full effects and costs of the Snake River dams. The predammed river is forgotten, like salmon running to Shoshone Falls. If we knew about the unregulated flow, biologists could begin to reconstruct a vision of what has been lost and per-

haps a realistic view of what could be regained. Though groundwater presents different variables, a hydrologist with a couple of
college courses can plot historic streamflow, yet I could locate no
one who has done it. What are the effects of the dams, flood reductions, flow depletions, and silt elimination on downstream cottonwoods? On riffle and pool sequence? On groundwater? No one has
studied these things along the Snake River. No one knows how
much farming is done with upstream irrigators' wastewater. Information is lacking for conjunctive management that integrates surface and groundwater users. The Swan Falls Technical Advisory
Committee published a twenty-five-page list of needed information regarding the Snake River.

The Bureau of Reclamation has authored 108 major documents
about the river, mostly reports on development projects. Yet bureau officials don't know what the total cost of Snake River development has been, and they have no idea of the costs incurred to
fish, wildlife, and the ecosystem. Congressman Miller asked the
bureau how much the water that was used on already subsidized
crops was worth in alternate uses. The bureau responded that it
didn't have the answer.

"We pay for our projects, we need the water, the nation needs
the food." Like a compass needle returning to north, the bureau
and the irrigation establishment have been saying those things for
so long that they—and most other people—believe them. For
years, critics have voiced concerns that the bureau and the Army
Corps do not monitor their developments. The agencies' occupa-
tional bias is not to look back when they could be building something. Likewise, the Geological Survey collects facts but shuns
political issues like the plague.

"There are so many interesting problems, but few people are
asking the questions," said Luna Leopold, who for years was the
director of Geological Survey research nationwide. "The management agencies show little concern for the long term or for the
effects of their works, whether it be damming, diverting, or clearcutting. The greatest problem is a lack of intellectual and scientific
curiosity." Grand Teton biologist Pete Hayden said, "I don't even
do biological studies anymore. Biologists have become paper-
pushing bureaucrats."

The Fish and Wildlife Service does important studies but is

lightly staffed and is criticized by state and agricultural interests. For that matter, any water reform by any federal agency in Idaho or Wyoming is undertaken as a suicidal endeavor and with full knowledge of the "fed-bashing" that emanates from individuals including three of the four U.S. senators in 1988.

At the state level, the Water Resource Board has had the limited curiosity one might expect from a policy body heavily weighted with agricultural interests, though this is changing. The Department of Health and Welfare—responsible for water quality—has discovered ominous problems and the potential for pollution that could change the face of Idaho, but the agency was hamstrung by budget limits and by threats of further cuts from the legislature. The three Idaho universities employ competent scientists, and other professionals have undertaken research projects, but in all areas potentially critical of the status quo in irrigation and reservoir management, the gaps of information are big enough to drive a cattle truck through. One agricultural scientist sadly admitted to me, "There's a lot we simply can't say. We need to work with the farmers, and if they perceive us as trying to prove they waste water, we won't get anywhere with them."

Elsewhere in the nation, conservation groups leverage investigations and goad publicly employed scientists into doing their jobs. But in Idaho the groups are small, poorly funded, and understandably preoccupied by wilderness issues at the headwaters of Snake River tributaries. A few private organizations, such as the Northern Rockies Conservation Cooperative, do research, but the complexity of the Snake River eludes and intimidates scientists and funding organizations alike.

Capable journalists work in Idaho, including Pat Ford of *High Country News*, Bill Loftus of the *Lewiston Tribune*, Stephen Stuebner of the *Idaho Statesman*, Rocky Barker of the *Idaho Falls Post–Register*, and Neils Nokkentved of the Twin Falls *Times–News*. Ken Robison won a Scripps-Howard Foundation award for natural resource writing before moving on to politics. But good journalism does not take the place of good science.

The greatest possibility for new information resulted from the Swan Falls agreement amendments (see Chapter 7). The Shoshone and Bannock tribes support scientific analysis, stating that adaptive

management "recognizes the dual role of information as a basis for
and product of action."

THE SNAKE RIVER AND THE REST OF THE WEST

The dams on the Snake River are big but are not the icons of giant-
ism built elsewhere. The reservoir behind the Colorado River's
Glen Canyon Dam, for example, is 186 miles long. Nor did the
Bureau of Reclamation's projects on the Snake attract the controversies of other rivers. New Melones Dam on the Stanislaus in California was the most intensely fought dam in America, but in 1982
the bureau flooded the most popular whitewater in the far West
and its deepest limestone canyon. Echo Park in the 1950s was one
of the earlier dam fights when conservationists prevented flooding of the Green River in Dinosaur National Monument. Some
people regard the bureau's alternative—Glen Canyon Dam—as
the West's most tragic loss of a wild river and canyon.

A few dams proposed by irrigators or by the Army Corps of Engineers on Snake River tributaries were opposed, such as on the
Bechler River and at Penny Cliffs on the Clearwater, but the bureau's dams on the main stem predated conservationists. If proposed today instead of 1910, Jackson Dam would surely not be
built at the base of the Tetons. Palisades might not be built, but no
one cared in 1950. The bureau's only contested project in the basin
was Teton Dam. The American Rivers Council clairvoyantly listed
it as one of twelve "disasters" in water development during appropriations fights in the early 1970s. The environmental impact report was fourteen pages long. Trout Unlimited sued, and geologists
warned of a rupture, yet the Idaho delegation wavered not at all in
support of the dam. Ironically, Teton Dam may have contributed
more to changes in the bureau and western water development
than any other recent project. "No single event in history changed
the bureau so quickly and dramatically," said John Keys. Overnight the agency gave priority to concerns for safety that had pre-
viously been muzzled.

Coming at the apex of river conservation efforts that stopped
other destructive projects, the Teton failure was a sixteenpenny
nail in the coffin of big water development. Dams had already

blocked every major river in the West but the Salmon. In the Columbia River basin, the federal government had built over 100
large water projects,[25] and people began to say, enough is enough.
The times had changed because of people's consciousness of river
values, tight money, and political reform that cracked the formerly
ironclad fortress of congressional pork barrel, seniority, and logroll-
ing that delivered dams and canals long after their construction
made economic sense. By the late 1970s, a practice of backroom
deals succumbed to an awareness that the nation was wasting bar-
rels of money on select groups of water recipients while destroying
irreplaceable resources. Teton was symbolic—the physical destruction of a dam at a time when large dams were being politically and
economically destroyed.

Eastern congressmembers, traditionally uninvolved in western
water, joined committees dealing with reclamation and represented
the taxpayers at large. Even a few western politicians led in the
frays against developments such as the Central Valley Project
in California, which taxed the temper and the humor of the
well-informed in Congress. As Secretary of the Interior during the
Carter administration Cecil Andrus said, "We are coming to the
end of the dam-building era in America." Speaking in 1982 of cuts
in funds to western water projects, New York Senator Daniel Moy-
nihan announced, "The Great Barbeque is over." Overseeing the
bureau, Chair George Miller of the Water and Power Subcommit-
tee said that he wouldn't trust the Bureau of Reclamation to "build
a doghouse." From 1976 to 1986 no new water projects were approved by Congress.

The turning point could have been Teton Dam, or President
Carter's "hit list" of wasteful water projects in 1977, or the Water
Resource Council's "Principals and Standards" recommending reforms in 1973, or the National Environmental Policy Act in 1969.
The pro-river, antidam attitude was more prevalent in other states
but grew in Idaho because large sections of rivers remain as natural
waterways or are salvageable, the amount of water used for irrigation per acre radically exceeds the norm worldwide, and the fisheries sacrificed for that excess are legendary.

With the demise of the dam-it-if-you-can approach, a new wave
of concerns is surfacing. The current issues on the Snake River and
throughout the West are those of healthy streamflows below dams,

management of fish and wildlife, protection of riparian habitat, recreation for an increasingly urban population and tourist economy, and agricultural reform for efficient use of water. Because the Snake River remains water-rich compared with the Colorado, Rio Grande, Arkansas, Platte, Missouri, and rivers in the Sierra and Southern California, it offers an opportunity for solutions; it also offers the possibility of a better way to manage the water and land of the West. It remains to be seen if the transitions can be made from old ways to new ways, but recent steps by the bureau offer hopeful clues.

THE NEW BUREAU

The Bureau of Reclamation's slogan had been "total use for greater wealth," but in 1975 the agency reported that new planning centered around "total water management, augmentation of water supplies, energy resource development, conservation and reuse of water, environmental quality improvement, water quality improvement, and development of Indian resources."[26]

At the bureau's Boise office, Bob Riley explained: "The bureau built irrigation projects to settle and develop this land. When the population increased, hydroelectricity was added as a purpose, then flood control. Only after urban growth in the 1960s have we seen interest in the river for recreation and amenity values. There was always an interest in fishing, but now that interest says, 'The Snake River is a resource for multiple use.' The river has become nationally important for fishing and rafting."

In 1988, after eighty-five years as a construction agency damming rivers and irrigating deserts, the Bureau of Reclamation announced that it had essentially accomplished those missions. It claimed victory and declared that the war was over. It embraced a new mission of making dams and water projects efficient and responsive to concerns broader than irrigation. The bureau reduced its staff, abandoned construction plans that were defunct anyway, and reported greater emphasis on "recreational and environmental concerns."

Westerners accepted reforms under the Reagan administration that they had bemoaned under President Carter. Perhaps that was because Jimmy Carter had to break the ice in the first serious challenge to a system of federal subsidies or perhaps because economic liabilities were undeniable in the 1980s. But more likely it was because westerners found Reagan appealing on horseback, even in California, while Carter had been seen as the loathed easterner. He of course "didn't understand" the West when he cut a tiny slice of the federal dollar drain to projects such as Fruitland Mesa in Colorado that would have served 100 ranchers at a cost of $1 million each.[27] Former Interior Secretary Cecil Andrus said, "Through those battles, people began to understand that there are other uses of rivers." Many individual farmers now support a broadened view of river management. They fish, hunt, and live with an ecosystem they would sooner see alive than dead, especially if it doesn't cost them anything. But the irrigation establishment viewed changes with skepticism. Reform is a liberal notion that will pass with the realization that the irrigators, after all, "own" the water. "We'll protect the facilities for the purposes for which they were built," said Sherl Chapman, executive director of the Idaho Water Users Association.

Conservation organizations applauded the new bureau policy but with caution. Good intentions did not prevent the bureau from cutting Palisades releases to 750 cfs and decimating fisheries again in 1989. Wanting results, not rhetoric, Trout Unlimited sued the bureau, lost under a local judge, and appealed to the federal district court in San Francisco. The bureau had resisted the Committee of Nine's vote to reduce Palisades releases to 550 cfs. "Some Committee of Nine members wanted us to go to zero," recalled the bureau's John Keys. Swans also died in 1989 with low flows in the Henry's Fork, but the bureau was credited with working hard to resolve that problem and helped to convince the irrigators to give up some water.

An acid test of the new bureau was the renewal of forty-year water contracts for the San Joaquin River in California. Much like Snake River dams, Friant Dam and its diversions had nearly dried up the riverbed, terminated salmon runs, eliminated riparian habitat, and polluted residual water into what a U.S. wildlife official called "the lower colon of California." The Natural Resources Defense Council (NRDC) saw the case as a precedent and argued that the bureau must prepare an environmental impact report on the contracts. The Environmental Protection Agency and the Fish and Wildlife Service concurred. The bureau responded that consideration was not needed because the contracts "do nothing more than retain the status quo."[28] Even though the law provides for new terms, the solicitor stated that the bureau had no discretion to negotiate a better deal for the United States. Karen Garrison of the NRDC likened the opinion to that of accepting a leaking toxic waste dump forever simply because it had been leaking for a number of years. "Other government contractors don't assume they'll have unchanged business in perpetuity just because they struck up a good deal at one time," she added. In 1989 the NRDC sued the bureau.

The "repayment" contracts on the Snake River give irrigators an "entitlement" to storage space and are somewhat different from the "water use" contracts on the San Joaquin and have not yet been challenged.

Some hardened resource professionals maintain that the bureau is only beginning to do what laws require it to do for fish, wildlife, and the environment, and that it will respond only as long as public pressure demands. A federal biologist said, "The bureau doesn't make a move without checking with the Committee of Nine. It's better in recent years, but as a federal agency, the bureau has public trust responsibilities for fish and wildlife that they've not paid much attention to."

The Bureau of Reclamation, in fact, *has* to reform. It has environmental responsibilities under the Fish and Wildlife Coordination Acts of 1934, 1946, and 1958, the National Environmental Policy Act of 1969, the Endangered Species Act of 1973, the Reclamation Reform Act of 1982, various clean water acts, and the Water Resources Development Act of 1986. If the bureau doesn't reform, lawsuits at every dam are about as likely as winter in Jackson Hole. "Slowly, the bureau is changing, not unlike the Forest Service's response to challenges over the last ten years," said Scott Reed, who pioneered reforms on the Idaho Water Resource Board.

"To make changes," John Keys said, "you take the first step, which Idaho has done in drafting a water plan. Through a new adjudication of water rights, they'll determine how much water is needed. Through an optimization study, we'll determine how much water is available. Then we can develop projects." Will water conservation studies be done? "Yes, absolutely."

Keys, himself, illustrates a change. He rows a raft and kayaks Class IV water. He speaks not with the slur of the western-born, but with the drawl of his native Alabama. A hydrologist and engineer, he worked on the politically polarized Central Utah Project, then the Garrison Diversion, lambasted with American and Canadian criticism and finally scaled back from 250,000 to 130,000 acres. A capable bureaucrat, he has adopted a reformist attitude without abandoning development. "Things *have* changed, but I still think Teton Dam could be rebuilt if the storage is needed." Yet he did not disagree with my hunch that the new appraisal of Teton wouldn't have a chance of economic justification. "Officially, I understand the irrigators' view, but part of my job is to provide instream flows. We're going to *solve* those problems below Palisades and Island Park. We have every intention of avoiding future losses of fish and swans. You'll find that all the regional directors have a new view now, a willingness to do things differently."

OPTIMIZATION

Good evidence of the broader view, responsive to the times, the public, and the law, is the Bureau of Reclamation's "optimization study." Max Van Den Berg said, "We feel there are a lot of nonirrigation benefits we can enhance without taking away from individuals who've paid for the projects." Bob Riley explained,

> We're looking at improving flow conditions in the streams, improving riparian systems, and providing water for the Indian tribes. We're looking at our 4.5 million acre feet of storage in the upper basin and asking, what are our obligations and what are the unallocated supplies? What part of the demand has been reduced in the last twenty years? There's a real need for hydroelectric power, irrigation, anadromous fish, and other uses. What's the marketplace for that water? Once we know, then willing buyers and sellers can get together.

Contrary to wishes of the Indians and fish and wildlife advocates, the study will not consider reintegration of this broken river by allowing water to pass Milner Dam. As the irrigators have chiseled in stone everywhere they go, the optimization outline repeats, "The established Snake River minimum flow at Milner Dam is zero cfs."

This study of the upper Snake was preceded by efforts on the Boise River, where the bureau modified hydropower releases at Anderson Ranch Dam to enhance trout. With goals similar to those in the optimization study, the bureau found that joint management of three reservoirs on Wyoming's North Platte River can reduce water shortages by 30 percent.[29]

Riley cautioned,

The optimization study is not the Snake River panacea study. When it's done, we might see what single irrigation districts can do. The bureau's only real latitude is with the uncontracted space in the reservoirs. We're looking at more than that, but we're not trying to manage everybody's water. We'll go out with new information and try for creative financing studies. Many interests are involved. We'll take a facilitator role in providing information and bringing those interests together. If the community in southern Idaho can be brought along with persuasion and understanding, something will happen. It's taken 100 years to get the water system for the upper Snake River to where it is now. It'll take another few decades to change that system, if in fact it ought to be changed.

The Snake River right now presents an opportunity to do something different from the past. People who enjoy the river have the opportunity to influence that. It's going to be their challenge to work out solutions with agencies that have the responsibilities for management. It will require a willingness to negotiate.

BUILDING AND REBUILDING

A cement-mixer's fantasy of new dams on the Snake River has been proposed over the years. Among them, the Bureau of Reclamation and other agencies have prepared a dozen schemes since 1963 to transfer water to the Southwest and California. One plan would divert 2.4 million acre feet from the Snake River near Twin Falls. Los Angeles County called for studies of Columbia River basin diversions in the 1960s. (Southern California houses eighteen times the population of Idaho, thirty-seven times that of Wyoming.) Averting water export had been a reason to form the Idaho Water Resource Board in the 1960s, and with a fear that seems to be a birthright, the board in 1976 forecast, "Idaho will see renewed efforts to divert Snake River water."[30] In the 1960s, however, California and the bureau had decided that the Eel and Klamath in California were the rivers of choice to be sent south—a decision that would be political and economic suicide today. To grasp now at the Columbia or Snake is even less likely. In 1986 Congress required agreement from the governors of all the affected states before any interbasin transfers can be studied. Wyoming had once plotted diversions southward to irrigate in the Green River basin and on the east slope of the Rockies, but under a compact agreement, Idaho must approve of diversions outside the basin.

No one promotes interbasin transfers now, and if they ever do resurface to supply a parched Southwest, a lavish overapplication on surplus crops in Idaho may be a poor defense. It's more likely that the spectre of transfer would be averted by the reservation of Idaho water for uses beneficial to the public at large and to national resources such as the salmon and steelhead.

In 1976 the Idaho Department of Water Resources had cited additional "major undeveloped storage" sites at Clear Lakes and Thousand Springs on the middle Snake River. The state had harbored illusions of building its own irrigation projects, and below Swan Falls, the Grindstone Butte, Sailor Creek, and Guffey Dam proposals were considered serious schemes.

The bureau had inventoried many dam sites in 1961, though Teton Dam lingers as the only active proposal. John Keys said, "We'd only need to build the embankment. It would certainly be a concrete structure, not earth-filled." The bureau director is astutely aware that concrete is a time-honored confidence builder to people living in the shadow of dams. This solution to Teton's muddy demise, however, overlooks the most poignant warnings of the U.S. Geological Survey—not that the dam would metamorphose to mush from the inside out, as it did, but that a strong earthquake could crack a concrete dam. The site is in the highest seismic risk zone identified by the Geological Survey.

Earl Corliss of the bureau said, "Though the original dam washed away, its purposes did not. The next time mother nature floods Rexburg, we'll see interest in Teton Dam." With bulldog tenacity, Fremont–Madison Irrigation District directors visit the bureau and state politicians every year with the message that the federal government has a "moral" responsibility to rebuild the dam (that district already receives all of the water from Island Park Dam). Support for Teton and other new dams has retreated from arguments that once stressed the practical imperatives, then the economic, then the political, and now the "moral."

With a Pavlovian response whenever it doesn't rain for a while, the Idaho House of Representatives in 1989 supported Teton Dam construction by a 69 to 3 vote. One legislator who voted for the resolution scoffed at it as "meaningless" and explained, "That dam's too expensive. No one would ever buy the water. We were in a drought and some legislators wanted to say something." At Idaho Senator James McClure's request, however, the bureau will spend $150,000 sifting through the files to see if the dam can be justified.

Keys reflected: "Idaho has a development mentality. I don't think that's bad. They wisely use their water with a development mentality. But I'll tell you, things *have* changed. The bureau at one time wanted to build Lynn Crandall. One of our men in the Burley office said, 'Come on up here, I want to show you something.' He took me down the river in a driftboat. Since then I publicly said, 'We don't want to build Lynn Crandall.' We would do it only if it were the sole alternative to meet real needs, and if the people of Idaho wanted it."

In a flagrant case of the state and irrigators as bedfellows, Committee of Nine chair Lester Saunders in 1979 signed a letter on stationery of the "State of Idaho Department of Water Resources, Water District No. 1, Idaho Falls" expressing the Committee of Nine's support for Lynn Crandall construction.[31] But the irrigators are starkly isolated. The House's resolution to rebuild Teton Dam had begun as a move by a Twin Falls legislator to build Lynn Crandall. Eastern Idaho representatives squelched the idea as explosively unpopular on their own turf, which indicates that attitudes are changing in Idaho and that many people with those attitudes will ultimately direct the activities of the bureau and temper the power of the irrigation industry.

About new dams, Reed Hansen said, "I believe that most people feel what we've done to the Snake River is good, but that we've done enough. Let's not diminish it any more." Farmer, legislator, and former Water Board chair, Hansen added, "Those who want more development are in a distinct minority."

Basinwide, the most realistic proposal is the Galloway Dam on the Weiser River northwest of Boise, studied by the Army Corps and the state for flood control and improved flows for salmon, though political pressure has mounted to use the dam for opening new irrigated land. It's a sign of the times that fish—regarded as largely worthless in the development and management of water projects until recently—are suddenly worth millions as justification for a new dam.

Upriver in Wyoming, politicians trip over one another in support of new dams, though none of the proposals lies in the Snake River basin. Supporting a dam, Richard Cheney of Wyoming voted with only fifteen other congressmen opposing the Endangered Species Act: "The act has been used to interfere with development in Wyoming." In 1989 Cheney became Secretary of Defense in charge of the Army Corps. Wyoming Senator Malcolm Wallop complained that western water development is impeded by a "funny and comfortable new camp developing in the east about water."[32]

Change may be occurring within the bureau, but how deep is the agency's commitment to reform? Under President Eisenhower, the bureau fell out of favor under the familiar ideology of "privatization." A few years later, new projects returned with a vengeance. Top managers now expound a philosophy of management, not construction, but is the rest of the organization changing? Earl Corliss of the bureau in Burley said, "Some people in the bureau think that everything's done. It reminds me of when they closed the patent office in the 1800s because everything was invented." Keys admitted, "The current shift away from construction is not permanent. We're going to build more projects, but all concerns will be addressed, concerns that were honestly not addressed in the old days."

During my discussion with Keys about Teton Dam, it occurred to me that 1988 was one of the driest years on record, following the dry year of 1987, but Minidoka Project deliveries ran with minimal cutbacks, even in spite of the fact that the bureau had drastically lowered the level of Jackson Reservoir for reconstruction. Likewise, for more than a decade, the bureau had drained either American Falls, Island Park, or Jackson reservoirs to low levels in order to do repairs. If new storage is needed, why was the decommissioning of those large dams even in the driest years felt no more than a fly on the back of irrigation?

Now that I've looked at the projects that make irrigation of the Snake River plain possible, what about irrigation itself? How is the water used? How much is needed? What really happens when water from the Snake River is diverted into canals and ditches?

4

Irrigation, Part I

A LIVELIHOOD

His grandfather raised potatoes, his father raised potatoes, and now Ken Mulberry raises potatoes. And other crops. "We have 400 acres here and 330 down the river. About half are in grains—red wheat for milling, barley, and other cow feed. Then there's the feedlot with 2,000 head of cattle, and the potato packing plant. We ship out a million bags a year to eastern markets." Each bag weighs 100 pounds.

Mulberry stood about six feet tall, strong in build, fair-haired under his ball cap, friendly and ready to share information. His farm lay just above the rim of the Snake River canyon near Twin Falls. Jenny Mulberry tended to five children, all blonde. "Another on the way," she said as she poured a row of orange juices. "Would you like a glass?"

"The family roots are up in the Idaho Falls area," Ken said. "It's colder up there, and the farming economy is depressed. It was time to make a move. Dad and I financed this operation, and it blossomed real fast." What I saw struck me as something that has gone beyond good farming and entered the early realms of agricultural empire. Ken Mulberry came here only seven years ago, when he was twenty-six.

"Let me show you the farm. I have some time now. I got some sleep last night." He slept nine hours for the last three nights, altogether. "We'll stay busy the rest of the season."

We left the wood-sided ranch house, crossed the dirt yard where landscaping was in process, stepped into the pickup, and rode down a lane to a ditch. "This is out of the Twin Falls Main Canal. Our water rights were established when the canal system was built in 1910. On a dry year, if anyone has to cut back, they cut out the users with the junior water rights. Down here, you hardly ever have to worry about managing your water. I watch it real close anyway, but you don't have to." We walked toward the ditch. "The live water is over there," Ken said, pointing to another ditch.

"Live?"

"Yes—clean water out of the canal. This ditch right here is a wastewater ditch. Anybody can take it, it's free."

For live water, farmers pay $14 a share, one share traditionally being enough to water an acre. "A share's really five-eighths of an inch, but they deliver more than that. They deliver about three-fourths of an inch as a constant flow." (Unlike a normal inch, a miner's inch is a measure of flow; 50 of them equal 1 cfs.) This much-removed channel of the Snake River was about 2 feet wide at the top, a foot or so deep, and carried about 50 miner's inches or 2 acre feet per day.

If the farmer pumps groundwater, it often costs less. "Pumping costs $20 an acre out of the ditches, plus canal charges, but if you have a well 200 feet deep, it costs about $25. That's cheaper than canal water. The cost of water and power are not a big factor in the operation. Over here we have a filter system." A mesh screen collected stubble and solids from someone else's wastewater. "We don't need to tap into the live water here at all, not now.

"Water quality is a big concern," Ken said as he kicked refuse from the screen. "Silty water is harder to use. It carries trash and stubble. It plugs up the sprinkler systems, damages the pumps, and enlarges the nozzles. Even the live water is silty by the time it gets down here. You can't afford to line these sod ditches, so the water picks up silt, and worse, we lose 3 to 4 inches of water to seepage for each mile of ditch. There's so much dirt in the water that we sprinkle 30 cubic yards of silt a day on a 13-acre field. You can see it on the plants when the water dries."

The problems of silty water cost money, but the main cost accrues at the front end of the siltation process. "The land erosion is terrible. Some fields, you'll notice, are kind of white at the top. It's hardpan—the topsoil washes off and leaves minerals. White soils produce hardly anything. A lot of fields won't grow 50 percent of what they did. Excess lime is the main problem." We drove up the road. "This farmer's one of the best farmers in the county. You can't see any color change on his fields. See, no white at the top."

Ken pulled over and we walked onto a whitish field he has just begun to farm, a part of Mulberry's chronic expansion program. "Look at this." He crumbled a handful of soil. "Crusted. We'll haul manure up here from the feedlot. With sprinklers, we can avoid this problem altogether because sprinklers save soil. We also cut back on erosion by using a chisel plow and ripper instead of the old moldboard plow. The new method leaves the fiber in the top 4 inches—it leaves the soil profile the same instead of turning it upside down. I'll tell you, farmers today are changing the whole way we do things."

We stopped at an overhead sprinkler—a pipe mounted on wheels powered by a motor. Water sprays downward as the pipe progresses slowly across the field. Evaporation consumes less water than in the old lines that sprayed the water upward. "By going to sprinklers and larger fields, we use one-third the water we used in furrow irrigation."

Furrows are just that—small ditches between rows of crops. From the supply ditch at the top of the field, the irrigator siphons water through short hoses and runs it down the furrows. The water washes topsoil to the bottom of the field, leaving whitish soil at the uphill end.

"Sprinklers save water, but the main advantage to us is the soil savings. Sprinklers wash almost no soil from the fields. Your crops do a lot better by getting the right amount of water. Production goes up. The use of fertilizer goes down because you're not flushing it off with all that excess water. That saves money. Having a tighter system pays all the way around. You save on labor, and we spend 50 percent of our man-hours on irrigation. It might not sound like a difficult job, but if you have unskilled labor setting siphon tubes for furrows and they run too much water, you can erode a furrow 6 inches too deep, right away. I went through sixty white kids before I got four Mexicans to do the job. You can't sprinkle without them.

"There are a lot of things you can do to save water if you try. See these hand lines? If you set five rows together, you have less evaporation than by allowing the wind to blow through single lines." Some crops, such as beans, do better with furrow irrigation. "We're improving on that, too. Let me show you this system my neighbor has."

Ken drove to the top of a furrowed field. "There are new things coming out of the research center at Kimberly, like this gated pipe." At the top of the field, perpendicular to the rows of crops, I didn't see a leaking, open, muddy ditch, but a large plastic pipe. At regular intervals, holes had been cut one-inch square. A roped device traveled down the inside of the pipe and opened and closed the holes—miniheadgates—to allow a precise amount of water to leave the pipe and flow down the furrow. "It saves soil, saves water, saves labor, and makes the field look nice. It's efficient." Wastewater that might flow to the bottom corner of the field was pumped back to the top. "That also carries the suspended soil back to the top, right where it ought to be.

"These guys have enough water rights to irrigate constantly, but that doesn't make sense. If you save water, you save soil and have efficient production." Ken looked at me and shrugged his shoulders, as if his statement was obvious to everyone.

"I think farmers are more open-minded now, and once you're open-minded you start asking questions. People used to tell us things were safe, like chemicals. Farmers doubt that now. I've gotten sick from chemicals. I think chemicals are in their prime now, and we'll see less of them in the future. They're developing biological controls, and I wish they could develop them faster.

"I used to say, 'Damn the conservationists,' but now I see the need to compromise. If we're going to have an organized society, we need some power plants and some irrigation, but some land should never have been put into production. Now they have this CRP program [Conservation Reserve Program]. I call it CPR [cardiopulmonary resuscitation]. It's giving farmers who are going out of business a chance to start something else."

"Isn't that just another subsidy?"

"Yes. I'd like to see an end to the subsidies; let the most efficient farmers win." Ken drove back toward the house.

"You're interested in the river, so I'll tell you, farmers are using less water, and marginal land is going out of production, so there's going to be more water in the river. Yet you won't see farmers giving up their water rights. That'd be like taking away their guns." Mulberry laughed. "You take away water rights and they'll go *get* their guns. Water rights were the basis of the settlement of this country. Even if farmers aren't using their water, they want to keep their rights so they won't go short in a dry year. That doesn't mean that agriculture and the river can't coexist. We definitely need minimum flows for fish. I hate to see the rivers get stagnant."

Ken Mulberry's tour introduced me to irrigation on the Snake River plain. He applied new solutions to old problems and personified the blending of the new and the old in the agriculture of the West.

US AND THEM

The cover of the Bureau of Reclamation's brochure, *How Water Won the West*, shows a weatherworn man and woman standing in the desert near Caldwell, not far from the Snake River. From their grim fundament the couple looks at a sign, "Desert Ranch, Have Faith in God and U.S. Reclamation." Faith, God, and the bureau strike to the core of attitudes about irrigation and the western land.

Attitudes still reflect the original fervor: to settle the West and to expand human and economic opportunities. Much of the settlement on the upper Snake River plain was by Mormon farmers, possessive of their land, having been so rudely dispossessed elsewhere. They prided themselves on conquering an area too hostile for others. To follow God meant to settle this land, to settle meant to farm, to farm meant to irrigate, to irrigate meant to dam and divert the Snake River. So, as if empowered by God, damming and diverting were sanctified as the foundation of a way of life—a righteous way by people having no doubts about the worthiness of what they did. Non-Mormon settlers participated fully in the development; as farmer and legislator Reed Hansen said, "The irrigation ethic is nondenominational."

Idaho, by the Federal Writers Project in 1937, appropriately spoke of towns such as Burley existing "through the miracle of water and irrigation." "Magic" is the catchword for irrigation in history after history. In its video, *The Snake: Jewel of the Gem State*, the Bureau of Reclamation announced, "Irrigation created a green garden in the desert . . . the Snake River translates into food, jobs, and the well-being of the region." Idaho public utility commissioner Perry Swisher reflected a common view, "It was a son-of-a-bitching desert until it was irrigated."

Reed Oldham, past president and a member of the Committee of Nine, called this a "forbidding land" that his Mormon ancestors settled. "I'm not sure there'd be much to quarrel about if it weren't for the irrigation that has made life here possible."

Indeed, how can anyone oppose what the pioneers did, what the government reinforced, what modern irrigators perpetuate? How can anyone question the foundation of this obviously proper existence? Except, of course, the Indians, who had been doing just fine before the settlers arrived. But how can white people question this civilization, especially when civilization elsewhere, in the eyes of southern Idahoans, is so undesirable? I speak of the neuroses of urban America, of inner-city blight, of drugs and crime, of hedonistic materialism, especially in California, which is economically a model that western states desperately seek to emulate but is rhetorically derided.

A good life has been established. There are differences, but irrigation has created somewhat of a transplanted eastern America in the West; the irrigated patchwork of fields and scattered homes is closer in appearance to Ohio than to the unirrigated desert. The society that has resulted floats like a raft on the waters of the Snake River. The question is, how can some small part of the wealth originating with the river be returned to the river to achieve a balance that allows a productive ecosystem to survive at the same time that a society built on the extraction of that wealth also survives? How can we have both?

Farmers are concerned about instream flows, fish, and wildlife, though I would never have suspected that when I talked to spokesmen for the agricultural establishment. Perhaps they agree but fear a weakening of their position. Perhaps they fear a loss of potential income if they lose their unused water rights. Of course they fear drought. And perhaps they fear the unknown now that a few people recognize the effects of the dams and diversions on the river and the ecosystem. From the very irrigated culture of Arizona, former Interior Secretary Stewart Udall said, "The irrigation issue in Idaho is a cultural issue. The grandfathers of those people built the canals. If you talk about changing *anything*, they fear for their livelihoods." This is the image of the Snake as a "working river," a two-word justification for dams, diversions, and pollution.

I spoke to Reed Oldham in his brick home on a 350-acre portion of his potato farm north of Idaho Falls. A likable man, Oldham and his contemporaries are the foundation upon which some better sides of western society are built. "Oldham is a good spokesman for the irrigators," I had been told, "not as conservative as many others along the upper Snake, and with lots of experience on the Committee of Nine." Sprinklers watered a vivid, green lawn. We sat in the comfortable living room next to an organ and a piano. With a clear tone of resistance, Oldham explained,

There's a feeling among irrigators that people coming from elsewhere are trying to remake us. We will resist that every way we can. We've got Jackson Lake, we've got Palisades, we've got American Falls, Henry's Lake, and the others. Farmers will support fish, but we don't want to subsidize low flows out of storage water.

We need to go back to the Book of Genesis. God told Adam that he was put on earth to go forth and cultivate it and subdue it. People are now trying to go back on that and quit doing that. They want to leave it alone.

Genesis 1:28 says, "Be fruitful and multiply; fill the earth and subdue it." But further into the Bible I find Ecclesiastes 3:19, "For the lot of man and of beast is one lot. . . . man has no advantage over the beast." Job, 12:7, advises, "But now ask the beasts to teach you and the birds of the air to tell you; or the reptiles on earth to instruct you, and the fish of the sea to inform you." An angry Jeremiah, 2:7, may have visited the dried-up Snake River at Milner Dam: "When I brought you into the garden land to eat its goodly fruits, you entered and defiled my land, you make my heritage loathsome."

"Those people," Oldham said of the environmentalist cabal, "are all from someplace else, and they bring their hangers-on from the East." This is a familiar theme, as if everyone's ancestors except the Shoshone and Bannock's and a few Mexican farmworkers didn't all come from the East. Until recent years, people testifying before an Idaho legislative committee had to say that they were "born and raised in this country," or they would be asked, and their answer was likely to be the gravamen of charges against them. But neither Cecil Andrus nor William Borah—arguably the two most success- ful politicians in the state's history—was born here. "I'm an Idaho- an by choice," is the response of the root-weary nonnative, many having come to Idaho for similar reasons as the grandfathers who are eulogized by those who were lucky enough to be born here.

In fact, many conservationists were born elsewhere. But as Linda Burke of the Idaho Conservation League (ICL) pointed out, she and many members have always been Idahoans. She took offense at the outsider stereotype. Former ICL director Pat Ford said, "The more crucial distinction in Idaho conservation is urban versus rural or recreation versus agriculture. It's not native versus nonnative, not new Idaho versus old Idaho."

Invariably, the irrigation establishment's bottom line is the same as Reed Oldham's. "Those people don't understand what goes on. They don't understand how this system works."

IRRIGATING IDAHO

Irrigated agriculture is no less a way of life than a big business. In Idaho, over 4 million acres (7.2 percent of the land) is irrigated; about 3.8 million of these acres lie in the Snake River basin and 3 million on the Snake River plain.[1] (Idaho farmland totals 6.5 mil- lion acres.) The Minidoka Project of 1 million acres represents most of the area served by the Bureau of Reclamation with water from the main stem and the Henry's Fork.

Idaho ranks third in the nation in production of sugar beets, hops, and mint; second in barley; and first in potatoes, a crop origi- nally cultivated by Peruvian Indians. Idaho now produces 24 per- cent of the nation's supply, and spuds are king. Governor Cecil Andrus filmed national television commercials promoting potatoes. The radio regularly advertises remedies for tuber rot and pink rot. Athletes compete in the Spudman Triathalon in Burley.

The only state close to Idaho's yield of 100 million hundred- weight in 1988 was Washington with 63 million. Several potato states, including Washington and Oregon, enjoy a growing season up to two months longer than the Snake River plain's 150 days, shortening to sixty in higher valleys.[2] One-third of Idaho's crop is sold fresh as the famed Idaho baker, a nutritious mainstay in the diets of many Americans. Two-thirds goes to processing for french fries and other deep-fried and kindred products. Vast quantities of potatoes bought by the J.R. Simplot Company are sold for the fast-food trade, McDonald's, etc.

Moisture-sensitive, the crop consumes 20 to 27 inches of irrigation water per year. Potatoes are often billed as Idaho's leading cash crop, but 1986 state data listed cattle and calves valued at $505 million, wheat at $314 million, milk at $290 million, and potatoes at $288 million.[3]

Spuds are widely regarded as the underpinning of southern Idaho society. Likewise, most people believe that the Bureau of Reclamation manages flows of the Snake River for potato farmers. But potatoes are not the major crop of the Minidoka Project. Cereals such as wheat and barley are grown on 376,000 acres. Forage including pasture and alfalfa hay covers 311,000 acres. Cattle are the chief beneficiary of Minidoka water, accounting for about 41 percent of the irrigated acreage. (It takes 3,430 gallons of water to produce one steak!) Farmers grow potatoes on 144,000 acres—14 percent of the land served by the federal dams.[4] On the entire plain, potatoes are grown on 8 percent of irrigated land and receive less than 14 percent of the water.[5] Rather than say that people dammed and diverted the Snake River for spuds, it's more accurate to say that it was done for alfalfa, a cattle feed that tops the list of water consumers, requiring six times as much water as a given unit of vegetables to produce the same product value.[6]

Agriculture and food processing are the number one industry in Idaho, accounting for perhaps one-fourth of the economy. The state ranks twenty-fourth in the nation in land in farms and twenty-seventh in marketings. Net farm income statewide was $354 million in 1986 on 24,000 farms. This was up $22 million from 1981, though the number of farms was down by 300.[7]

Water from the Snake River is diverted by 100 entities in the basin: by community ditches run by groups of farmers, by ditch companies with bylaws, by corporations owned by irrigators, by quasi-municipal irrigation districts with taxing authority, by farmers who place pumps along the river, by farmers who pump groundwater, and by groups of irrigators with batteries of pumps.

Large supplies are delivered by canal "companies" organized under the 1894 Carey Act and by irrigation "districts" with contracts for Bureau of Reclamation water.

ENOUGH AGRICULTURE

In the 1970s, agriculture had been subject to the optimism infecting boomtowns of the mining era. To bring more land into production, the state sued the federal government to release federal land for private farming under the Carey Act. The court denied the state's right to some of the contested 3 million acres, but many tracts remained available. By 1977 farmers had filed for 600,000 new acres and 400,000 under a similar act, the Desert Lands Entry Act (some acres overlapped).[8]

As recently as 1978 the Department of Water Resources moved to reserve another 1.7 million acre feet of Snake River water to irrigate 347,000 acres as the Bruneau Project in spite of counterproductive effects that this would have had on existing Idaho farmers. In Washington state's Columbia basin, for example, the Army Corps had found that new irrigation accelerated the decline in farm numbers and population because corporations worked new land at an industrial scale.[9] Idaho farmers banded together to halt construction of the second half of the bureau's Columbia Basin Project, not in Idaho but in Washington.[10]

The draft of Idaho's water plan in 1976 had recognized impacts that new irrigation would have on the Snake River, yet chose to increase agricultural acreage anyway. There was, as Department of Water Resources director Keith Higginson explained, "an urgency expressed in the state to divert all the water in all the streams to prevent export of water to California." To nip any water transfer plans at an early stage, Washington Senator Henry Jackson had an amendment passed banning so much as the study of water export, Oregon laughed at the California bogeyman and elected environmentalist Tom McCall as governor, Canada eventually adopted a national policy of no water export, and even California had its northern rivers added to the national wild and scenic rivers system to ban diversions to Southern California. Idaho, in contrast, took a burn-Moscow approach to the Snake River. The Russians, however, had the good sense to make sure Napolean's army was really coming before they torched their city. Idaho's use-it-all rationale did not subside with legal bans on the study of water export.

A state report proposed no minimum flows in the Snake River because "the range of flows identified for the main stem if adopted would essentially eliminate all future agricultural development in the basins." Then pressed by a citizen's initiative, the Water Resource Board set a minimum flow, though it is far below the lowest flows ever experienced and abysmally below amounts needed for healthy ecosystems (see Chapter 6).

From 1975 to 1983, farmers developed 140,000 new acres of irrigated land in the basin. The 1986 water plan further recognized that up to 700,000 acres of new land could be developed, though constraints "will undoubtedly" limit development to less than that amount.

Meanwhile, the economy of agriculture was turned on its head. The boom of the 1970s turned to a near-bust. As Governor Cecil Andrus stated in Idaho's 1987 manual of agricultural statistics, "The power and capacity of Idaho's agricultural industry is well known; however, the shortcoming has been in selling what we produce."

"Many farmers are bitter," said Bob Burks, past president of the Idaho Water Users Association. "We're getting the prices we got in the 1930s with the expenses of the 1980s."

While grandiose expansion plans were still on state government's books, the federal government spent extravagant amounts of money to take Idaho farmland *out* of production. In 1988, 770,000 acres were idled under "set-aside" subsidies, and another 668,000 acres were idled under the Conservation Reserve Program, for a reduction of 1.4 million acres. People who didn't plant barley, which is the third highest acreage crop in the Minidoka Project (behind only alfalfa and wheat, which is also subsidized), received 92 percent of the value of the ungrown crop. The Agricultural Stabilization and Conservation Service reported that an astounding $767 million in federal funds were disbursed from 1983 through 1987 to Idaho farmers to reduce production. Federal taxpayers spend more than $153 million a year to *not grow crops* in Idaho.

This subsidy to curb production is equal to 20 percent of the budget of the state of Idaho. One irony is that the program encourages farmers to collect payments and then take their unregulated acreage and grow even more of the surplus crops, accomplished through saturation applications of pesticides and fertilizers. The subsidy programs are a boon to the chemical companies and in some cases fail to reduce the surpluses swamping the market. About half of the crops (chiefly barley and wheat) that are heavily subsidized through the Minidoka Project received price supports. Most of the lands actually retired from production were in nonirrigated areas, but had grown the same types of crops.[11]

To the set-aside programs' credit, the government pays for "conservation" treatment of the idled land to retard erosion. Hundreds of millions are being spent to "restore" land that had at no cost supported diverse stocks of wildlife until the Bureau of Land Management (BLM) divested the land for private use. The Soil Conservation Service (SCS) stated that because of erosion problems, 489,000 acres in the Snake basin should be converted from cropland back to wildlife habitat.

While the government pays farmers to take hundreds of thousands of acres out of production, other new acreage is going into production, including tens of thousands of acres in eastern Idaho. Near Rupert, 9,400 acres may be opened for farming through a congressional appropriation of $16 million to the Bureau of Reclamation. As a "unique concept," irrigators could obtain federal land if they agree to allow hunting of Chinese ringneck pheasants.[12] Native wildlife habitat of 5,360 acres would be lost to gain 1,090 acres of farmer-created pheasant habitat for sports purposes.

A case of sorts can be made for new farmland because developers can be counted on to convert open space to urban use if given half the chance. It seems that the only idea that arouses a more vehement reaction than the threat to water rights—guarded to keep land *in* farming use—is the threat of regulations limiting the farmer's ability to take land *out* of farming use. As a result, suburban sprawl in Idaho gobbles 9,900 acres of farmland a year. The SCS stated, "Losing our prime farmland to other uses will move Idaho's agriculture onto marginal lands and will greatly increase land management and crop production costs for future generations." Neon-strip development radiates from every town in the farmbelt of this state that bows to agriculture as its number one industry and has sanctified almost any policy you can name to further agricultural enterprises, except for a policy of encouraging that the best farmland remain for farming.

Because of a nationwide drought, Idaho farmers had very profitable years in 1988 and 1989, yet no one predicted another long-term boom. The economy and the Swan Falls agreement (see Chapter 6) have dictated that limited new acreage will be cleared for agriculture. Idled and urbanized land means that water could be available so that the Snake River could once again be a real river instead of a desiccated monument to surplus crops. But will the river ever see this water?

THE ISSUE OF WATER RIGHTS

Water rights are fundamental to irrigation in the West. Farmers secured access to the natural flow of streams by simply diverting water as a "constitutional" right. No permit or demonstration of need was required. Having once taken the water, the users had the right to continue. They could also apply to the state for a "statutory right." Since 1971, Idaho has required applications for new or increased diversions. The state does not grant ownership of water but rather the right to use it for "beneficial purposes." Theoretically, the water, streams, and aquifers remain public resources subject to state control.

Unlike property rights, which are usually acquired by paying for them, water rights are free from the state as a constitutional give-away. But once secured, water rights are somewhat like real estate and can be bought and sold, with limitations.

The right depends on when the person applied for it. The oldest are the best—the first to be honored in dry years—the first-in-time, first-in-right gospel. In 1935 the governor called out the National Guard to enforce this provision in the Teton basin, where junior irrigators took all the upstream water.[13] In 1988 one ditch rider told me, "It's a low water year, but these are old rights and we're delivering water as usual. One farmer said he was going to cut back on account of the drought, but he's rare. If they don't have to cut back, they won't."

When all the flow has been given away, the river is "fully appropriated." At that point, the streambed may be dry.

Storage rights are different from natural flow rights. For storage rights, applicants contract with the agency that built the dams—the Bureau of Reclamation, for example—and pay for the rights to storage space in the reservoir. The contracts do not guarantee a water supply, which depends on runoff and management of the reservoir, but only the use of water should the reserved space be filled. Rights to store water are usually junior to natural flow rights; water is typically stored when no one is irrigating or when flows are high. Storage is often used as "supplemental" water to help guarantee late season or dry-year deliveries.

Ron Carlson, the water master for the upper basin, with authority regarding the distribution of the water, said, "The perception by the public, given from the water users themselves, is that if you own rights to water, you can have it. That's not true. The water must be put to beneficial use. If you don't need the water, you have no right to it." The Idaho constitution mentions only domestic, agricultural, manufacturing, and power as beneficial uses.

As for the first-in-time, first-in-right argument, the fish, of course, were here first. Fish, wildlife, and cottonwoods predate the irrigators' legal and rhetorical bedrock of the state constitution by several million years. But God's creatures had no rights under Idaho law for most of history. Even if they wanted to, state administrators were precluded by law from considering the public interest.

In 1974 the Idaho Supreme Court cracked open a legal door to instream flows at Malad Canyon by ruling that there can be beneficial uses of water other than those perceived by writers of the constitution in 1890.[14] Justice J. Bakes ruled that "the concept of what is or is not a beneficial use must change with the changing conditions." The same year, the Water Resource Board adopted a policy that wildlife, recreation, aquatic life, and water quality have equal desirability with irrigation and other uses. Opinion polls had revealed that the public valued preservation more than new development.[15] Further rulings required the state to consider the public interest in new appropriations of water. In 1978, after a bizarre chain of events forcing the legislature's hand (see Chapter 6), Idaho passed a minimum streamflow law establishing a procedure for licensing water rights for instream flows.

Water remains subject to a policy of free development, comparable with the 1862 Homestead Act for land. The reservation of water for public uses—corresponding in a way to President Benjamin Harrison's withdrawal of the first national forests in 1891— did not begin until 1974. Only the minimum—not optimum— flows may be approved for instream uses.

Unlike rights for irrigation, the law does not provide for individuals or organizations to claim an instream flow; that would have opened the arena to possibilities such as sportsmen's groups securing water for fish. To guard this legal beast otherwise having the potential to protect a lot of rivers, only the Water Resource Board may apply for instream water (other state agencies send requests to the board). To guard against an overenthusiastic board, the Department of Water Resources must approve applications. To guard against excessive protection by the department, the legislature may veto approvals. To guard against excessive protection by any one legislature and to consider consumptive requests that might arise at any time, instream permits may be subject to review in fifteen years, a condition frequently imposed by the department. This measure was considered great progress for fish and wildlife, though a similar process for irrigators would probably touch off a revolution. Wyoming also passed a law for limited recognition of instream flows in 1986.

The Idaho water plan reported that the Water Resource Board "should seek to appropriate waters in the state for instream flow purposes," yet since 1978 only a few minimum flows have been set per year.[16] Information and sponsorship are not lacking. The Department of Fish and Game forwarded recommendations for flows on dozens of streams; in 1988, eighteen requests were pending. Minimum flow recommendations were proposed for the Snake River below Idaho Falls and Blackfoot.[17] Progress after ten years shows that thirty-four different streams are designated involving only a few thousand cfs on 213 waterway miles out of a state total of 40,000 (not counting Snake River flows below Swan Falls, which were established in a separate process). This means that the worst historic conditions (often a streambed of cracked mud) will not get even worse on less than 0.5 percent of Idaho's streams. In contrast, Colorado obtained rights for 700 stream reaches. Even though the board spends "a lot of time" on the instream issue, according to Keith Higginson, director of the Department of Water Resources, the result remains a few crumbs in a booming bakery of

water use. Fish and Game sits on additional requests because un-
resolved applications are already on the table. "More should be
done," said a Fish and Game official, "but our department will not
take strong action on anything dealing with water users. The legislature perceives us as obstructing all those good uses of water. To
take a high profile would be suicide."

Higginson has had state water rights experience in Utah and Idaho since 1957 and served as commissioner of the Bureau of Reclamation under Interior Secretary Cecil Andrus. I asked him, why
aren't more minimum flows established in Idaho? "I guess the Water Resource Board hasn't seen the need," he responded.

A Department of Water Resources staff member explained that
the board is composed of working people who have only so much
time. The governor appoints its members, who in 1988 included
four farmers, three members from agricultural families or farming
communities, and a retired academic in forestry. In the past, this
policymaking group was called "the Idaho Irrigation Board" and "a
captured agency" by some people, though Higginson called those
people "grossly misinformed." (The board has in fact changed in
recent years.)

For all the shortcomings, Idaho has an instream flow provision,
and Higginson stood up to hostile questioning by the legislature. In
1989, the department set minimum flows for nine creeks, springs,
or small rivers, and the membership of the board was broadened to
include people such as riparian authority William Platts. "We had
to start somewhere," said board chair Gene Gray. "Idaho had hell
to pay to get any instream law to begin with."

Water lawyer Jeff Fereday said, "We don't have the level of controversy that we used to have over new minimum flow designations. I think that many irrigators know they have sufficient water
supplies and that a junior right to a minimum flow poses no
threat."

"For supporting minimum flows, I was under a dark cloud from
my own industry," said former board chair Reed Hansen. "Now
you have to be pretty narrow-sighted to not recognize other values
of water."

"Minimum flows are now more acceptable," said Pat Ford.
"Elected officials see both sides of this issue. But the record of designations is still poor."

Perhaps most limiting: an instream water right beginning in 1978 is pointless in dry years—when the flows are really needed—because the right is subordinate to older irrigation rights that take every drop. Scott Reed wrote, "There is virtually no place in the West that a water right with a date of 1988 would be of the slightest value." Widely seen as progress in stream protection, the minimum flows simply keep terrible conditions from getting worse. We could also claim victory over toxic wastes because there aren't any *new* Love Canals.

Supporting better instream flows, the Soil Conservation Service (SCS) recommended that "future enactments should promote a more intensive use of existing supplies and reallocating of preempted water to other contemporary uses. . . . needs have changed since the initial claims were filed. Water management technology has advanced considerably. Yet the estimates of usage that established the early rights are still in effect today. To a major extent, these rights . . . hamper attempts to more efficiently use and manage water."[18]

In contrast to the East, western land is plentiful but water is not. Long known to irrigators, this fact gains new urgency among conservationists who see that protection and restoration of habitat depends on the control of water. The battles over parks, forests, and wilderness will be replaced by battles over the appropriation of water in rivers and wetlands.

Idaho's minimum streamflow statute presumably offers the only means to use state law to establish an instream water right for fish, wildlife, or recreation. However, there are other ways to keep water in the streams. The concept of "public interest," which appears in the Idaho water code, and the public trust doctrine (see Chapter 1) could be used to limit diversions, but securing instream flows is more likely under federal law. While irrigators wage arguments based on water rights that have state constitutional protection, the management of the federal reservoirs is a different issue and is the most likely source of improved instream flows. Also, the Federal Energy Regulatory Commission can require flow releases as a condition of hydroelectric project licensing. The federal clean water acts have been invoked to limit or condition diversions. Federal reserve water rights can also provide instream flows (see Chapter 6).

Resources consultant Ed Chaney and his rancher client are breaking legal ground by seeking to convert diversion rights into a minimum streamflow for salmon. Chaney predicted that water-rights holders will not permit the state to dictate which of several beneficial uses must be pursued and that changing public values and market prices will sweep away the anti–instream flow bias within a decade.

The day may come when the state, federal agencies, or private conservancies will buy water rights to return flows to rivers. Montana considered paying irrigators the value of their crops during dry years in order to keep water in streams. Ed Chaney's Resources Information Center has started an Idaho Fish and Wildlife Water Bank to buy or broker water rights. The Water Heritage Trust was created in 1988 to buy western water rights for fish and wildlife and then give or resell the rights to resource agencies. Compared with land preservation, the water rights business is "institutional chess compared to checkers," according to the trust's founder, Huey Johnson.

Why should water rights be bought if an irrigator is not using all his water rights or if he is not meeting the beneficial use requirement? The law requires that those rights revert to the state. So far, the definition of "beneficial use" has little to do with "efficiency of use." Ron Carlson said, "The amount of water diverted doesn't really relate to beneficial use. In some areas of the Snake River, 20 acre feet per acre are applied where consumptive use is 2 acre feet. That's still a beneficial use." In one area, alfalfa is subirrigated by literally raising the level of groundwater to meet the root zone. Whether or not the beneficial use requirement assumes wise, reasonable, or efficient use raises nettlesome legal questions, but the attitude throughout the West is evolving toward a "reasonable" use requirement.

It's a simpler situation, theoretically, when the irrigator doesn't use some of his water rights at all. He could lose that portion under a "use-it-or-lose-it" doctrine. Are the irrigators in fact using all the water to which they hold rights? Advocates of instream flows say that if the irrigators want to adhere to the letter of the law as they are always claiming in defense of their water rights, then let them prove that they are using all of their diverted water, which could be a substantial challenge.

No one understands the complete picture of the water that is claimed, withdrawn, used, or returned to the river unused. Awarded water rights in the West sometimes exceed the actual flow of the rivers by 200 percent. This occurs partly because diverted water returns to the stream and is diverted again, but this also reveals a difference between "wet" water and "paper" water. The situation is not unlike the West described in 1899 by Elwood Mead, later an illustrious commissioner of the Bureau of Reclamation: "Ditches diverted more water than could be used, their owners claimed more than they could divert, while decrees gave appropriators title to more water than ditches could carry and many times what the highest flood could supply. Little was known of the quantity of water needed to irrigate an acre."[19]

To learn how much water is validly claimed and thus be able to plan ahead, the state is adjudicating the water rights. In this decade-long undertaking, holders are required to submit claims specifying the amount of their rights. Irrigators will apply for the maximum they can "justify."

The Idaho Department of Water Resources' adjudication responsibilities involve evaluating the actual beneficial use—the measure and limit of a water right under a long-standing rule in western water law. "If they're actually using less than indicated on paper, they can't have the extra water rights," Higginson said. Yet the state faces a dilemma. Should an irrigator who saves water be penalized for cutting use while a neighbor who wastes water receive his requested rights?

Will the paper rights for irrigators who have converted to sprinklers be cut back because they use one-third the previous amount of water? Will water rights to land converted to urban use be retracted from irrigation companies that continue to divert the unused water? The department's adjudications chief, David Shaw, answered with statements such as, "I can't tell you that if one portion of the right changes, the right will change." Shaw said that policies for the adjudication have not been set and that the "courts are likely to decide" on many of the questions.

One decision that the department *has* made is that adjudicated rights will assume that every acre grows alfalfa—the most water-consumptive crop. Nobody working on the adjudication gave me the slightest indication that they would look carefully at beneficial use in a way that might scale irrigators' paper rights back to amounts that are actually being applied to the land.

Knowing the department's position, Sherl Chapman said, "The use-it-or-lose-it provision was once frightening to many farmers, but now there's less concern. They're reassured by the state that they'll have adequate water rights."

The legislature appropriated $800,000 to begin the adjudication in 1985. About one-third of the costs will be borne by irrigators, though the lion's share of the work is done regarding their rights. Hydropower producers, whose rights are clearly defined and tightly regulated under federal law, will pay for one-third, ultimately a cost borne by all electric ratepayers. Public instream flows already approved by the Department of Water Resources require minimal work in the adjudication but are charged $100 per cfs or ten times the rate of fish farming. State taxpayers will pay this $2.8 million in fees, a figure based on instream flows of 28,000 cfs, which counts water in the Snake River three different times. The state has charged the federal government $100 per cfs for instream claims to maintain federal wildlife refuges and fisheries, though the Justice Department is challenging the fee. The Idaho public is paying for most of the adjudication, yet involvement by public interest groups—if it occurs—may be impossible without state supreme court or legislative action.

Is the adjudication simply a great "paper chase," as one Water Resources official suggested? It's legally clear that users can lose their rights if they don't use the water; on the other hand, it seems that the state will award irrigators any amount they claim regardless of beneficial use. The adjudication could, however, have extraordinary potential to release water rights for nonconsumptive uses and could be the finest opportunity of the century to correct some of the ecological damage of the past.

A PERSPECTIVE ON USE

In 1987, 3.8 million acres in the Snake River basin were irrigated by withdrawing 25.1 million acre feet of surface and groundwater, averaging 6.6 acre feet per acre according to Idaho Department of Water Resources (DWR) data sheets. Consumptive use of 2.2 acre feet per acre accounted for 8.2 million acre feet (water withdrawn for irrigation and never returned to the river), accounting for 99 percent of all consumptive use in the state. (Data reported by the U.S. Geological Survey are somewhat lower in volume.)[20] Municipal and industrial withdrawals totaled 0.4 million acre feet, a negligible portion of which was consumed. In many areas, withdrawals from the river average about 8 acre feet per acre irrigated.[21] Above Idaho Falls, irrigators withdrew much more water per acre than elsewhere. (One acre foot equals 325,851 gallons or 43,560 cubic feet. Irrigators measure water in miner's inches; 1 inch equals 9 gallons a minute, also called a share.)

Idaho's withdrawals rank fourth among states in water used for all purposes including hydroelectric power, behind only the enormous populations of California, Florida, and Texas.[22] In irrigation, Idaho ranks second only to California, where 8.6 million acres are irrigated. Idaho leads the nation by a wide margin in the per capita amount of water withdrawn for all uses—about 19,000 gallons per day (gpd) in 1980, which means it probably has the highest rate of use on the planet, by far. The nationwide average is 2,000 gpd. The Water Resources Council listed only four subbasins in the nation where per capita use exceeded even 5,000 gpd: the Southern California, Sacramento, and San Joaquin districts in California and the upper Snake River in Idaho.[23]

Idaho does not suffer from the domestic and industrial water supply problems of Arizona, California, and Colorado. Likewise, adequate instream flows for the ecosystem were long ago abandoned in the West's heavily depleted basins such as the Colorado and Rio Grande. In Idaho, an opportunity exists to do things differently—to have all the urban use that can be expected, to have at least all the farming use that now exists, and to also have a healthy river.

USING LESS WATER

To increase crop yields, halt erosion, and cut labor costs, farmers began converting from inefficient surface irrigation (furrows or flood) to sprinklers in the late 1960s. Incidental are water savings of 50 to 70 percent. "There's been a dramatic cutback in use," said

Hal Anderson, technical services chief for the Department of Water Resources. "Farmers realized they didn't need to apply as much water as they had thought."

A study by the Soil Conservation Service (SCS) for the Bureau of Reclamation in 1988 reported "greatly reduced diversion requirements" in three areas of the upper basin between 1977 and 1987. Farm deliveries fell by 47 *percent*—an annual savings of 389,600 acre feet on 153,000 gross acres within the areas—an impressive decrease of 2.5 acre feet per acre. Sprinkling increased from 10,571 to 55,730 acres while surface irrigation was reduced; however, this accounts for only 35 percent of the savings. Improved furrow irrigation, improved canals and ditches, and especially laser leveling of land also saved great amounts of water. These figures are not projected, proposed, or theoretical—the reductions are what the SCS reported happening in the last decade. Furthermore, crop yields in many areas increased *because of* less watering.

The savings in applied water in the three areas is significant—equivalent to 67 percent of the Shoshone and Bannock water claims, for example—but if reductions on all irrigated lands in the Snake River basin were as great as on the Burley District, Minidoka District, and Idaho Canal Company lands, savings would total an utterly amazing 9.5 million acre feet a year. This equals 38 percent of basin withdrawals in 1987 and 1.2 times the basin's total consumptive use (using DWR figures).

Basinwide, 1.7 out of 3.8 million acres were irrigated by sprinklers in 1986.[24] Assuming sprinklers cut applied water from 5 to 2 acre feet per acre, the conversion to sprinklers over the last twenty years saved at least 2.9 million acre feet of applied water a year. New land irrigated mostly by sprinklers in the twenty years used an additional 0.86 million acre feet,[25] still leaving a sprinkler-induced savings of 2 million acre feet. This already-saved amount is *twenty-seven times* the water needed to increase winter flows below Palisades Dam from 750 to 1,000 cfs. To put the savings in perspective, the total capacity of Palisades Dam is 1.4 million acre feet and the combined usable capacity of all eight reservoirs in the upper basin is 5 million.[26] Sprinklers installed since completion of Palisades Dam are saving river and groundwater equivalent to about four times the greatest amount used from Jackson Dam since Palisades was built. Tremendous amounts of water are being saved through many other techniques, land idling programs, and urbanization, which requires far less water.

Conversion to sprinklers drawing from the river or canals clearly reduces the needed withdrawals from the river. Other sprinklers would represent an even greater reduction of withdrawals because some farmers abandoned surface supplies and shifted to groundwater when they converted to sprinklers. All sprinklers represent a savings from a complex of surface and underground sources that is one interrelated system—fundamentally one pool.

The voluminous amount of water that is saved is largely an unintentional byproduct of other farm efficiencies. The potential for even more water savings is enormous. Surface irrigation is still used on 55 percent of the acreage. The SCS recommended irrigation improvements that would save water on 931,000 acres.[27]

Under a Bureau of Reclamation contract, a hydrology firm, Bio/West, studied water conservation potential in four of the upper basin areas accounting for 498,000 acres using 2.8 million acre feet a year, less than the typical amount.[28] For the North Side Canal Company, seepage from canals was 268,000 acre feet in 1977, or 34 percent of the annual diversion. The "conservative" estimate of total canal seepage for the four areas was 686,000 acre feet. *Canal leakage alone accounted for 25 percent of Snake River diversions investigated by Bio/West.* Considering only three forms of water conservation—eliminating canal leaks, scheduling irrigation, and converting to sprinklers—Bio/West reported that 979,000 acre feet of diversions could be saved. Ditch seepage is also substantial; farmers told me that they see flows of 60 miner's inches reduced to 45 inches between canal and field—a 25 percent loss.

Even more startling, Department of Water Resources data sheets in 1987 reported a 9.8 million acre feet "pre-headgate loss"—water lost in transit between the river and the farmer's ditches—equal to 59 percent of surface water withdrawals.

Bio/West noted that by converting from unscheduled surface irrigation to scheduled sprinkler irrigation, farmers can save 0.9 acre feet per acre. This, too, appears conservative; an Environmental Protection Agency (EPA) study found that 1.1 acre feet per acre could be saved by scheduling. Bio/West suggested an initial economic savings of 236,400 acre feet. No one has studied the basinwide potential, but if the four areas are comparable with other irrigated acreage, 1.8 million acre feet could economically be saved by merely lining some canals so that water doesn't leak directly into the soil, by installing sprinklers, and by scheduling irrigation.

"We do canal improvements each year, dynamiting out ledges that back water up and cause seepage," said Bob Burks of the North Side Canal Company. "But it's expensive. Lining canals *sounds* good, but concrete doesn't work here like it does in California. Here, it freezes and cracks." Because of that problem, Bio/West used PVC liners at $8 a square yard.

Neil Wilton of the SCS said that a decrease of 25 to 50 percent in water diversions can be accomplished through sprinklers and other improvements such as lined ditches and gated pipes that release only a specified amount of water. And much more could be done. To measure the soil's moisture needs and fine-tune applications, tensiometers can be used with impressive water savings. Irrigation scientists at the Kimberly, Idaho, research station stated that significant savings could result by cutting a month off the irrigation season without damaging crops in most years; irrigators in other areas do it routinely.

"Water availability to most farmers is not a problem," said Thomas Trout of the U.S. Department of Agriculture Snake River Conservation Research Center. "Irrigators from the main Snake River system very seldom have to deal with a shortage of water. In the last twenty years, canal companies cut back to their contractual amount once. Otherwise, they deliver 20 percent more water than their own bylaws call for."

When confronted with the problem of minimum flows being inadequate for the ecosystem, Keith Higginson said, "The other permitted uses of water are also for a minimum, not an optimum." Yet up to 20 acre feet per acre are applied in the Egin Bench area, canal companies that converted to sprinklers continue to flush their full water rights amounts through their canals, and less than 1 percent of the surface-irrigated fields have pumped unconsumed runoff back to the tops of the fields.

Sprinklers depend on electricity to pump water, and some people fear that rising power rates could reverse the sprinkler revolution. Department of Water Resources and Idaho Power Company spokespeople, however, agree that those kinds of increases are unlikely, and a lot of electricity can be saved. The department reported that a 25 percent energy savings can result through low-pressure nozzles, efficient motors, larger mainline pipes, and scheduling. Some farms reported a 50 percent energy cutback.[29] Agricultural energy could be cut 30 percent in the next twenty years.[30] New technologies are being developed for low-pressure and drip irrigation that will save even more water while reducing energy use. Leaving water in the river would likewise increase hydroelectric production.

Sherl Chapman agreed. "We'll see continued decreases in water use." In many interviews and meetings with irrigators and their spokespeople along the Snake River, I constantly heard of concerns that irrigators' rights to water be retained, but I rarely heard concern for the need for full amounts of paper rights.

In yet another study, the Idaho Water Resources Research Institute reported that farm efficiencies of 11 to 62 percent could be improved to 60 to 70 percent and that "large decreases in river diversions could be obtained." Feasible efficiencies on 252,000 acres could result in 960,000 acre feet of water remaining in the river. But author Brent Claiborn recognized that farmers have "little reason to alter their current practices and operating levels."[31]

Lining canals and rebuilding systems to require less carrying water costs money. Could the subsidies for dams and set-aside programs be spent on efficiency improvements rather than on destroying more rivers and paying farmers to not grow crops?

WHERE DOES THE WATER GO?

One might think that less water applied by irrigators would mean more water left in the river, a scenario that seems to have a "Who's buried in Grant's tomb?" simplicity. But where the saved water goes is a mystery. The water master's records show a 0.8 million acre foot reduction in water ordered by the irrigators from 1975 to 1987—an amount that is held in the reservoirs, adding to the irrigators' insurance against a dry year and sometimes sold at a profit for hydroelectric production—but it is not nearly the full amount of the reduced application on farms. All indications are that farmers apply *far* less water then they applied in the past, but that they divert only *somewhat* less water from the river. Sherl Chapman

agreed. "There's certainly less water applied to fields than is reflected in the decreased amount of water diverted in the ditches."

Measurements are not made of water that runs through the irrigation systems and spills back into the river without being applied
to crops. The state reported, "The lack of a systematic irrigation
return flow measurement program prevents . . . efficient management of Snake River flows."[32] The Department of Water Resources
had no data on unused water flowing through the canal systems.
The Geological Survey monitored some of the return flows in
1980, but the state did not support continuation of the program.
"They didn't see a need for the information," a Geological Survey
hydrologist said.

In an amazing affront to contrary evidence, Keith Higginson
said, "We can't assume that less water is being applied to farmland. Diversions are down 800,000 acre feet, but I'm not sure the
applied amount has decreased that much." He credited the reduction in diversions not to sprinklers and efficiencies but to compu-
terization of the water master's services. David Shaw, chief of the
adjudication for the Department of Water Resources, was the only
other person in the water and agriculture industry who would not
admit that farmers are applying less water per acre than they used
to apply.

To protect their water rights under the use-it-or-lose-it doctrine,
it behooves irrigation companies to order water even if they don't
use it. This is no defense against forfeiture of water rights unused
on the farms, according to water lawyers I talked to. Yet not to
order the water is to invite scrutiny. If the Department of Water
Resources knows that less water is applied, then it would have a
legal obligation to cut back on irrigators' rights in the adjudication.
This is a political incendiary bomb, and so the fact that far less
water is being applied on farmland is not officially recognized by
the agency in charge of monitoring the use.

Strategically, everyone is on a tightrope. If irrigators "lose" paper
water rights because they saved water, they'll be less likely to save
it, and under Idaho law, no one can force them to use water wisely.
The state accepts even flagrant overapplication of water as "beneficial" and even the most gaping leaks in canals as a constitutionally
protected part of irrigators' rights. To curb unapplied diversions of
water, should the state prove that irrigators don't beneficially use

all of their diversions and thus "force" the users to cease taking water unnecessarily? Or should the state reward the users for efficiency by allowing them to establish rights to the unused water even though they are legally not entitled to it? Some users hope that they will be able to sell those rights, though benefiting a bank account is not a "beneficial use" under the revered constitutional right.

A tremendous amount of unused water would be discovered if the department does an accurate job in the adjudication by looking at amounts of water that are actually applied on fields. Lawyer Jeff Fereday said, "A strict adjudication will not affect an irrigator's water right; it will only affect what he *thought* his right was. No one has rights to water he doesn't place to beneficial use. The appropriation doctrine is oddly elegant here. Strictly interpreted, it protects present water rights holders and still maximizes the amount that is in the river." That doesn't mean the "new" water would benefit the river; a state commitment would have to be made to that effect (in Oregon, 25 percent of reverted water rights go to enhance instream flows). Idaho has not addressed the question of what it will do with the newfound water, assuming it shows up in the adjudication's paperwork.

Another destination of the mystery water is unauthorized fields. Water rights usually include a specified amount of water and land to be irrigated, but undocumented acres—and the amount may be extensive—have been brought into production illegally. Rules for the adjudication protect many of these expansions.

Perhaps most important, the irrigation systems—the canals, ditches, headgates, pumps, and siphons—all run with fewer problems given a large head of "carrying water." And it's convenient when a lot of water runs through the system; if a farmer wants water on short notice, a gate can simply be opened rather than waiting for water to arrive from far above. Sherl Chapman said that half the water in many canals is not applied to fields but taken for the custodial convenience of carrying water. Few canals have a "low profile" design for minimal carrying water. Bob Burks admitted, "Okay, let's say one-fifth of the water is not needed. But if you take that water out of the ditch system, the cost of building lower checks and headgates would be horrendous. That water running through the system is needed." Reed Oldham confirmed that "quite a bit" of water runs straight through the ditches and back into the river. "With lots of head, you don't need a fancy distribution system."

"We don't know how much water we're spilling," said Jack Eakin, general manager of the Twin Falls Canal Company. "But it's considerable. You have to run a lot of water for people at the lower end to get their share. Distribution is pretty much like it was in 1905. A new, efficient system could operate with a lot less water. We did the engineering for an $80 million federal loan to upgrade, but that turned everybody off. Instead, we're upgrading slowly. We're putting in measuring weirs so water isn't run just by guess and by golly." Incentives to consider the loan and maintain the system came in 1979 when a judge ruled that the company had to pay damages resulting from ruptures in a canal.

In its river basin study, the SCS recommended a "comprehensive" approach rather than the current "crisis" approach to replace irrigation structures to allow fewer diversions and improve use.[33] Out of 110,000 structures such as headgates in the upper basin, the SCS recommended replacement of 37,000 as obsolete. The companies have to build new hardware anyway, so why not do it in a way that will waste less water?

To improve the canal systems so they require less carrying water and thereby allow more water to stay in the river is federal policy. The Bureau of Reclamation called for the "lining of conveyance and distribution systems, more exact timing of water deliveries, avoidance of overdeliveries, use of new water-saving methods of irrigation such as drip irrigation, and overall better management of irrigated agriculture."[34] But the government has largely ignored the distribution of water it stores.

Quite simply, the canal companies don't want to save water. "If we don't use the water, it just goes to the next junior water right holder," said Jack Eakin. "We wouldn't get a dime. There's no monetary incentive to save water."

Reed Oldham explained, "You could save water from leaking out of the canals, but *anything you save flows down the river and is gone.*" His what-you-save-you-lose argument is based on the belief that, first, undiverted water in the river is wasted; second, that excessive irrigation augments the groundwater in a beneficial way; and, third, that the water saved would not augment water stored in dams but instead would be added to the high streamflows of the early season, which are untrapped by dams and "lost" if not diverted by irrigators.

Having dealt with the first item elsewhere, I will ignore the point that water in a river is useless except to serve irrigation.

Shortly I will look at the fascinating point about groundwater. As to the third point, in years when reservoirs fill, subsequent flows do escape the upper basin by flowing over Milner Dam (one of few things keeping salmon and steelhead populations nominally intact—see Chapter 9). But in low water years, when the reservoirs do not fill, an acre foot saved from leaking canals—even in the high runoff month of May—is an acre foot added to the reservoirs and available for later use by irrigators or anyone else. In May 1988, irrigators were drawing 9,000 cfs from Palisades Reservoir when it was obvious that it would not fill and that a low water "crisis" was upon Idaho. Even in normal years, stored water is being used by mid-June.[35] That means that the reservoirs are being drawn upon for 70 percent of the irrigation season. During that time, water saved in the irrigation system would be saved in the reservoirs as well.

The efficient use of water, which can profoundly benefit the Snake River and its ecosystem, will also benefit irrigation in the low water years that concern farmers so much. Like the sprinklers installed in the 1970s, every new water-saving device and practice adds to agriculture's insurance against drought.

Irrigation, Part II

THE EROSION OF THE WEST

Controlling soil loss is one reason irrigators convert to sprinklers and improve water efficiency. The Soil Conservation Service (SCS) reported that as a rule of thumb, one inch of topsoil takes thirty years to form from subsoil. Because that inch weighs 150 tons per acre, a tolerable loss is 5 tons per acre per year (it would take thirty years to lose an inch while new soil forms at the same pace). But Snake River farmland erodes at a much greater rate.

Irrigated cropland in the basin lost 8.9 tons of soil per acre per year; dry cropland lost 6.6. The cultivated plateaus of southeastern Idaho were worst, losing 14.8 tons per acre. Idaho is among the worst ten states for agricultural erosion.

Does the irrigation of Idaho hold the seeds of its own destruction? Is this the "fabulous but deceptive richness" of which historian and novelist Wallace Stegner wrote regarding irrigation? Will the agricultural West be tomorrow's Appalachia? That first mountain society of North America began with a wealth of resources but fell into a depressed and chronic welfare state. Mesopotamia and dry regions of the Middle East, Africa, Far East, and southern Europe had also appeared as endless sources of wealth before they were made wastelands. Erosion of soil and buildup of salt and minerals have been the unavoidable epitaphs of many societies in regions with the same amount of rainfall as southern Idaho.

For furrow irrigation, David Carter at the Department of Agriculture's research station near Kimberly, Idaho, found that 50 percent of the water applied at the head of Idaho fields runs off as wastewater, carrying soil with it.[1] Topsoil depths of 15 inches had been reduced to white, calcified soil at the upper ends of 75 percent of surveyed fields; a third of the area of those fields showed white minerals where crop yields were "drastically reduced." The whitish soils are plainly evident to anyone who simply drives across southern Idaho on Interstate 84 in the spring. Counting not just whitened areas but all fields in his study area, Carter found a decrease in agricultural productivity of 25 percent.[2]

In 1983 the Council on Environmental Quality reported that desertification—the transformation of productive lands to deserts—proceeds faster in western America than in Africa. As early as 1886, E. W. Hilgard of the University of California wrote of erosion and salinity problems accompanying irrigation: "To expect them not to increase unless the proper remedies are applied is to hope that natural laws will be waived in favor of California." One could as easily read, "in favor of Idaho."

Proper remedies were not applied in the Central Valley of California, now plagued by mineral buildup and foul runoff that poisons land, wildlife, and water supplies. The Bureau of Reclamation stated that more than a million acres in the valley "may become a barren salt flat." Over $300 million in annual crop losses may occur by 2000.[3]

For Snake River areas, no one has calculated the economic losses. But if I accept the bureau's figure that gross crop value for the Minidoka Project was $383 million in 1981 and Carter's 25 percent loss figure as typical (he took many samples), then soil erosion could represent a $96 million a year loss. At those rates, farmers have lost $364 million a year basinwide because of erosion by inefficient surface irrigation. Whatever the figures really are, soil erosion is stalking the agricultural economy of Idaho and translates into a significant dollar drain. Today's rate of fertility decline in the West may dwarf the indulgent soil squandering of the East and South where history has ridiculed short-sighted agricultural practices of the previous century.

Saving soil is one of the most crosscutting and irrefutable arguments for saving water in the Snake River basin. Overirrigation is insidiously self-destructive of agriculture itself, putting farmers on the frontline of injury resulting from excessive water use.

Thomas Trout of the U.S. Department of Agriculture said that great amounts of soil can be saved at little cost by pumping tailwater back to the tops of the fields. "This is not done because water is very cheap." Organic residue coverage through conservation tillage can curb erosion by 70 percent while reducing diesel fuel requirements by one-half and cutting water use from 6 to 4.5 acre feet per acre.[4] Most important, the SCS reported that farmers can cut soil losses from furrow irrigation up to 90 percent by using sprinklers.

THE QUALITY OF THE WATER

Snake River water comes to the fields as some of the cleanest large-river water anywhere, far cleaner than the Colorado, Missouri, and other major streams. Running through the fields, it picks up silt, minerals, pesticides, and fertilizer. Excess irrigation is a double-edged sword: Erosion washes soil away, and at the other end of the process the water-borne silt contaminates the rest of the irrigation system, the river, and the groundwater.

Much of the washed-away soil ends up in the bottom of the next reservoir. Nationwide, the U.S. Geological Survey reported that sediment causes over $100 million in lost reservoir capacities annually; another $125 million is spent dredging 38 million cubic yards from harbors and waterways—enough for 2 million railroad cars.[5] Sediment deposition in Snake River reservoirs has been studied little or not at all; one handwritten note in bureau files indicated 85,000 acre feet of sediment may be accumulated behind American Falls Dam. Black Canyon Reservoir on the Payette River may be half full of silt. The capacities of reservoirs are decreasing; ultimately they will decrease to nothing, and sharply reduced hydroelectric capability will accompany their demise. In Austin Reservoir, Texas, siltation cut storage by 96 percent in thirteen years. Steward Udall presided at the Interior Department during construction of Glen Canyon Dam on the Colorado River but now regrets the loss of that canyon. "It's going to fill up with silt in a hundred years, and what is the judgment of posterity then? That's the down side of the big dams—the rivers are not renewable."[6]

The silt carries polluting residues. The Fish and Wildlife Service called American Falls Reservoir "a sump for many toxics, including pesticides, heavy metals, PCBs, etc."[7] The SCS reported that one-third of $6 billion in damage from all pollution nationwide originates on croplands.

While silt in irrigation wastewater is on its way to become mud in the next reservoir, it pollutes the river. The 1988 nonpoint water quality report of the Idaho Department of Health and Welfare stated, "Agricultural irrigation return flows and runoff contaminated with herbicides, pesticides, and their suspected breakdown products [including] the heavy metals copper and mercury, have contaminated waters in the agricultural regions of the state. Toxics of agricultural origin have contaminated 300 miles of stream." (Toxics from all municipal discharges have affected 73 miles.) In the upper basin, 2,913 of 5,732 stream miles were "impacted by agricultural activities." In southwestern Idaho, 63 percent or 1,700 miles of rivers may not be swimmable or fishable because of agricultural contamination. Deteriorating water is intercepted by reservoirs—giant septic tanks that retain silt and pollutants. In the longest free-flowing section, Swan Falls to Weiser, water quality during the irrigation season plummets to a soup of foam and suspended organics. This continues in spite of the 1972 Water Pollution Control Act, which called for the elimination of pollutants by 1985. The target date is now 1995.

Health and Welfare staff said that the Farm Bureau "blasted" their study. Retaliation was seldom necessary; on top of chronic underfunding of water quality programs, the legislature periodically raided the pollution control account for things such as fire fighting, thus increasing the timidity of department officials. In 1988, an act that Governor Cecil Andrus would not sign ordered $2 million to be shifted from pollution control to the general fund. (In 1990, additional funding was made available to the department.)

Even though the state document reported that "primary pollutants" in the Snake River are "nutrients, sediment, organic enrichment, pathogens, and ammonia from agricultural activities," the agency incongruously listed overall water quality as "good" or "fair." The reason may be that no state standards are set for agricultural sediment—the industry is exempt—and it is a well-known quirk of the analysts' profession that where a standard does not exist, a "problem" does not exist. Fine print beneath the "good" and "fair" ratings for the recreational Snake River in Hagerman Valley flatly stated, "Beneficial uses are threatened for domestic water supply, agricultural water supply, cold water biota, and secondary contact recreation." Attempts at source reduction of chemicals encounter intense opposition from agribusiness. The Bush administration's Environmental Protection Agency (EPA) called for a ban on the fungicide EBDC, reporting that it caused cancer in animals and would probably be carcinogenic in humans if lifelong exposure is significant (an alternative pesticide was available).[8] Idaho Senator Steve Symms responded, "We've got to address this problem with more science instead of the scare tactics of these eco-terrorists."[9] Agribusiness defended the pesticide as a necessity, and the same week, the Idaho Potato Commission announced a new marketing strategy because it had found that American women thought a comparable spud could be grown elsewhere. A television ad capitalized on Idaho's pristine environment by combining images of mountains, clear streams, and buttered bakers.

The state quit monitoring the ambient water quality of the Snake River in 1983. This had involved regular sampling to determine overall conditions (the money was to be spent on tributaries). The data void makes further knowledge of trends, particularly in a legal arena, about as good as throwing darts at data sheets, except that anyone with eyes can tell that the quality in agricultural reaches is abysmal. For Idaho's 773 miles of river, the state monitors data at two stations, Heise and King Hill—just below the clean water discharge from Wyoming and just below the clean water discharge from Thousand Springs. The abandonment of monitoring is a curious step since the federal Water Quality Act directed all states to update their inventory of affected waters and to focus on management of nonpoint source pollution including agriculture. (The state hoped to persuade the Geological Survey to adopt some of the stations.) In 1988, Idaho was the only state failing to enact an anti-degradation plan for high quality waters.[10] After years of negotiation, the legislature passed a bill in 1989 addressing nonpoint contamination; however, lawmakers excluded the means of monitoring farm pollution and made agriculture—the chief source of nonpoint problems—exempt from state enforcement. To the credit of Health and Welfare, the SCS, and certain farmers, the state has a successful program of technical and financial assistance for farmers who chose to improve the quality of their wastewater.

Idaho's point sources of pollution—municipal treatment plants and industries—are regulated by the EPA and are considered largely in compliance. Ninety percent of the water quality problems emanate from nonpoint sources.

"Federal law is now driving the system, and we have to clean up the problems," said farmer and Water Board member Don Kramer. The state's water planning program is addressing a ban on new dams for the Milner to the King Hill reach of the river, and water quality is the primary concern because more impoundments would mean higher temperatures, less oxygen, and more algae. Regardless of everything else that might be done, additional flows may be necessary to meet federal water quality standards. Water Board chair Gene Gray said, "We'll eventually see more water being run down the river, if only to flush the pollution, which is now a stagnant mess."

About water quality, irrigation specialist Wilford Gardner wrote, "This issue will take its place alongside the issue of water rights as the greatest threat to the long-term survivability of irrigated agriculture."[11]

GROUNDWATER

The questions of groundwater are inextricably related to the questions of irrigation, water quantity, and water quality. The Snake River plain aquifer is one of the world's most productive; its upper 500 feet holds 200 to 300 million acre feet, enough to flood a flattened Idaho 4 feet deep.[12] The aquifer can be imagined as an extension of the river, mostly north of it and running beneath the ground as much as 900 feet. The state estimated that 8 million acre feet a year flow out of the aquifer or are pumped out while 7.8 million flow in.[13]

Basinwide, state data showed 8.5 million acre feet of groundwater withdrawals in 1986 while surface withdrawals were 16.6 million acre feet.[14] One-third of the irrigated acreage on the Snake River plain is served by groundwater from 5,300 wells, according to the Geological Survey.[15] Irrigation accounts for 95 percent of Idaho's groundwater use, industry 3 percent, and domestic use 2 percent.[16]

Groundwater problems here reflect the problems of the nation. Half of the United States' population drinks groundwater, which constitutes 96 percent of the total water resource. Two-thirds of all groundwater withdrawals are for irrigation.[17]

The irrigation industry's response to suggestions about water conservation along the Snake River is that the flow of groundwater depends on excessive diversions; water leaking from canals or un-used by crops seeps into the ground. This argument is the hydro-logic equivalent of apple pie and motherhood. Bob Burks, former president of the Water Users Association, said, "You can't say we're wasting water if it's going in for groundwater." Some irriga-tors pumping groundwater established their farms in areas remote from canals. Others can obtain surface water, but as farmer Ken Mulberry said, it's often cheaper to pump from the "free" aquifer than to buy surface water. "If we line the canals," Reed Oldham of the Committee of Nine cautioned, "there will be less flow into the groundwater. If we save that water it will just stay in the river and be gone."

Keith Higginson said, "People used to get upset at what ap-peared to be excessive irrigation practices in the Snake River basin, but that excess water is preserved in the aquifer. That water is not wasted. From Idaho's standpoint, water is wasted when it flows under the Lewiston-Clarkston bridge." This reference by Idaho's chief water officer was to the state's downstream boundary with neighboring Washington.

Instead of going down the river, some 4 million acre feet spilled from the irrigation systems seeps underground for a slower jour-ney.[18] By sending water through the aquifer, the pumpers benefit; by sending some of it down the river, the river and instream users would benefit.

There is little doubt that the practices of upstream farmers bene-fit other farmers who pump, but the upstream benefactors have no legal obligation to deliver the excess water. How many farmers benefit? Do they grow needed crops or surplus crops? How much do they depend on the conveniently excessive habits of their up-stream neighbors compared with natural flows? How do irrigators justify continuation of this incidental "benefit" of overirrigation when they have neither sought nor obtained a right for the inci-dental recharge?

What would be the effect on groundwater of leaving half a mil-lion acre feet in the river? That's a small percentage of what could easily be saved, but it is the full amount drawn from Jackson Dam in its most used year since Palisades Dam was built in 1958. Assuming that half of the saved water had otherwise seeped underground (the true amount is probably far less), that amount is only 3.2 percent of the total aquifer inflow on the Snake River plain. And the volume of water needed to raise flows below Palisades Dam from 750 to 1,000 cfs in winter is less than 1 percent of aquifer inflow.

Idaho's water plan states that pumped depletions in an aquifer should not exceed recharge, yet new groundwater withdrawals are being approved by the Department of Water Resources even when a department report states that extractions on the plain already exceed inflow by 250,000 acre feet.[19] The accusing finger by some people fearing groundwater depletion is not pointed at irrigators who are known to pump 2.3 million acre feet directly from the plain's water table, according to Geological Survey data, but at the potential groundwater "losses" resulting from reduced river diversions even if they are only a few thousand acre feet.

Agricultural spokesmen always say that their irrigation practices keep Thousand Springs running. This is like defending Old Faithful. If it's good for Thousand Springs, it's good for Idaho. Historically, the springs may have flowed at 4,000 cfs; they now run at 6,000, presumably reflecting excess irrigation water. Yet many irrigated acres lie on the south side of the river—water unavailable to Thousand Springs. Water saved there would not affect the major springs. Furthermore, some staff at the Department of Water Resources believe that substantial amounts of applied water may be lost to deep percolation in inaccessible water tables; after all, igneous rocks of the Snake River plain are many miles thick. Furthermore, would anyone "lose" Thousand Springs if it reverts to its natural flow? Is there a public obligation to maintain artificially elevated levels regardless of costs to the river elsewhere? Are the unknown groundwater supplies that are accidental to the leaking of canals more important than the rights of the Indians who claim water under the Winters Doctrine? Are artificial groundwater levels more important than instream flows for a modicum of fish and wildlife?

The central underpinning of the irrigation industry against reducing waste of irrigation water is that groundwater will suffer. At great public cost, the people of Idaho, Wyoming, the Northwest, and the nation forego the benefits of a living river so that some unknown number of farmers may receive a small amount of free water that spills out of a leaking and excessive irrigation system that drains the Snake River dry.

QUALITY AND SPECULATION

On the Snake River plain, 99 percent of the residents drink from the aquifer. Nine in ten people statewide drink groundwater; Idaho ranks fourth in percentage of population relying on underground supplies, behind only New Mexico, Florida, and Mississippi. Statewide, the groundwater basin considered most vulnerable to pollution is the lower Boise. The second most vulnerable is the Snake River plain.[20]

While many problems from sewage were solved after the 1972 Water Pollution Control Act, concentrations of toxic wastes increased dramatically, especially in groundwater where many chemicals are colorless, tasteless, odorless, expensive to test, unregulated, and unmonitored. Included are pesticides. Nobody has reliable data on the volume applied in Idaho; growers are not required to report their use. The state lists fifty-seven pesticides in use on the plain.[21] The Department of Health and Welfare estimated that farmers also applied hundreds of thousands of tons of chemical fertilizers. The agency stated, "Monitoring data for these chemicals in Idaho's groundwater are practically nonexistent. At this time it is impossible to evaluate whether agricultural practices are a significant source of groundwater contaminants."[22]

Considering what is added to irrigation wastewater, the case of maintaining groundwater levels through irrigation return flows calls up the classic hydrologist's analysis: "The good news is that your well will never go dry; the bad news is that you've got to keep flushing your toilet."

Health and Welfare reported 357 "incidents" of actual or potential groundwater contamination from all sources in 1988. These were just the ones the department knew about. In the Ontario area, pollution of drinking water wells exceeded acceptable levels of nitrogen. Problems were reported on the south side of the river from

Murphy to Marsing, and agricultural chemicals were suspected in the pollution of Boise Valley groundwater.[23] Dissolved solids of 200 to 300 parts per million increase by two or three times after irrigation is begun.[24] Groundwater quality seems subject to a great amount of trial and error with substantial opportunity for error.

Authorities say that problems remain localized. Most groundwater migrates about 10 feet per day.[25] It will take some years for radioactive effluent from the Idaho National Engineering Laboratory to reach the river, and perhaps years for plumes of localized pollution to mix with the larger flow and materialize somewhere. On the other hand, a measurement of flow called "transmissivity" is among the highest known in North America, allowing little time for filtration and decomposition; hydrogeologists consider the plain one of the most permeable large aquifers in the world.[26]

People used to think that the separation of shallow from deep groundwater strata kept pollutants out of the deeper regional supplies, but recent studies by the Geological Survey found that the separations are not continuous and that deep wells provide conduits for polluted water to reach underlying reservoirs.

People used to think that pesticides remained in the root zones of the plants. Then regulations forced farmers to abandon abhorrent chemicals such as DDT for pesticides that dissolve in water. Forty-three chemicals in common usage are mobile in water. Without bacterial action, nitrogen fertilizer is persistent; it does not break down. Elsewhere, nitrogen has caused increased infant mortality; blue baby syndrome is found in the agricultural Platte River Valley. Nitrate concentrations in Idaho groundwater are thirty times those in surface water. Health and Welfare found that 67 percent of sampled wells in the Burley Irrigation District and 31 percent in the Minidoka District exceeded 5 milligrams of nitrate per liter, causing agency "concern." Maximums of 30 and 76 milligrams were detected; the drinking water standard is 10.[27]

Few samples exceed drinking water standards; thus, concerned people have been called "alarmists." But once the standards are exceeded, it's too late. The standard, in effect, becomes an expectation, and the margin of error shrinks to zero in what has been termed the "falling-bodies" approach to water quality evaluation. For a state that rejects legalized gambling, people in southern

Idaho engage in one of the largest imaginable games of chance with the one resource they hold most sacred.

People used to think that dilution with the enormous volume of groundwater was the reason that nitrate problems are not as serious as in Iowa or Nebraska. Keith Higginson said, "In certain areas there will be problems, but the Snake River aquifer is so large that water quality will not be a major issue." Most pollution seems to disappear when it enters the tremendous volume of groundwater, but dilution as water enters the aquifer could be friend or foe. Health and Welfare stated, "Where considerable water is applied to the land surface in the form of precipitation or irrigation water, the potential [of pollution] is greater because additional water is available to leach contaminants below the root zone."[28] Thomas Trout said, "We need to manage systems to cut overapplication of water, which leaches nitrogen into the groundwater."

The horrifying problems of selenium, more poisonous than arsenic and infamous for deaths and deformities of birds living in irrigation return flows in California, Nevada, and elsewhere in the West, have not been seen in Idaho, though selenium naturally occurs through irrigated areas in far eastern Idaho, in a belt west of Idaho Falls, and across a wide swath in the west central area. Selenium problems are typically delayed in colder climates and aggravated by high pH in soil, which is common on the Snake River plain. No one knows if irrigation wastewater could contaminate Idaho groundwater with selenium; studies are just beginning.[29]

Those who argue for dilution of pollution are out of step with the state's water plan: "It is the policy of Idaho that the use of water to dilute pollution is not a beneficial use."[30] The plan bans instream allocations for dilution, which could coincidentally aid other instream uses as well, but specifies nothing about the dilution of pollution by injecting it into groundwater. The thin difference here—twisted as it sounds—is that it's illegal to add clean water to dilute dirty surface water, but it's legal to dilute dirty water by adding it to clean groundwater. In fact, dilution of pollution by dumping it in the aquifer is a common practice.

Wastewater is deliberately injected into the groundwater by irrigators who own land that does not drain to streams. They simply drill wells and channel wastewater into them. Each year, the Snake River aquifer, as a pollution sump, receives 25,000 acre feet of wastewater—8,125,000,000 gallons. The estimate is probably low. "We have trouble just counting all the older wells," said Frank Sherman of the Department of Water Resources. "We still don't know where they all are." Though Health and Welfare is the state agency charged with water quality, the irrigators' waste-injection wells are monitored by the Department of Water Resources. Staff assured me that drinking water standards are met in the untreated wells except for turbidity (silt), phosphorus, nitrogen, and bacteria. These are notable exceptions. The most common herbicide, 2,4-D—some forms of it were banned from use on lawns—was found in 79 percent of the samples, with 36.5 parts per billion being the highest concentration. One hundred parts is the state-accepted limit for drinking water. Studies of wastewater wells in 1982 found eighteen pesticides and breakdown products, the most frequent tailwater additives being 2,4-D, PCP, PCNB, and dicamba.[31]

Health and Welfare formed a groundwater unit only in 1983. Cheryl Brower of the department said, "Most groundwater is good or excellent with only localized problems. But to believe in that analysis in a thorough sense is folly because so little is known. What we *haven't* tested for is greater than what we *have* tested for." One page in a report lists samplings for chemicals in groundwater. "The fact that we can list all the information on one page is probably more significant than any of the information listed."

Senior water quality engineer Dick Rogers said, "If I were in the trout-rearing business at Thousand Springs, I'd be watching that water carefully. Toxins could easily get into that water." Ample illustrations justify concern. In Iowa, 50 percent of public water supplies in alluvial aquifers were tainted by pesticides; in Kansas, 28 percent of tested wells exceeded nitrate standards; in California, fifty-four pesticides have contaminated wells.[32]

Like the irrigators, the Idaho National Engineering Laboratory (INEL) deliberately injected wastes into wells as recently as 1984. Tritium contaminated 42 square miles of Idaho's aquifer. Though found at ten times the drinking water standard, tritium does not concern officials greatly because of its short half-life. Other radioactive isotopes were detected in groundwater: iodine 129 and strontium 90 at three times the standard. The Water Users Association opposed INEL's injections.

The aquifer is the only water supply for most residents of the plain—over 200,000 people—a fact making the underground river eligible for protection as a "sole source" under federal law. In 1982, residents who had organized as the Hagerman Valley Citizen Alert petitioned the U.S. Environmental Protection Agency (EPA) to designate the aquifer and thereby ban federal funds from programs contaminating the water. The law clearly exempts the Bureau of Reclamation and water development activities, but that was not enough assurance to agricultural interests and the state. "If that were called a sole source aquifer, there's no telling what they'd require on the regulation of chemicals," said Bob Burks, expressing a fear of the agribusiness lobby. "People say, 'Why wait for trouble with the groundwater?' but farming would become uneconomic. If those people want the farmer to stop using pesticides and fertilizers, they'd better be prepared to pay a lot more for groceries." In Wyoming, Senator Malcolm Wallop expressed similar disdain for federal interest in keeping groundwater clean, calling this "the new and more dangerous spectrum of federal involvement."[33]

Idaho blocked the EPA-recommended status; the Idaho Water Users Association brochure boasted, "IWUA stimulated significant opposition." Sherl Chapman said, "We're concerned about water quality. What we oppose are people who speculate on the problem." One side speculates that groundwater quality could turn bad and the other side speculates that it won't.

It appeared that the only people seriously concerned about groundwater quality were members of a group who actually live in the Hagerman Valley and employees of the agency that's actually responsible for water quality. In an *Idaho Clean Water* article titled "Snake Plain Aquifer Susceptible to Groundwater Contamination," Health and Welfare stated in the spring of 1988, "It is important to realize that groundwater is not immune to pollution, and practices once thought to be quite benign are now known to threaten this valuable source." Cheryl Brower was hopeful that concern was growing. "Farmers have their own wells in the middle of all this and are looking at better management practices." The legislature passed a bill in 1989 authorizing the state to prepare a groundwater protection plan. "I don't believe in waiting for the threat to materialize," said Reed Hansen, who carried the bill on the floor.

Speculating for a moment that the groundwater problems of

INEL, Minidoka, Burley, Ontario, and the Boise Valley are regarded seriously, and considering that the problems could become more widespread, the question is, what could be done? Once an aquifer is polluted, it cannot be cleaned up.

To eliminate the pollutants is unlikely. To eliminate the quantity of pollutants, however, is eminently feasible, and the method is identical to the method of returning water to the Snake River, of seeing more water in years of drought, of preventing soil loss, of protecting and restoring fisheries, of awarding the Shoshone and Bannock their treaty rights, and of obviating the "need" for Teton Dam. The method is to apply water efficiently to crops and therefore have less runoff and groundwater contamination with sediment, nitrogen, and pesticides.

THE RESPONSE

I've seen what some individual farmers are doing to conserve water. Some are doing a lot. I've seen, on the other hand, what the irrigation establishment says about water conservation—that the point is somewhat moot and counterproductive, a product of distorted and unworkable views of outsiders. Have the irrigators ever felt as threatened as they do now?

"No," said Reed Oldham. "When Palisades was planned, everybody was behind it, but now we have a vast population of non-Idahoans." Indeed, according to the U.S. Census Bureau, only 46 percent of the state's residents were born here. The percentage of nonnatives was probably even greater, however, when the original irrigation projects were built.

Sherl Chapman said, "We used to look at problems as local things. Now, it doesn't matter what the problem is, it's a system-wide problem. That's been a difficult adjustment for us to make. The natural thing is to duck hard and wait for the problem to go away, but it won't." A geologist specializing in hydrology, Chapman spent seven years at the Department of Water Resources; he was the agency's assistant director before taking his job as director of the Water Users Association. "It's foolish to say that agriculture is the only important use of water, but there seems to be a lack of recognition that water rights are a property right. We're not used to the competing pressures, the growing public perception about other uses of the river. The concerns for water quality, recreation, fish, and wildlife are seen by agriculture as an attack on water use. The irrigation groups have become stronger as a result. Each side thinks that it knows what the other thinks, but that's not necessarily so. Everyone needs to work on this problem. I think the level of cooperation will become better in the future."

The Bureau of Reclamation officially supports water conservation efforts. The *Westwide* study stated, "It is expected that total water management increasingly will become a most important means of satisfying new water demands."[34] Max Van Den Berg of the bureau said, "I like to think that we're always promoting efficiencies; that has been our policy."

The Reclamation Reform Act of 1982 required that irrigators receiving federal water prepare conservation plans by 1988. Meeting the deadline were forty-seven of sixty-seven districts in the basin. No review tells if the plans are any good, and no monitoring tells if anything is being done to conserve water.

The bureau's Water Management and Conservation Program is to provide nonstructural solutions for efficiency; Hydromet, for example, is a computerized network of weather stations to allow better scheduling of reservoir operations and irrigation. In theory, the program incorporated the bureau's old Irrigation Management Service, which advised farmers on ways to cut water waste. Nominally staffed in the 1970s, this function received no funds in 1988. The bureau has used money from the Bonneville Power Administration for conservation involving two districts, but there is no budgetary evidence that bureau staff time is now spent on conservation. Nationwide, the program received $120,302 in the bureau's $1 billion budget.

"Water conservation is a program that we'd like to see grow in this corner of the nation," said Robert Barbo of the bureau, "but at the present time, we're not devoting a lot of staff time to it." The Boise office has started conservation studies of three areas—all in Oregon, outside the Snake River basin.

The bureau's Rehabilitation and Betterment (R&B) Program loans money for improvement of irrigation systems—precisely what is needed to reduce carrying water requirements. The terms, however, are far less desirable than the formulas that delivered the

dams to irrigators in the past. In 1989, the bureau allocated
$2 million to the nationwide R&B Program, 0.2 percent of the bud-
get, in spite of congressional directives for water conservation. In
the rare instance where R&B work is done, the irrigation companies
do not strive to reduce unneeded withdrawals, and the bureau
does not require it.

The Idaho Department of Water Resources has a "statutory obligation" to promote efficient use of water but no identifiable program dealing with water conservation. In the past, it loaned money
for sprinkler conversions and canal improvements, though not
with conservation in mind. One of the more explicit references I
found to the "C" word surfaced in a letter from Governor Cecil
Andrus to Michigan Congressman John Dingell when the state
fended off wildlife interests during the Swan Falls debates in
Congress. "We are considering new reservoir projects and management techniques as well as water conservation programs to make
more water available for downstream migration of anadromous
fish."[35]

Like a flash of light in the night, the 1974 *Objectives* report of the
Water Board had called for beneficial *and* efficient use as conditions of water rights, and for "maximum efficiency. . . . steps
must be taken to overcome this waste of a natural resource." But
fourteen years later I found no evidence that the board was doing
anything on conservation. Buried in policy 11, item 3, of the 1986
water plan, the board stated, "Investigate methods of encouraging
more efficient use of water," which is not a policy at all but simply
a job for staff to do if they have time, which they don't under their
current orders.

Offering some hope, Governor Andrus announced the pursuit of
conservation and efficiency as one of six new river protection goals
at a 1989 Idaho rivers conference. He called for state bonding authority to encourage the lining of ditches and other improvements.
"To those who are consumption-oriented, we have a responsibility
to see that water is available, but we also have to see that water is
used in the best manner possible. In the future, water conservation
will make the difference."

To find a written proposal for conservation of water, I had to
uncover an obscure document under the Swan Falls agreement
calling for analysis of "potentially useful approaches in water con-

servation to improve flows for anadromous fish."[36] Disagreeing with the scope of the studies, the state walked out on the process.

Among seven state and federal water agencies I visited, only the SCS had water conservation information on display. In short, the government agencies that are entrusted with the waters of the Snake River are doing almost nothing to promote the efficient use of the water in spite of congressional directives and ample evidence that there is plenty of water for everybody if the existing supplies were only managed efficiently.

The Bureau of Reclamation's optimization study offers a hint of hope. Could the subsidies of the future go toward "production" of water through efficient canals instead of new dams? "Yes," Bob Riley of the bureau said. "Our program is going in the direction of management and efficiency improvements. But this is a complicated matter. We might go out to a district and say, 'We want you to be more efficient.' The first thing it asks is, 'Who pays?' Then, 'Who gets the water that's saved?' 'What about the guy who's irrigating with wastewater?' It all sounds like a big cloud of obstacles, so let's take one case and see if we can work something out with the state and the users and everybody. But first we have to identify a district that wants to participate."

No one has studied the potential of water conservation basinwide. No studies have considered rehabilitation of irrigation systems to save water. Agencies are responding to the issue slowly or not at all. While attitudes, mandates, and work programs evolve in what might be called creeping reform, perhaps economics will catch up to the profligate use of water in the Snake River basin.

THE COST OF WATER

Economists say something that every post-Christmas-sale shopper knows: the lower the price of a product, the higher the volume of sales. Snake River water is among the world's cheapest water supplies since the time of Noah.

Storage for irrigation water purchased from the Bureau of Reclamation has cost as little as 12 cents an acre foot, paid to the government. An acre foot fills a municipal swimming pool or supplies a family of five for a year. A University of Idaho study found that the "hypothetical average total cost" of irrigation water was $28 per acre foot, much more than irrigators pay. "At present, water is a quasi-free good in Idaho."[37] Counting delivery charges that go to canal companies or districts, Minidoka Project farmers pay $11 to $30 per acre, which translates to $1.30 to $6 an acre foot, with most bills at the lower end of this scale. Payments of $12.50 an acre, equivalent to $2.50 an acre foot, are typical—incredibly cheap water. In contrast, Central Valley Project water in California averages $6 an acre foot, a price that is often criticized because it represents only 10 percent of the government's expense.

It's bewildering that a resource so coveted, so guarded by those who hold rights to it, so argued about, and so essential for the entire web of life in the West can be valued so lowly in an economic world and in a free enterprise way of life held as dear as the flag. In other words, it seems absurd that water in the desert is almost free.

Sherl Chapman called Snake River water "real cheap," but added, "People will be as efficient as they want to be regardless of how much they pay for water." Striving for efficient use while paying by the acre farmed instead of by the acre foot of water used is like trying to lose weight at an all-you-can-eat restaurant. Flat-rate customers in cities use two times the water of metered customers. Chapman added, "It would be a nightmare to meter irrigation water. The system is simply not set up that way." The bureau in fact sells storage rights on an acre foot basis, but the cost to the irrigator is so low that there is no incentive for him to save.

The SCS helps farmers with irrigation systems. "We'll talk about less carrying water being needed with a new system," said the SCS's technical adviser Rod Alt, "but the response we get is, 'I have a right and I'm going to take it.' When I started working here, I talked about wastewater return systems and I was laughed out of the room. When water is that cheap, why recycle?"

A lot of water is never requested by the irrigators even though they own rights to it. It's stored in federal reservoirs as a Water Bank whose administration is entrusted to the Committee of Nine, which rents the water out on a yearly basis. Much of this goes to the Idaho Power Company. The price of the water—even in the searingly dry year of 1988—was $2.50 an acre foot. That's 1,300 gallons *per penny*. This is the same water about which the irrigation establishment expounds the not-over-our-dead-bodies attitude regarding winter releases to keep entire fisheries alive. This was the price of water in a year so "critically short" that the state of Idaho planned the resurrection of Teton Dam. (In some other areas, such as the Wood River basin, irrigators did run out of water in 1988.) When state officials say that Snake River storage is so valuable that releases for the survival of salmon and steelhead cannot even be considered, they're talking about a "real world" price of 1,300 gallons per penny, and this is over five times what many irrigators pay the government for their coveted storage rights. If the irrigators are running out of water, why are they selling it for almost nothing? In a similar water banking arrangement in California, purchasers during the 1977 drought paid an average of $61 and as high as $142 per acre foot.

Is rental income a beneficial use of this publicly owned resource whose development demanded enormous subsidies? Or should the unused water, under the use-it-or-lose-it doctrine, be reassigned by the state according to public interest criteria, which include hydropower and instream flows? A technical advisory committee to the state reported that the present Water Bank operation is "probably lawful," but recommended that the bank be "critically examined" for "better utilization."[38] Can the irrigators logically oppose the Shoshone and Bannock's plan to use *their* water as instream flows for fish when the irrigators are renting their *own* water for instream flows for hydropower?

Some water rights can now be sold, but a net of regulations prohibits the functioning of a market economy and thus prevents profiteering of this supposedly public resource. Irrigators can sell only the amount they consume, not the amount they withdraw. They must prove that other users will be unharmed.

Marketing elsewhere has yielded an enticing flow of cash. An extreme case, Utah's Intermountain Power Project paid farmers $1,750 an acre foot. Water from the Colorado–Big Thompson Project was sold for urban use at $2,895 an acre foot.[39] An Idaho governor's statement announced, "The state should encourage the establishment of an effective water marketing system."[40]

By resisting efforts to reappropriate water, irrigators may be sitting on a gold mine. Not prepared to give away unused water to the fishery below Palisades, the irrigators say that if anyone wants water, it's available at $2.50 an acre foot. In the interest of political expediency, federal agencies are preparing to pay irrigators to get water for the swans at Island Park.

When hydropower demand rises or when the Bonneville Power Administration pays for enhancement of fish runs ruined by hydropower dams, windfalls could accrue to anyone with water rights to sell. This prospect may have something to do with the irrigators' fear about losing rights to instream flow improvements, not to mention the fear of an adjudication process that reduces the paper rights, not to mention agriculture's opposition to the Indians selling *their* water for fisheries flows and thereby beating other people to the money. Regardless of the economic possibilities, Sherl Chapman said, "We'll not see wholesale selling of water rights." With a differing opinion from the same organization, Bob Burks warned, "If it's easy to sell, farmers will do it."

Water marketing is a two-edged idea. Without it, the irrigators' unused water would be nearly worthless and therefore its reassignment under the use-it-or-lose-it doctrine to other purposes might be less politically volatile. With marketing, rights can be bought and put to new uses with minimal political strife because the irrigators will make money by selling rights that they received from the state for free. It's an outrage to some people that a select group would be paid for water rights they received at no charge and that they do not use. Hopeful about combining reforms, lawyer Jeff Fereday thinks the new adjudication process, if properly done, will limit irrigators to the water they actually use for beneficial purposes. "Then, a water market can further refine the redistribution of water."

Consultant Ed Chaney added, "If users can contravene state law to keep unused water rights, they'll do it with or without a market economy. If you want reform in wasteful practices, follow the money." Chaney predicts a "public trust program" of the state whereby unused water rights that will presumably surface in the adjudication can be reassigned to public uses.

Some people, including lawyers with the Environmental Defense Fund, say that the irrigators will remain politically protected and water rights will not be reassigned even if the irrigators are not using them, and that marketing is the only way to redistribute this natural wealth. Another idea has vast potential. An irrigation district could have the option of paying for its own improvements and doing what it wants with the saved water, or paying nothing while someone else improves the system and receives the saved water. This could be done by fisheries agencies or hydroelectric producers. Casper, Wyoming, paid for the lining of the Casper–Alcova Irrigation District's canals and received 7,000 acre feet a year from the water saved. The Metropolitan Water District of Southern California plans to fund improvements at the Imperial Irrigation District where 437,000 acre feet can be conserved for $8 to $115 an acre foot—far below the cost of new development. Federal incentives for rehabilitation of irrigation systems either by the project owners or by outside parties could speed the process dramatically, as shown by incentives for small hydropower development through tax breaks and similar advantages.

With responsibilities that would make irrigators blanch, hydropower users *must* make efficient use of their project sites. Otherwise their federal permits might not be renewed but reassigned to applicants who propose more efficient use of the water.

Water marketing will be pursued throughout the West as economic forces inevitably grow more important. The transition represents no less than a shifting of thought: Water is not free, it's worth money. Much of our culture may not understand or attach importance to rivers, or fish, or riparian habitat, but it understands money quite well, and if wasted water means wasted money, less will be squandered.

SEEING THE FUTURE

"Growing food seemed like a worthwhile thing to do," said Gary Nelson, a farmer of 1,800 acres. "There was a purpose, a need in 1974. All that has changed. The economics of it now force you to be a meticulous businessman." At food and at business, I would say Nelson's success is remarkable. He has built a new enterprise, a new farm, a new home.

Unlike many farmers in the Bell Rapids Project, Nelson, his wife, and children live on their farm—a dry, windy plain that stretches south toward Nevada. The site offers the feeling of great height because the drive up requires low-gear out of Hagerman Valley. In fact, the 3,200 foot elevation is lower than the city of Twin Falls.

The bench had only been grazed upon until the technology for
high-lift pumps evolved in the 1960s. Nelson, now thirty-eight,
had done little farming but saw an opportunity. He now raises
sugar beets, potatoes, and grains. Unlike water in other farming
regions along the Snake River, water here costs a lot because of the
expense of pumping from the river—$35 an acre foot.

"The cost encourages you to save water," Nelson said. "When
we installed meters, farmers' use dropped 15 percent. With operation and maintenance charges and 2 acre feet an acre, water costs
about $95 per acre per year. At Twin Falls, $14 is typical. We irrigate only when it's absolutely necessary. We installed our own
weather station and use tables to determine the exact irrigation we
need."

Some other farmers deride high-lift projects as unnecessary energy consumption on marginal lands. Yet Nelson's farm is something
of a model because he's earning a very good living while using
water very efficiently. Canals and ditches lose almost no water. All
irrigation is by sprinklers.

"And in the future," Nelson said, "we'll see tremendous advantages through drip irrigation." This occurs through tubing set in the
root zone of the plants, supplying the precise amount of water in
the precise place. Ideally, the surface of the ground is not even
wetted; evaporative losses are nil. Drip systems irrigate only the
plant. "The potential for drip irrigation of potatoes is great, and it
can be used for any crop, really. The technology is not yet here—
they need to perfect the tubing—but a lot of people are working on
it. This is exciting to me. We'll be able to cut water use to a third of
that used by sprinklers, which automatically lose 30 percent to
evaporation. Drip systems will change the face of agriculture.
There are other benefits too. With no water for weeds, we can cut
our use of herbicides. The quality and yield of potatoes can be
increased by one-third because you lack the variable effect of
sprinklers, such as wet and dry patches when the wind blows."
Drip systems face formidable economic and technological problems, but Nelson is hopeful. "Drip irrigation can't get here fast
enough."

With or without drip, efficiencies will result in newly available
water. Will more lands come into production? "No. In the last six
years, 2,000 acres up here have gone *out* of production. That trend

will probably continue. In Idaho, we overproduce just about everything we grow. The water we save will be available for other uses. That river is not here so I can grow potatoes. That river is the lifeblood of Idaho. If we don't take care of it, it won't take care of us. It's a valuable, fragile resource. It has many facets, and people need to work together to maintain it. We need to manage that water as best we can for the benefits of all people, not just select groups.

"I think most farmers agree. Some say, 'I have a water right and I'm going to take it all even if it means the last drop in the river,' but I don't think that's a typical attitude. Most farmers are sportsmen, they live in Idaho because we have a good way of life. When they're not working, they're enjoying the benefits that the river provides—fishing, boating, a healthy environment. The economy of southern Idaho is agriculturally based, but this is tightly intertwined with everything else. In growing food, we can't afford to ignore everything else."

SEEING WHAT IS POSSIBLE

The myth of unlimited agricultural expansion died in the Snake River basin. The trend has reversed, with marginal land going out of production. Other farming regions of the West are following this path as water-wasting, energy-consumptive, subsidy-supported agriculture clashes with the modern world of limits—economic and natural.

Ask an eastern farmer about irrigating the arid West and he'll respond with the same confoundedness with which he might respond to whitewater rafting: "Why would anyone want to *do* that?" he asks about trying to settle and cultivate in an area so poorly suited to settlement and farming when compared to his own land of rainfall, greenery, and fruitfulness having nothing to do with miner's inches or second feet. Will the economics of agriculture shift back eastward when a desert of mineralized soil constitutes the residual West of the twenty-first century? The timber industry is already returning east. Is western agriculture eroding from the inside-out, much as Teton Dam eroded when it failed so conclusively?

On the other hand, the Snake River basin remains water-rich relative to the rest of the interior West, and the problems of mineral buildup are not as severe as in California's Central Valley or the Colorado basin. While Idaho's climate is not the best, it's better than the high plains and the valleys of the Rockies that are doomed to a short growing season.

Can this rich resource be managed to minimize the fatal problems of nearly every irrigated society known to man? In 1988 Stewart Udall said, "All over the West the changes will be happening. A new balance and a new outlook is developing for the resources of the West." Changes occur, but do they occur fast enough? Back in 1974 the Water Resource Board called for "maximum efficiency of water use" and for efficient use of electricity, control of erosion, and designation of wild and scenic rivers. During the intervening years, some progress has occurred, but the gaps are enormous. Ed Marston of *High Country News* wrote that resistance is institutionalized by the seniority system of water rights, which "locks out the future rather than includes it."

Scott Reed likened the irrigators' dominance to that of a glacier that has slowly ground to a halt. "When you talk about what's *perceived* to be taking livelihoods away and undoing what the forefathers did, that glacier does not recede very fast. Irrigating supremacy will continue, but one hundred years of legal water-right apartheid have ended."

Ed Chaney said, "The system today is a product of thought from the turn of the century. People have built their lives around some one-line articles of faith. Those people are not going to change. But the system will change around them."

Evidence of the evolution is apparent on the State Water Board, still composed of irrigators but also including biologists. Nearly all members reflect new receptivity to other uses of the river. Indeed, the board is sometimes viewed as pulling a foot-dragging Department of Water Resources toward reform. Chair Gene Gray said, "It took the board from 1964 to 1977 to go from strictly agriculture to multiple use. What we're seeing now is a total change in the way people think. Public interest is the new term. When the board was started, 52 percent of the Idaho legislature worked in agriculture; in 1988, the percentage is 32. Our society must come together as an integrated unit. If we don't, no one will be able to afford the lawyers."

Board Member Bill Platts said, "We're not shifting to protection, but simply to the view that we should get the best use out of the river, and that means to include a river with natural values. The change is occurring because the people of Idaho have changed in their outlook."

Senator and rancher John Peavey said, "The state has come leaps and bounds. There's a strong political climate to protect the Snake and other rivers."

Farmer and legislator Reed Hansen elaborated, "The farmers are not part of a mindless group that wants to dry up the river. The majority have a concern. Irrigators are maturing in today's world. No longer can we close our eyes and say, 'It's always been this way.' We can't say, 'Get out of here and leave us alone.' I say to my Republican friends, 'If we don't change, someday they'll clobber us politically and we'll lose it all.' We do feel threatened and fear that what we have will be taken away. We need to accommodate each other, knowing it won't be perfect. I'm confident we can solve a lot of these things if we talk and have patience."

There are still times such as the Water Users Association's seminar for irrigators and water attorneys in 1989 with rabble-rousing by Roger Ling of Burley. One of the busier water lawyers in Idaho, he insisted that the irrigators' water is like gold, and now that farmers have done all the mining, other people are coming along and saying, "Hey, that's nice. I'd like to have that gold. *Give* it to me." One of his many implications seemed to be that farmers own the water as a miner owns an ore deposit, which is not true. "Why should we share?" One irrigator responded. "They want it all for fish." Opposing a plan of mitigation of fish and wildlife losses resulting from hydroelectric dams that didn't really affect irrigation at all, the Users Association decided "to provide a coordinated front of opposition to the proposed plan." Digging itself into an archaic hole that most of Idaho seems to have abandoned with distaste, the Users called for construction of not only Teton but also Lynn Crandall Dam.

John Keys had preceded Roger Ling with a nonthreatening appeal for irrigators to cooperate in seeking solutions to problems on the river. "If we don't make serious attempts to deal with instream flows on behalf of the public, I can assure you that the issue will be dealt with before a judge, and I don't think we're going to like the results. No one has to give up water they need. No one has to lose." Ling, not Keys, got the applause.

I later asked Keys, What it will take to get better cooperation from the irrigation establishment? "Maybe they'll just have to lose once or twice."

Irrigation with Snake River water created a productive agricultural economy. Nobody says it's necessary to alter the society held tightly by people who benefit from livelihoods based on irrigation. What people do say is that the system of water and resource use that has made the irrigation society possible should be reconsidered in light of what has been lost, and should be regarded with a new concern for the future of the river, the fish, the wildlife, the recreation, the environmental vitality, and the people of Idaho. Also with new concern for the long-term health of the agricultural enterprise itself.

The Shoshone and Bannock stated the need for a new approach. "We can pretend that other interests on the Snake River do not exist in which case we, at best, work at cross purposes and, at worst, create layers upon layers of unnecessary conflicts. The Tribes believe that cooperation and adaptive responses to conflicts over water resources is a workable approach."

A religious zeal can be seen in irrigation and farming—the righteousness of the founding of the West, of the pioneers settling a hostile land, of people maintaining homes and communities. Today, there is another religious view—a reverence for life, a reverence held by people who want to protect and restore the river and the land. Belonging to the Shoshone and Bannock and their ancestors long before history, this belief is older than that of any white settler. Belonging to people concerned about the river, this view is also younger—a product of Idaho's conservation movement, of modern pioneers, and of the emerging, broader-based economy here and throughout the West.

Just because water rights were given to irrigators, should a river and a public resource be destroyed? Beyond this ethical bent, evidence is clear that the river and the public resources don't *need* to be destroyed for even short-term economic viability. With reasonable management that many people maintain is essential for the health of agriculture itself, there can be enough water in the Snake River for everybody and for all creatures.

This cannot be said for many other rivers of the West. Right here, the Snake River offers the brilliant potential that the society we've created can solve its own problems and restore much of what is cherished in old ideas and new ideas about Idaho and the American land. I speak of quality, livelihood, opportunity, health, freedom, a reverence for life, and a realization that if we and our children are to remain, we must be caretakers and not exploiters.

What had appeared to be unlikely is in fact waiting to happen. The changes toward a living river are not only eminently feasible but perhaps inevitable as more people become aware of what is possible.

Milner Dam to Swan Falls

MILNER GORGE

Where water should have been running, I walked downstream from Milner Dam. My amazement at the desiccated scene increased when I considered that this river has run 87 miles longer than the entire Delaware and that the basin above Milner encompasses an enormous 17,180 square miles.

The Snake River ranks as America's foremost example of a large river dried up by diversions. Others are the Colorado River in Mexico, the Rio Grande in New Mexico, and the San Joaquin and Kings rivers of California, but only the Snake is reduced from such a massive river to nothing at a single dam site.

Milner Dam causes the ultimate low flow, though irrigators accomplished nearly the same thing as far up as Jackson Dam where flows were cut to nothing in the 1960s. At Lorenzo and Blackfoot, flows at times approach zero. In recent years, Milner has not been as dry as it was. Decreased diversions have resulted in an addition of 0.8 million acre feet passing the dam on average years since the mid-1970s. The water appears as hydroelectric flow bought by the Idaho Power Company from the Water Bank after June and as springtime floods uncontainable in upstream dams. Is there a value in having water in the river at Milner?

"No," said Reed Oldham of the Committee of Nine. "The state's water plan says zero flow at Milner. The Snake River above Milner is *fully appropriated.*"

In resource planning, the concept of minimum flow is to maintain a small amount of water for fish, wildlife, and uses that require water in the river. But here, a state water plan—presumably with the weight of science and public interest behind it—proclaims a flow of zero, not just tolerating but formally sanctioning this dry-riverbed embarrassment to the very essence and profession of planning.[1]

"That minimum," said Keith Higginson, director of the Idaho Department of Water Resources in 1988, "is a matter of state policy. We do not require, expect, need, or want any flow to pass Milner. We do not foresee a change in current policy. We consider the Snake a new river below Milner."

It's easy to get the idea that nobody cares about the Snake River in this gutted canyon while the most powerful lobby in Idaho calls for zero flow—nothing else will do.

Another local view is presented by Rob Lesser, who has lived in Boise all his life, excepting travels to whitewater rivers of the world. It is fitting that this man, growing up near the Snake River tributaries of the Payette, Lochsa, and Selway, would become one of the country's preeminent kayakers of big whitewater, breaking through barriers intimidating to other boaters. He has pushed the sport beyond what was thought possible.

> When you grow up in the West, in the middle of all this, you don't realize the effects of what we've done. We saw this happy-faced Reddy Kilowatt, the building of the Hells Canyon dams, and we said, "Isn't this great?" You didn't think about what had been lost. Then something opens your eyes. It was in the early eighties when the water was high that we went up and looked at Milner Gorge.
>
> The rapid below Milner Dam is undoubtedly the longest big rapid in Idaho, probably in the American West. I think you'd have to go to Niagara Gorge or British Columbia to find a comparable drop in North America. Milner is several times the length, and tougher than Lava Falls.

Lesser speaks of the big rapid in the Grand Canyon, regarded in much literature as the preeminent rapid of North America. Until now. "I don't know who ran Milner first, probably people from Pocatello. Some friends and I drove up there and were pleasantly surprised. Here in southern Idaho is world-class whitewater, undiscovered into the 1980s." Lesser featured the 1.6-mile rapid, "The Milner," in a commercial video that shows one roaring mayhem whose upper layer consists more of air than water. The camera loses the kayakers beneath foam. Maybe twenty people a year run the Milner. But not many climb Mount Everest either, and Milner Gorge is the Everest of big whitewater in North America.

Beyond the big drop, repeated wonders unfold. Seven miles below Milner Dam lies Caldron Linn (*Linn* is Scottish for waterfall) where, only five years after Lewis and Clark's journey, the Hunt expedition abandoned its attempt to reach Astoria by water when a boat crashed and a man drowned. A party member wrote that the river's "terrific appearance beggars all description." The Snake River's first pioneers got out and walked, and based on their humbling experience, travelers shunned this canyon until the time of Lesser. From Caldron Linn to Twin Falls, 14 miles, the Murtaugh section lacks the extremes of the Milner but challenges advanced paddlers. Kayakers delight on scores of waves for river surfing; the wave of their dreams is 6 feet high and 100 feet wide. Ron Watters at Idaho State University said, "The Murtaugh reminds me of the Grand Canyon, only the rapids are close together."

Glimpses of this gorge, which is more significant than anyone imagined, can be caught from the dizzying height of the Hansen bridge east of Twin Falls. You don't even see the canyon until you walk to its edge and then stop suddenly at the chasm between the field you are in and the next one, a quarter mile away. In its natural state, Milner Gorge would be one of the more extraordinary canyons in the West. Much of this fascinating though water-robbed landmark is public property, administered by the Bureau of Land Management. Four outfitters raft the Murtaugh section commercially, but activity is limited by the short season to 2,000 customers in a good year. In dry years, such as 1988 when the upstream reservoirs didn't drink their fill and therefore didn't spill, boating exists not at all. Even during wet years, the gorges lie in sun-baked stillness in June because of diversions.

Lesser's passion and the outfitters' livelihoods are seen as frivolous pursuits to water rights owners. Whitewater, however, is only one potential use of the river. Al Van Vooren of the Department of Fish and Game said, "With even a few hundred cfs, we could have a fishery. Zero flow at Milner is not the way it's always going to be."

"The elimination of the river for most of the year is a sacrilege,"

Lesser said. "There's a future in the Snake River that's not being realized. We're not talking about taking water rights away from anyone, but we are saying that the system should be studied to see if there's a way to release water at certain times and realize a tremendous recreational value. With 10,000 cfs on summer weekends, we'd have a world-class attraction in Twin Falls, Idaho." Indeed, that chamber of commerce could quit reminiscing about "Evel" Knievel's dud "skycycle" of 1974 and get around to really promoting something. "A sociological change is happening in this state," Lesser added. "People are more conscious of natural resources and discovering they can enjoy these places. This section of the Snake River was seen as beyond reach, not something people could participate in, but now rafting and paddling are growing in popularity. Maybe it'll take ten years, but eventually, other uses of the river will not be totally at the mercy of the irrigation system."

The Twin Falls and North Side Canal companies proposed to further reduce the season of high water by diverting winter flows to a hydroelectric plant 1.6 miles below the dam. They had a hard time believing it when Lesser and his colleagues objected. "It was amazing," the Boise native recalled, "to walk into a hearing room full of sixty-five- to eighty-year-old men who had no idea what I was doing there. We're dealing here with a total cultural difference." The boaters asked for releases from Milner as a condition to the new development. Fishing interests likewise argued that if the irrigators want to divert yet more water, they should be willing to compromise.

Bob Burks of the Water Users Association recalled, "Some kayakers showed up and wanted releases. Those people have no authority to get a minimum flow past Milner. That's licensed water."

In a pathbreaking environmental impact statement, the Federal Energy Regulatory Commission (FERC) staff, with a one-sided, sixty-eight-year heritage of development, recommended a 300 cfs minimum from Milner as a condition of the new hydro plan in 1987, and a release of 1,260 cfs in the nonirrigation season—enough to wet 60 percent of the channel.[2] An agreement was struck whereby the Idaho Power Company—a cooperator with the canal companies—will release a "target" flow of 200 cfs when it's available for purchase from the irrigators' Water Bank, which typically begins in July. Though that amount is not nearly enough for kayaking, it will support a modest fishery. "We weren't that pleased with the agreement," said Jack Eakin of the Twin Falls Canal Company, "but, we will not be giving up any of *our* water; it will all be from the Water Bank." With the ink hardly dry on the agreement, the irrigators considered changing the distressingly malleable rules of the Water Bank to penalize farmers who sell water for Idaho Power's use over Milner Dam.

Another development was proposed at Caldron Linn, a nationally registered historic site, but raucous objection surfaced to the entrepreneur's plan to divert all but 160 cfs for half a mile. FERC staff called the project "not preferred." The Bureau of Land Management (BLM) refrained from opposition but reported that the Murtaugh section is "likely to be studied under the wild and scenic rivers act."

THE FALLS

Driving on roads as flat and gridded as in Illinois, I arrived at Twin Falls—not the city, but the falls. Signs for a scenic overlook lured me to an oasis watered by the Idaho Power Company where, camera in hand, I walked to the place identified as a scenic view. A chain-link fence topped by barbed wire provided complete protection, and the view of Twin Falls, 180 feet high, was like a view from a prisoner-of-war camp, except that a hole had been cut in the fence for cameras.

Some people call Twin Falls "TF," but the city's other nickname, Double Drip, is not just figurative. Green algae flowed more plentifully than water where the river dribbled over the landmark cataract. The chamber of commerce's seal says, "Magic of Resources" beneath a drawing of the falls, depicted, of course, when it ran, unlike what exists much of the time. Even when Twin Falls is actually a falls, it is no longer a *twin* falls because Idaho Power has blocked one side for hydroelectricity.

In the shade of the picnic area I cooked burritos while a neighboring foursome aired Tina Turner full blast. A shirtless boy sauntered over to my van. "This music bother you?" It didn't, especially "Be good to me," but he listened for a moment as we talked. "I think maybe I'll turn it down a little anyway." Then, what I heard was the snarl of a speedboat that returned again and again as young men must do with fast boats in small reservoirs—the dam above the falls backs up water for 1.6 miles. As I ate, the boy and a slender girl waged a soda battle, spraying their beverages from shaken bottles, then washing under the faucet.

I drove downriver several miles to Shoshone Falls (sho-SHONE), 212 feet high—higher than Niagara and a phenomenal thousand feet wide when Milner Dam's spigot is turned on. Chamber of commerce brochures label this the "Niagara of the West." Niagara—the continent's greatest tourist attraction—was the object of North America's first major conservation cause. A park was established in 1885 and power development was restricted.[3] No less striking to preirrigation visitors, Shoshone Falls was visited by photographer Timothy O'Sullivan of the Geologic Survey of the Fortieth Parallel in 1868, who called this "one of the most sublime of the Rocky Mountain scenes." In 1901 a congressional bill would have designated a Snake River Canyon National Park here, but the bill died and the irrigation systems were built instead.[4] Signs on Interstate 84 identify the falls as a "Scenic Attraction," but on most days, a slimy trickle is all you see. Having been to Milner, I took this in stride, though I remembered my first view of the Snake River nineteen years before, when I wondered where the water had gone, and stood puzzled, feeling that nature had been warped in a sinister way, as if I had seen a three-legged deer or a toothless squirrel. An older couple from the East shared the overlook with me. Indignant, the woman said, "This is *nothing* like Niagara Falls!"

Also spying the limestone view were a short-haired, clean-cut boy and his chunky girlfriend. "Yeah," the boy said to the woman, "they need all the water for irrigation."

"Humph," said the woman who obviously, as the irrigators say, just didn't understand the way the Snake River works.

Something Rob Lesser has not done—in 1929 Al Fawsett ran this impressive drop in a canvas boat for $733. He broke his right hand. Along this vein, Evel Knievel attempted to jump the Snake River canyon near here in a rocketlike skycycle, but when the craft sputtered, Evel had to parachute. In the chamber's brochure, his photo precedes all other wonders of the "Magic Valley," as the region is known.

Before any dams were built, Shoshone Falls was the most significant division of an upper and lower Snake River. This marked the upper limit for spawning salmon and steelhead.

Twin Falls (population 27,750) is veneered by miles of land use kindly described as "strip commercial." Beyond the flashy armor of neon, fast food, and gas, I tripped upon the city center and strolled through a pleasant downtown.

Below the city, Rock Creek gained notoriety as a "wildlife habitat obituary." Challenged by that inglorious label, the Soil Conservation Service (SCS) and other agencies worked to retard farmland erosion, and the stream now supports wild trout, proof that restoration is possible in unlikely places. The Snake River murmurs through quiet stretches and tumbles over the rapids of Pillar Falls, Auger Falls, and Kanaka Rapids. The startling fact is that from the trickle below Milner Dam, the river is reborn with 6,000 cfs of groundwater entering through a 10-mile length of perforated cliffs known as Thousand Springs.

THOUSAND SPRINGS

There probably *are* 1,000 springs bursting with water believed to come from the Lost River, which sinks mysteriously into the lava, 150 miles away in eastern Idaho. (The Lost River has its own set of "Thousand Springs" between the Lemhi and Lost River mountains.) Runoff from Birch Creek, Silver Creek, additional streams, and unconsumed irrigation water add to a spring flow rivaled in the United States only by Missouri's Current River. Eleven of the nation's sixty-five largest springs flow from these cliffs.[5] Some single outlets yield 300,000 acre feet a year[6]—enough to supply all of Idaho with domestic water (the same amount would serve 1.5 percent of the irrigated farmland at 5 acre feet per acre).[7] The water discharges steadily at 58 degrees.

Sounding like Niagara, for which it was named, one spring erupts from the canyon's face with 300 cfs—enough for a canoeing-sized river—and sprays across a sieved slope of lava, impenetrable with greenery in the desert canyon. Other spring flows are born at the 400-foot canyon rim opposite Highway 30 and leap from waterfalls. Four creatures here are candidates for the endangered species list. The Shoshone sculpin is a fish endemic to two spring branches; the giant Columbia River limpet, Snake River physa (a snail), and Bliss Rapid snail are found in a few other places. Like Milner Gorge and Shoshone Falls, an undisturbed Thousand Springs would surely possess national park qualities.

But it is not undisturbed. All springs but one are affected by hydropower diversions, fish farm withdrawals, or irrigation. The one remaining spring—a falls frothing from multiple fissures—has been saved by The Nature Conservancy of Idaho, which is to say, by Guy Bonnivier.

"An estate was going to be sold, and it included 3 miles of river frontage and more springs than I could count," Bonnivier explained. "We had a chance to protect Idaho's largest great blue heron rookery, a golden eagle's nest, and bald eagles in winter." The property also houses the world's largest colony of Shoshone sculpins and the finest riparian habitat along the Snake River below the Fort Hall Bottoms.

"There was a serious problem," Bonnivier added. "I needed $1.2 million. Developers wanted to build houses, fish farms, and hydro projects. They offered $2 million, but we offered cash. The judge decided in our favor and slammed the gavel down. I walked out not knowing how I was going to pay for the place. The Nature Conservancy was just a bank account; I had to raise my own money. Three attorneys and I finished the loan agreements one hour before the closing."

In addition to the real estate problems, Bonnivier saw the need to secure the flow of Minnie Miller and persuaded the Idaho Parks and Recreation Department to file for a minimum streamflow. "The whole thing was an extreme longshot." We had been talking in the living room of the Thousand Springs farmhouse. "Let's go look at the land."

Bonnivier yanked the starter, the Zodiac coughed into a hum, and we motored down the tributary river created by the springs. A vivid green algae called veronica blanketed the bed. Schools of fish darted from us. We passed Minnie Miller with its extravagance of waterfalls and mattresses of moss and entered the Snake, now recharged with springwater 52 miles below the big dry at Milner. We cruised east through upper reaches of the 9-mile impoundment behind Upper Salmon Falls Dam. Springs spilled from cliffs, though the largest was enclosed in an Idaho Power Company pipe that dropped from rim to buzzing power plant. At Blue Heart Spring, beyond the conservancy's boundary, we stared into aquamarine depths of tropical beauty, a color defying what I had thought possible in the realms of light. At Box Canyon, we walked up to waterfalls and spring flows that made an instant river at a semicircular cliff face, the eleventh largest spring in North America, supporting several rare species. The conservancy's action at Thousand Springs is one of the success stories of conservation along the Snake River, but like suckers in spawning season, the threats just keep on coming.

Aquacultural entrepreneur Earl Hardy wanted to divert much of the water from Box Canyon for another fish farm, though his plan has been challenged in court.

FISH FARMS

Scores of fish farms are wedged onto floodplains and into canyon crannies and produce 90 percent of the commercially processed trout in the United States—25 million pounds. Serving a Clear Springs fish farm, a siphon tube dives under the river from Box Canyon and emerges to disgorge 300 cfs on the other side. A network of raceways—18-by-160-foot feedlots—houses rainbow trout from fingerling size to dinner plate diameter. "The water is of top quality and quantity," said Duane Wilson, manager of the Clear Springs Hatchery near Thousand Springs. "Even in winter, the temperature drops only one degree." Twenty people worked at the hatchery full time.

Fish feces are not much to carp about in normal situations, but imagine the excretion of half a million trout in the equivalent of a farm pond. Employees rake the bottoms of raceways, vacuum waste into a settling vat, and haul it away. Dead fish, uneaten fish food, chemicals from cleaning, and tons and tons of pharmaceuticals for diseases in the Thousand Springs anthills of aquaculture are troublesome additives to the Snake River.

The U.S. Environmental Protection Agency (EPA) did not require pollution discharge permits of the hatcheries until 1984. "Residents complained," said the EPA's Wally Scarburgh. "That's what it takes to get an agency's attention. We now require permits for farms producing 20,000 pounds of fish. We're also trying to check on smaller operations." Compliance is based on an operators' honor system. Until 1988, the EPA telephoned ahead to schedule visits and were accused of "contrived" enforcement. "Now," said Scarburgh, "we frequently inspect unannounced." After one firm released belching loads of fish food and manure into Billingsly Creek, the EPA intended to fine the company $23,000.

The Idaho Department of Health and Welfare reported that while many fish farms are meeting requirements, water is still being polluted. Below the 10-mile aquaculture complex, algae blankets so much of the Snake River that ducks can nearly walk across. Has anyone considered the effect of seventy large and unknown numbers of small hatcheries growing many millions of fish? "No," Scarburgh said. "A cumulative analysis would be a good thing to do."

The Fish and Wildlife Service wrote that further aquaculture development will have "adverse impacts on fish, wildlife, and recreation."[8] Bob Burks, adamant defender of irrigation, opposed new fish farms. "They've taken up nearly all the springs. Some of those people just don't care about the public resources."

THE PEOPLE AND THE EARTH

Bill Chisholm inherited what he called a "local outlook" by growing up on the Snake River plain, where his father owned a farm equipment business. "In college, I enrolled in business, and a teacher in a government class said, 'Take your values system apart brick by brick and look at it. Keep it or don't keep it, but decide for yourself.' He taught me to think. Then I fought forest fires for seventeen seasons and saw Idaho from a helicopter. Things look different from up there. You get a larger view of the land. You see what's happening to it."

Today, Chisholm fights to keep southern Idaho "livable" by halting more hydropower dams and the development of plutonium for nuclear weapons. "If you pollute the aquifer at the Idaho National Engineering Laboratory, you pollute the Snake River the whole way to the ocean. Officials say what they do is safe. Sure, it's *all* safe. The Nevada test site was safe. Agent Orange was safe. People don't believe that anymore. There's something in the conservative mind-set that works for us—a distrust of 'Big.' Big business, big government, big weapons, big anything."

Chisholm has a reputation as an "environmental activist," though he dislikes the label. He dislikes the use of all labels except the opprobrious "big." "There are people who want development at all costs, but a lot of people want quality, they live in Idaho because of the environment. So when somebody talks about altering the balance of life around here, a lot of people get upset.

"There are those who would unrecognizably change the face of this land, suck this river dry, pollute the groundwater. I feel we're at war, not using guns, but still battling for our lives, for our existence, for the way of life that has been Idaho."

This man's hair was tied in a ponytail. He lived in a teepee year round. And he won the 1988 primary election for state senator. He received 43 percent of the vote in the general election, a good showing considering that his county last elected a Democratic legislator in 1936 and that his opponent benefited from a Mormon get-out-the-vote drive aimed at defeating a state lottery.

"I believe in stable-state economics. The alternative is the steroid state. Like steroids in the body, it might seem to do good for awhile, but it causes the system to break down. We should provide for everybody's life but not destroy the basis for life. The river is the basis for life in this valley, but look at what we're doing to it. We needed to make the changes years ago."

Chisholm sells T-shirts emblazoned, "Idaho, it's not for sale." Each comes with a card written by Bill: "Idaho—it can be seen, felt and breathed, but it is *not for sale*—it is a gift from God—a part of the Earth Mother. . . . We have a beautiful thing going for us here in Idaho, but as with most beauty, it is fragile. The earth, the sky, the water, the lifestyle have a connection—they are interdependent. We must live our lives and make our decisions in a way that acknowledges the relationship and promotes the balance between the people and the earth."

THE HAGERMAN REACH

At the base of Lower Salmon Falls Dam, Jeff Jarvis, his wife Donita Cotter, and I embarked in his raft. Phoenix-like, the Snake had been recharged by springwater; 6,000 cfs rolls in green waves. Perhaps no other river in North America is revived so well after such wretched abuse.

A recreation planner with the Bureau of Land Management (BLM), Jarvis guided the raft and interpreted the 7-mile canyon called the Hagerman reach. He pointed to the hackberry, a small tree of the Southern Rockies that appears at the Snake because the climate is warm. "We have a river that runs through four states," Jeff said, "and when I see a few acres of good riparian habitat, I get excited. What's that say about the balance of development and protection?"

Commercial rafting is destined to underpin the valley's recreation industry; three outfitters and over 5,000 people run this river, which can be done all summer. We were passed by five boats brimming with laughing families.

We avoided wading fishermen; rainbow and brown trout draw many thousands of anglers a year. Jarvis pivoted the raft into a roller coaster of breaking waves. Consumed by his pastime and profession, he said, "This is one of the finest recreation areas in southern Idaho."

The Hagerman reach will not stay this way if Wiley Dam is built. The city of Tacoma, Washington, applied to dam the entire section. The Idaho Power Company had proposed the same project in 1983; the FERC dismissed it because of a lack of power needs.

From Milner to Swan Falls, developers have filed FERC applications at Milner Dam, Star Falls (Caldron Linn), Kanaka Rapids, Auger Falls, Wiley, and Dike. Auger Falls would eliminate prime mallard duck habitat.[9] Dike Dam would bury 7 miles of remote canyon below Bliss Dam. And so forth. I asked Jarvis which section of the river he would sacrifice for hydropower. He did not hesitate. "So you have six kids; which of them would you allow somebody to shoot?"

The individual losses would hurt, but the cumulative effect would obliterate values that doggedly survived a century of assault on the river. Water quality would plummet without rapids that maintain oxygen levels. Tim Litke of Idaho's Department of Health and Welfare said, "The river is stretched right now. It's loading up with agricultural materials, and it can't purify itself."[10]

White sturgeon, the largest freshwater fish on the continent, survive in several sections, and Idaho Fish and Game plans to reintroduce them in reaches including Hagerman. Dike Dam threatens one of only three reaches where sturgeon reproduce, and Al Van Vooren, of the Department of Fish and Game, regarded maintenance of their habitat as the foremost issue in resident fisheries of the river.

The power is not needed in Idaho. The Idaho Power Company sells 23 percent of its electricity to California and other states and dropped plans for new dams because of sagging local demand. Other developers persist because they can force Idaho Power to buy the electricity at high rates governed by the Public Utility Regulatory Policies Act (1978). Congressional intent was to develop power sources other than foreign oil; the effect is to destroy rivers without a justification of need. "People object to sending Idaho water out of state," Jarvis said. "Is it any different if we dam our rivers to send electricity south? Speaking for myself, since this is my day off, I find that hard to accept."

Fish and Game director Jerry Conley asked, "If these developments are done by out-of-state interests, then when we need electricity, will we go to other sites that are more damaging, or will we have to buy power out of state at higher prices?" The state's water plan raises the same concern: If *they* build dams now, then *we* won't be able to build them later. Is state opposition to river destruction only a deposit in Idaho's bank account of future dam sites?

The U.S. Fish and Wildlife Service flatly opposed all additional dams on the Snake and regarded main-stem threats as "high priority." Is any other agency looking at the whole river?

"No one," Jarvis answered, "is looking at the Snake in a cumulative sense." The FERC had done "cluster impact assessments" on Washington's Snohomish River, the Salmon River, and the eastern Sierra Nevada, though that agency's sense of cumulative impacts falls short of others' expectations. But investigating four of the Snake River proposals, the FERC reported "significant cumulative adverse impacts," and called Star Falls and Auger Falls "unique visual resources" as the last two undeveloped waterfalls on the river.

Floating along in Jarvis's boat, I slowly raised my eyes from the water to the riparian edge, to grassy slopes, to rock faces, and to the sky. Stripping civilization away, I imagined the Snake River of 1901. From Milner to King Hill, 91 miles of canyons were bursting with whitewater, plunging over waterfalls, garnering the Thousand Springs, nurturing the sturgeon, hosting salmon and steelhead below Shoshone Falls. It was a desert river unexcelled in North America, comparable in some ways with the Grand Canyon, though far surpassing it in diversity and biological value. This whole section of the Snake River clearly possessed national park quality. If we could acquire another Grand Canyon today, would we do it? Will we want another Grand Canyon in the future?

"When does something become important enough to protect?" Jarvis asked. "When half of it's gone? When 90 percent is gone? Once a species is down to a few surviving pairs, the genetic pool is not enough. Let's look at the whole Snake River and ask, how much should be developed? Only cumulative studies will address those kinds of questions."

Idaho has taken a step in the right direction. In 1988 the legislature passed the Rivers Planning and Protection Act. The Water Resource Board will consider protection for sections of six streams: this reach of the Snake, the Priest in northern Idaho, the Henry's Fork, the South Fork Boise, and the Payette's North Fork, South Fork, and main stem. The act's genesis came twelve years before; during his previous term at Water Resources, Keith Higginson said, "We've gone very extensively into public opinion surveys . . . and they're telling us very loud and clear that they want wild and scenic river systems, they want minimum streamflows established, they want our streams, our quality streams in Idaho protected, but also want a continued growth of the economy."[11] The draft water plan reported that eighty-one stream segments of 3,100 miles "could be preserved for their natural beauty."[12] The entire Snake River was considered a "greenbelt" for recreation development by local governments. No action was taken, though the water plan of 1986 recommended a "natural and recreational rivers system." Part of the motivation was to sidestep federal protection; a state system would be more responsive to the needs and desires of Idahoans.

Likewise, legislative action in 1988 was intended "to limit the scope" of protection by the Northwest Power Planning Council (see Chapter 7).

The Department of Water Resources will study the six rivers. If designations are enacted, Idaho will become the thirty-second state with a scenic rivers program. Meanwhile the law prohibits new dams for two years. Lawmakers, however, made one exception in the Milner–King Hill reach. The Milner hydroelectric diversion, proposed not by out-of-state interests but by the irrigators of the Twin Falls and North Side Canal companies, is exempt from all requirements.

THREE ISLAND CROSSING

Below Bliss dam the river chops through two rapids and winds through a wild canyon threatened by Dike Dam. Beyond, the village called King Hill is shaded by cottonwoods, and farther downstream, at Glenns Ferry, I rattled over railroad tracks and coasted to Three Island Crossing State Park, exactly halfway down the Snake River, headwaters to the Columbia. Here is the most historic site on the river. From 1841 until the Civil War, settlers traveled through the Twin Falls area, then forded here—water level permitting—because the north side trail to Fort Boise was the most direct.

Kit Carson helped John Frémont cross the Snake in 1843, losing a cannon in the process. Quite early in the technology of river running, they claimed to have constructed an inflatable boat: "We had a resource in a boat, which was filled with air and launched." Narcissa Whitman crossed in 1863. "The last branch we rode as much as half a mile in crossing. . . . Both cart and mules were turned upside down in the river and entangled in the harness. The mules would have been drowned but for a desperate struggle to get them ashore."[13] Peter Burnett wrote, "In crossing we killed a salmon weighing twenty-three pounds, one of our wagons running over it as it lay on the bottom of the pebbly stream." Frémont stated that the depth was 6 to 8 feet; others reported 2 to 4 feet. In 1869 a ferry was started at Glenns Ferry; for 119 years no one has needed to ford here, but I decided to try.

Like a good Oregon Trail pioneer, I prepared well on that cool day in June. They caulked wagons; I put on a wet suit, zipped my best life jacket, and clutched a ski pole. The bottom was not pebbly but robed in algae whose biomass is surely greater than that of all the potatoes in Idaho. Fifty feet from shore, water lapped at my waist; at 100 feet it rippled chest deep and entered my wet suit with quite a cooling sensation felt the whole way down. I took one more step and began floating toward Fort Boise. My feet felt nothing but the spooky tangle of algae. According to Frémont's estimate, it was 950 feet to the other side, and as to my own estimate, I couldn't *see* the other side. I swam back to the north shore, untied my boat from the van, and paddled across this ford the way anyone with sense in 1843 would have done given the possession of two canoes.

THE BRUNEAU RIVER

The river entered its second longest reservoir where Idaho Power's C.J. Strike Dam flooded 44 miles and 1,125 acres of riparian forest along with whitewater that must have been impressive; steamboats were unable to ascend one of the rapids. The Bureau of Reclamation wanted to build dams here and at Bliss, but the Idaho Power Company beat them to it.[14]

From the south, the Bruneau River, averaging 411 cfs, trickles into the reservoir during the irrigation season. This river and its tributary, the Jarbidge, spectacularly incise a horizon-reaching plateau of sagebrush. The rivers' capricious beauty is available to boaters risking a short season of high water, vehicle-wasting roads, knuckle-banging rapids, no exit for days, and buzzing dens of rattlesnakes that can effectively aim low on sandal-clad invaders. These qualities make the Bruneau one of the few truly wild desert rivers. The Interior Department recommended 121 miles for the national rivers system.[15]

Driving to a Bruneau overlook, I passed a sign bearing this cryptic message: "Warning, this road crosses a U.S. Air Force bombing range. For the next 12 miles dangerous objects may drop from aircraft." The bombers came but spared me.

Downstream, the sun-dried community of Grand View sits along the Snake, and Highway 67 crosses the languid river, 430 feet wide according to my pacing on the bridge. I paused in astonishment to photograph J.R. Simplot's feedlot, 50,000 head strong, back-to-back feedlots that stretch down the valley as far as the eye can see. Also near Grand View is Envirosafe Services' repository where 41,000 tons of hazardous waste were disposed in 1987, three-quarters of it from other states.[16] Electricity is shipped out of Idaho and toxic wastes are shipped in.

THE BIRDS OF PREY NATURAL AREA

The Birds of Prey Natural Area spans both sides of the river and Swan Falls Reservoir for 81 miles with the greatest density of nesting raptors on the continent, including several hundred pairs of hawks, eagles, falcons, and owls.[17] Morlan Nelson of Boise, an authority on raptors, knew of the canyon's importance in 1967 when he spoke with Edward Booker, Bill Meiners, and Hugh Harper— Bureau of Land Management officials who moved the designation of the federal lands through a governmental maze.

Harper, now retired from a thirty-five-year career in wildlife management, launched his Boston Whaler motorboat above Swan Falls Dam, and the wind blew his shock of snow-white hair as we motored upriver. On the cliffs fronting the river, nesting sites were visible by splays of whitewash below them. "The time to see birds is early May," Harper said. "By June the young have fledged and it gets so hot up there they can't stand it." With binoculars, we located an occasional hawk. Beyond the rim, sage and greasewood plains are home of the Townsend ground squirrel and black-tailed jackrabbit, food for the raptors that forage up to 15 miles away. While much of the Snake River plain supported small mammals in great numbers, Birds of Prey is a rare remaining section where raptors can both nest and feed.

Within the study boundaries, 159,000 acres had already been divested by the government under the Desert Lands Act for irrigation, which eliminated small mammal habitat from the best soils. Another 111,000 acres were under application. Supporting the giveaway, Sagebrush Rebellion, Inc., sued without success to halt the use of federal lands for the natural area.[18] Interior Secretary Cecil Andrus agreed to expansion of the 26,000-acre area in 1979, but not without one compromise that cut the size from a study area of 833,000 acres to 482,000 and another that allowed reconsideration of protection in the 1990s.

THE SWAN FALLS AGREEMENT

Swan Falls Dam, named for trumpeter swans of long ago, is the Snake River's oldest dam. In 1901 salmon were blocked from 157 miles of river by the hydroelectric project, built for a mine that folded before the power arrived. Rehabilitated in 1987, the dam is the subject of one of the more important decisions regarding the river. The Swan Falls agreement enmeshes hydropower, irrigation, water rights, agricultural development, wildlife, fish, governors, congresspeople, and state and federal agencies, though this has occurred through accident more than through any vision of integrated management or commitment to a basinwide view. Too complex for most of the media, the controversy has eluded all but the experts.

The unlikely root of the agreement lay in a coal-fired power plant called Pioneer, proposed by the Idaho Power Company near Boise in the 1970s. Energy use had been booming in Idaho. A primary reason was the pumping of irrigation water to benches high above the river, done as though there were no tomorrow. Idaho Power foresaw demands increasing 7 percent a year, doubling in a decade. The 1976 draft water plan projected generation requirements growing from 1,300 to 10,630 megawatts in 2020; coal-fired plants—of which there were none in Idaho—were to yield most of the new power. The company, agricultural industry, and Republican politicians all lined up behind Pioneer, but this came at an apex of environmental and consumer awareness. Pioneer represented no less than a turning point in the use of water and power in Idaho—a symbolic end of hydropower and the beginning of thermal generation.

State Senator John Peavey was one of few people who saw beyond the veneer of rising demand dictating rising production and spoke out with bedrock reasoning: Water taken from the river to irrigate new land would reduce the amount of water available for hydroelectricity, while at the same time it would increase the need for electricity through pumping. Coal-fired electricity would send rates soaring, making farming less economic at the same time newly cultivated lands flooded the market. By expanding, the agricultural industry was cutting its own throat. Coal generation would cost seven times that of hydropower. Idaho Power admitted that with one coal plant, everyone's rates would more than double.

Most farmers didn't hear Peavey very well because of their vociferous approval as they stepped into the arc of this double-edged sword. Life had been based on more, more, more, but as Pat Ford wrote in his excellent article on the subject, "the biggest threat to southern Idaho farms was now more farms."[19]

The 1976 state water plan projected irrigation of another 860,000 acres and delivery of supplemental water to 379,000. Lost hydropower revenues from irrigating 450,000 new acres were conservatively estimated at $66 million a year.[20] Residential ratepayers would subsidize the high-lift farms, typically corporate- and absentee-owned.[21] An Interior Department study found that irrigators would pay 13 percent of the pumping costs; residential ratepayers would cover the rest. New diversions would have completely dried up the river below Swan Falls, repeating the insult of Milner Dam without the alibi of a nineteenth-century consciousness.

Like other utilities, Idaho Power was enamored of mega-projects such as the Hells Canyon dams. Big was better, and no one denied the inevitability of thermal power if new land continued to be irrigated. But Pioneer was defeated in a three-county vote, and the Public Utility Commission (PUC) disapproved the application in 1976 because of environmental problems and rate increases.

The case rattled a system set on consuming water, land, and power for growth at any cost. Not stopping here, Senator Peavey introduced a bill to place a moratorium on new water allocations. During a hearing, the senator heard something very interesting. A farmer said, "If you want to stop taking water out of the river, just go to Idaho Power. They have a water right dated 1906." It had been assumed that hydropower was subordinate to later diversions by upstream irrigators, hydro being a second-class use of water. But with an ingenious lawyer, Matt Mullaney, Peavey found that, unlike at other power projects, Idaho Power's water right at Swan Falls was not subordinate. The company, however, had failed to defend its right and thereby lost hydro flows to irrigation. Peavey's team reasoned that Idaho Power had forfeited generation capability through negligence and owed the consumers for the lost water.

In 1977 ratepayers filed a complaint before the PUC charging Idaho Power with giving away 2,400 cfs (flows had dropped from 8,500 to 6,000). Literally taken, the challenge meant that rights of late-coming irrigators could be invalid. An intricate chain of events unfolded. Idaho Power funded Peavey's opponent, and though the incumbent was a rancher of rock-solid Republican family, he was beaten. Four years later the mettlesome Peavey switched parties and regained his seat. (People agreed he was more or less a Democrat anyway.)

Separate efforts were launched to establish a minimum Snake River flow below Swan Falls. The 1976 draft water plan had recognized 3,300 as a feasible low flow, but threw in the towel on the Snake River's fish and wildlife before the fight even began by stating, "Because this flow is only about 40 percent of identified fish and wildlife flow needs, no instream flow designation for fish and wildlife is proposed." Conservationists launched a state initiative in 1978 to pass a minimum flow law—instream rights had not been recognized in Idaho. The effort would have failed because of a lack of qualifying signatures, but legislators didn't know that, and fearing a citizen takeover of water law, they passed a weaker minimum flow act. With it came a requirement of 3,300 cfs below Swan Falls—simply the amount remaining in the river if existing water rights were used. The Department of Water Resources acknowledged that this was "less than the amount identified as needed for fish, wildlife, and recreational purposes."[22] Under the same pressure, the Water Resource Board had enacted a minimum after failing to do so in its draft plan.

Meanwhile, the Idaho Supreme Court agreed with the ratepayers in 1982 and found that subsequent rights for irrigation were indeed subordinate to Idaho Power's hydroelectric flow. This brought down an avalanche of new alignments in the politics of Idaho water. The fraternity of irrigation, hydropower, and state government collapsed as Idaho Power and the irrigators found themselves contestants thrown into a gladiator's pit by Peavey's band of ratepayers and post-Pioneer environmentalists. In this twisted way, an awareness dawned on electric producers and conservationists that their interests were the same; hydropower requires instream flows and so does the ecosystem. That fact had been obscured from political strategists by years of ill will over power versus fisheries—especially at the Hells Canyon dams. But now, with no *new* dams being proposed by Idaho Power, an uneasy coalition gelled between these strange bedfellows. Larry Taylor of Idaho Power said, "An alliance with conservationists exists when we have the same interests. It was a big shake-up of the old order."

Idaho Power, caught between its own agricultural promotion schemes and its ratepayers, notified farmers with junior water rights that their supplies were in jeopardy. This intensified political mobilization all the way around. "It was unfortunate that the farmers were sued," Senator Peavey said. "I believe an early compromise could have been agreed upon if Governor [John] Evans hadn't supported subordination of Idaho Power's right." To escape the unthinkable relinquishment of water rights, the irrigators had to resort to legal loopholes or brute political force, and as usual in the West, they turned to the latter.

A group in the legislature became incensed that agriculture could lose even one round in this heavyweight bout over the remnants of a river, and to protect irrigators, they threatened to legislate the court's ruling out of existence. This failed in a close vote. Irrigators were desperate for protection from Idaho Power, and Idaho Power was desperate for protection from its ratepayers whose lawsuit called not only for reform but for money. "Our solution was to get a law passed protecting us from the legal complaint," Larry Taylor explained.

In closed-door sessions, the state and the power company negotiated the Swan Falls agreement, ratified by the legislature in 1984, establishing a minimum of 3,900 cfs during the irrigation season and 5,600 in winter. The extent of Idaho Power's relinquishment to the irrigators is apparent: The Supreme Court had found that the company's unsubordinated right was 8,400 cfs, and 4,500 was the actual low flow. Idaho Power thus agreed to 600 cfs below the existing low flow. Scott Reed wrote, "Ultimately that controversy was settled in the same manner in which Idaho water conflicts have always been resolved. The Power Company and the water users struck a deal, and the conservationists and fish and wildlife interests were cast adrift, ignored like so much flotsam."[23]

After all these machinations, some things just never changed;
Governor Evans's "framework" statement announced, "The state
can allow a significant amount of further development of water
uses without violating the minimum streamflow." But development should be "carefully scrutinized against express public interest criteria."[24] These included consideration of the water's value at
all hydroelectric dams downstream rather than just at Swan Falls—
a requirement that made new withdrawals unlikely. The limitation
on new development is held up as a gift to river conservationists; in
fact, new development was an economic fiasco and would have cut
the throat of existing agriculture.

Nobody knew just how much water was being used by whom,
so the Swan Falls agreement called for an adjudication of water
rights in the basin, a substantial undertaking. Every user was required to submit claims with justification on beneficial use. It didn't
make sense to act on these while the Shoshone and Bannock's
claim—the largest—is based on prior reserved rights, so the state
and Indians agreed to negotiate first.

As far as the health of the Snake River goes, a critical part of the
Swan Falls agreement was yet to come. Because Swan Falls Dam
operates under federal permits, the FERC had to ratify the agreement and became mired in its own set of problems, ironically offering a crack of light to environmentalists—the FERC had to write an
environmental impact statement. Frightened by what a scientific
analysis promised, the Idaho political powers and state government lobbied Congress to preempt the FERC and to ratify the
agreement itself, dispensing with the environmental statement.
Chair of the committee, however, was John Dingell, a friend of fish
and wildlife.

For all the lip service about "better citizen access" at the state
level, it was only with the federal government that people other
than power company executives and state water officials were allowed meaningful participation in this process so vital to the future
of everybody's river. Harold Miles of the Golden Eagle Audubon
Society informed Dingell that the minimum flow was not enough
to sustain the Deer Flat National Wildlife Refuge downstream of
Swan Falls. The Idaho Wildlife Federation lobbied against the minimum, basing their position on Fish and Wildlife Service studies
showing that half the Deer Flat islands would be severely im-

pacted.[25] The group argued for a year-round minimum of 5,500 to protect the refuge and the white sturgeon. Fish and Game studies had shown that both the water plan's 3,300 level and the agreement's 3,900 would be devastating.[26]

Adding fuel to environmental opposition, the National Marine Fisheries Service reported that the minimum would be contrary to the Northwest Power Planning Council's goal of increasing salmon and steelhead. The Fish and Wildlife Service raised the vexing issue of federal reserved water rights implicitly attached to federal lands: The refuge was created in 1937, and it was assumed that the government had the right to enough water to sustain its viability.[27] (Courts held that the government has an implied water right on public lands set aside for purposes such as refuges, national forests, and wilderness.)

The state opposed the conservation groups and federal agencies wanting more water. In one policy statement—difficult to take seriously given contrary evidence from the Department of Water Resources itself—the state water plan reported that the minimum flows "are sufficient and necessary to meet the minimum requirements for aquatic life, fish, and wildlife, and to provide water for recreation. . . . " State agencies had already admitted that flows were inadequate. The policy also conflicted with the plan's objective to give "equal consideration" to "fish, wildlife, and recreation."

Congress's Swan Falls ratification act finally confirmed the flows as agreed by Idaho Power and the state but called for a study of the environmental issues. The House Energy and Commerce Committee report did not limit the studies to the minimum flow but called for analysis of the "considerable environmental concerns" and for mitigation proposals. As observers on a study committee, the Shoshone and Bannock argued to consider the river above Milner Dam; the Interior Department and National Marine Fisheries Service agreed. But like the irrigators, the state was adamant that the river "began" at Milner Dam and sought to perpetuate the fractured-river syndrome. In a heated meeting, the Indians' Howard Funke said, "You guys are not really even interested in finding out what is wrong with that river, or in cleaning it up, or in anadromous fish or any of the other resources. It's basically whether those turbines turn or the farmers pump water. Nobody is really interested in how to truly manage the river in its proper fashion. Nobody is looking fifty years down the road."[28]

Sherl Chapman of the Idaho Water Users Association said, "We quickly got the impression that the federal agencies believed the fisheries need the water. The agencies have a single purpose with little concern for the impacts on agriculture." Keith Higginson echoed Chapman, "We felt the federal agencies were going beyond the scope of the agreement. They are attempting to expand base-line data to assist federal parties to assert claims on the Snake River." The state walked out on the negotiations.

Important work will be done anyway. Water quality, operation of dams, and effects of low flows on habitat, fish, and wildlife will be considered. For the first time, water conservation strategies will be investigated. Few efforts have attempted to define the effects of low flows on a large ecosystem so completely. (Montana studied the Yellowstone River and granted it a healthy instream reservation of 5.5 million acre feet per year.)

The studies have landmark potential in river science but will address primarily the reach from Milner to Brownlee—the most degraded free-flowing section. Studies of the river in Idaho from Jackson Dam to American Falls and Hells Canyon Dam to Lewiston could revolutionize management of those reaches with world-class qualities of fish, wildlife, and whitewater. Opening the door, the FERC's joint agreement on the studies recognized "significant federal interests in fish and wildlife . . . above Milner Dam." The Interior Department will consider the need for "additional studies necessary to protect those values."[29]

Already, people knew that the minimum flow below Swan Falls was not enough for the ecosystem. "It is expected that sturgeon would be adversely impacted," the Fish and Wildlife Service reported. The agency predicted reduced smallmouth bass habitat, warmer water temperatures, dewatered sloughs, decreased rearing habitat for all fish, increased catfish predation, wildlife impacts for 80 miles, loss of island integrity, diminished geese production, depletion of turkeys and deer, and adverse affects on hunting and fishing.[30]

The cynical view is that the Swan Falls agreement will be devastating to the river's ecosystem and that the studies, which in final analysis mandate nothing, are a bone thrown to river supporters.

The work will, however, be considered by the FERC when relicensing hydroelectric dams. Roy Heberger, chair of the Interior Department effort, thinks that the weight of the studies will be substantial, especially if recognized as part of a plan for the basin, which the FERC is required to respect. Perhaps the FERC will readjust the minimum levels or call for better fish and wildlife management in the future. For all its shortcomings, the agreement caused a halt to agricultural development before the river ran out of water, not after.

Keith Higginson said, "Swan Falls represents the abrupt ending of a history of unfettered development."

John Peavey reflected, "The Snake River would have been completely dry at Swan Falls the way it was going. I saw the case as a wrench thrown in the works for a few years, thinking that, when the system of development is turned loose again, there will be a more mature attitude."

Pat Ford concluded, "The Swan Falls issue shows that we're in a changing world of water use. Fish and wildlife are now on the list of concerns. The system is politically more open than it used to be. Where we once encountered a wall, we don't anymore. A lot of the people who built that wall are now gone from the legislature. It is not a matter of confronting agriculture; we can have both. We've stopped the momentum of a process that was robbing the Snake River of all its natural values. The question is, can we move forward to the next step?"

With new limits on withdrawals, a surplus of electricity, and few demands for new cropland after the recession hit in 1979, a window has opened to the future of the Snake River. Few people, however, sought to seize the moment in this decade of new expectations or to advance the cause of river protection into a positive arena and not just one of stagnated development. "We're making progress protecting the Salmon and Payette," Pat Ford said, "but if we don't take better advantage of this opportunity on the Snake River, we haven't done enough."

At a 1990 Idaho rivers conference, Governor Cecil Andrus recognized, "Now there are legitimate uses of water other than application on the ground," and he called for recommendation of sixty wild and scenic rivers to Congress, higher minimum flows on 130 streams, and a state role addressing fish and wildlife mitigation on the relicensing of existing hydroelectric dams. "We need a balanced view of water. In Idaho we can have the best of both worlds."

With an open-mindedness emanating from the Swan Falls controversy and the times themselves, with new tools of science, and with a national mood to protect the environment, corrective steps are possible to restore the Snake River. An accurate adjudication of water rights is the opportunity of the century to correct some inequities. Involvement in that process is tiresome and abstract to most citizen activists, but it is the next logical step beyond the Swan Falls agreement. To influence the future of the Snake River, the window of opportunity may be open for only a short while.

Snake River in Grand Teton National Park

*Howard Funke, lawyer for the
Shoshone and Bannock tribes*

*Dick Schwarz of the South
Fork Coalition*

Cottonwood forest along the Snake River above Heise

The Great Feeder diversion structure and canal

American Falls Reservoir and recreation area

The dry Snake River bed below Milner Dam

The Twin Falls Main Canal above Milner Dam

Furrow irrigation, the Snake River plain

Milner Gorge above the Hansen Bridge, with 1,000 cfs in the river in November

Bob Burks, past president, Idaho Water Users Association

Ken Mulberry at his farm near the Snake River

Irrigation return water in the middle Snake River

Shoshone Falls when irrigation flows are diverted from the river

Guy Bonnivier, director of the
Idaho Nature Conservancy,
at Thousand Springs

State Senator and rancher
John Peavey

Swan Falls Dam

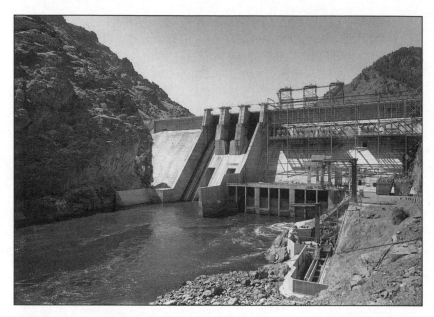

Hells Canyon Dam

Great River Journeys' dory in Hells Canyon

Wild Sheep Rapid, Hells Canyon

Jet boat, Hells Canyon

Hells Canyon below the Salmon River confluence

Hugh Harper in Hells Canyon

Mulberry tree with roots exposed because of eroding sand and degrading riverbed below Hells Canyon dams

Fish ladder, Ice Harbor Dam, lower Snake River

Hydroelectric generators at Ice Harbor Dam

Fish trap for the salmon and steelhead barging facility, Lower Granite Dam

Mouth of the Snake River, impounded with the Columbia River behind McNary Dam

Bison and the Tetons, Grand Teton National Park

Snake River below Flagg Ranch

Jackson Lake Dam in Grand Teton National Park

The Gros Ventre River in Grand Teton National Park; all the water is diverted for pasture in late summer

Roger Smith and students of the Teton Science School along the Snake River

Hydrologist Luna Leopold at the Teton Science School

Wildlife biologist Frank Craighead at his home in Moose

The Jackson Hole levee above the Wilson Bridge

Alpine Canyon, below Jackson Hole

*Len Carlman at the spring that creates the highest year-round flow of
the Snake River*

The upper Snake River in the Bridger–Teton Wilderness

The Middle River and Hydropower

BELOW SWAN FALLS DAM

On a hot evening in June, I loaded my canoe for another Snake River journey. I planned to paddle from Swan Falls Dam to the town of Weiser, covering most of the longest free-flowing reach on the river, which runs 116 miles to the backwater of Brownlee Dam.

Desert light shone golden on the cliffs when I loaded my canoe and entered the water at the swirling outwash of the Swan Falls Dam. Its power plant, two stories and brick, with rows of windows, could represent hydropower's early days in New England. Half a dozen fishermen stood on shore or slumped in lawn chairs at eddys reached by dirt road. This reach was classified a "highest value fishery resource" by the Department of Fish and Game, mainly because of its sturgeon.

One white sturgeon hauled from the Columbia River topped out at 1,285 pounds. In recent years, 300-pound, 8-foot behemoths have been caught. Considered one of our most "primitive" fish, their heads are armored with bony plates, their bodies with five rows of scutes. Many spend part time in the ocean; others, including these, are barred by dams into rivers. A choice food fish and a source of roe, the sturgeon is the most valuable species in the entire Columbia's commercial harvest. In San Francisco Bay, these are the most sought fish by sport anglers, which would be true on the Snake if populations were healthy enough to allow fishermen to keep what they hook. Sturgeon live an impressive 100 years and grow the whole time. The Fish and Wildlife Service is striving to keep the Snake River population off the endangered species list.

Sturgeon eat clams, which are sensitive to water quality and appear in only a fraction of historic numbers, once blanketing the riverbed like gravel. For spawning, many fishes require clean gravel washed by flowing water, but the sturgeon has an additional demand: Eggs must be suspended in tumbling water during incubation, requiring miles of current without reservoirs. The only sections with enough free-flowing length for reproduction are between Bliss and C.J. Strike Reservoir, Hells Canyon, and along this middle reach of the Snake River.

I bobbed on the flanks of waves and paddled past a basalt boulder, probably rolled here during the Bonneville flood, which resulted from a shoreline rupture of Lake Bonneville. The size of Lake Michigan, it had covered the Salt Lake area in Utah. About 15,000 years ago, the flood raged as a 400-foot-high wall of water—10 million cfs—carving canyons as it went. Earlier, this was the bed of Payette Lake, sometimes called Idaho Lake, dammed by Hells Canyon lava, with water 2,000 feet deep and covering the valley for 300 miles, even above Hagerman.[1]

I paddled through a rapid and landed at a stone dwelling that looked as if built by people who had just upgraded from a cave. Only the tin roof was twentieth century, camouflaged under heaps of dirt. I imagined the Shoshone settling in this canyon in November to eat fish, cattails, and rabbits through the winter. Archaeological sites, in fact, are plentiful.

Gnawing on my lunch, drifting on water, I spotted the wake of a snake. Not shy, the reptile aimed straight toward the canoe, perhaps for a rest. Taken by surprise, I dropped my sandwich, grabbed my paddle, and splashed urgently, "Down, boy, down!" I was once chased by a bull elk and once by a grizzly bear, but somehow this harmless creature's pursuit was the strangest.

On my second day on the river, the canyon ended abruptly, though the valley, several miles wide, was enclosed by steep slopes to Homedale. Through this Swan Falls–Brownlee reach, eighty-six islands compose the Deer Flat National Wildlife Refuge, a wintering home for waterfowl. I lugged the boat onto the steep bank of an island. Shielded from the highway by brush, the campsite seemed remote except for a pump hammering on the shore, lifting water hundreds of feet to the bench.

DEGRADED RIVERBED

The next morning I strolled to the upper end of the island where rivers normally form gravel bars when the water is slowed and separated by the land, but I found only a crumbling embankment. The mainland shores were matched in steepness and erosion. The channel appeared to be "degraded"—water erodes the bed, deepening it without depositing new gravel and sand. A healthy river is "in-grade," balancing cut with fill, eroding on the outside of bends and depositing new material on the inside.

The hydrologic shambles of a degrading riverbed is one of the more insidious problems resulting from dams. In the impounded flatwater, silt and sand settles to the bottom. Up to 99 percent of a river's silt can be trapped in reservoirs; Garrison Dam on the Missouri River traps 90 percent; Glen Canyon Dam swallows 87 percent of the Colorado River's silt. As a result, water below the dams runs silt-free or "hungry," capable of eroding soil at a greater rate while depositing nothing. Streambeds have been lowered as much as 25 feet. Sandbars disappear. Banks are undercut, cave in, and wash away, resulting in a voracious erosion of the floodplain itself. The cottonwoods are flushed to oblivion with no chance for recovery because the soil is gone. Like a ditch draining a swamp, the undercut banks drain groundwater, lowering the water table of the floodplain, drying it out. The biological bonanza of the riparian zone turns into a biological desert. The pattern of steep banks, few sandbars, and drained shorelines continues to the Boise River, which dumps silt into the Snake and forms a maze of islands.

Biologist William Platts suspects that cottonwoods once lined many shorelines of this middle river but died after silt deposition and regular flood overflows were stopped. Degrading riverbeds will cut deeper, limited only by nonerosive checkpoints downstream, such as shelves of bedrock. Irrigation wastewater does not restore equilibrium to the degrading river; its silt is too fine to replicate the natural movement of sand and only serves to pollute the water. The day may come when pipelines are installed at reservoirs to flush silt from the upper ends—where it's deposited—to the dam's outflow. The degrading river's death knell to wildlife can ironically benefit localized fisheries, at least in the short term. In rivers otherwise plagued by silty irrigation flows, fish thrive below dams such as Swan Falls because the water is clear.

In foam-speckled pools I heard the slop of fish lips—feeding frenzies of suckers and catfish. Normally bottom feeders, these adaptable creatures—countless numbers—gulped detritus and a snow-flurry hatch of mayflies.

I saw broken barbed-wire fences that had collected tumbleweed, burned fields with gnarled skeletons of sagebrush, fields white with alkali from years of irrigation, scars of power lines and pipelines angling to lava bluffs, fields overgrazed until denuded to rocks showing like zits, water tanks squatting on hills, pipes gridding fields, metal farm buildings, old Fords half-buried in river banks, sprinklers spraying water that became one with the sky in the stiff upstream wind, and soil billowing in dustbowl clouds from newly plowed fields.

At the town of Marsing I beached at a refreshing riverfront park. Except here and at a similar park downstream in Homedale, people mostly ignore the middle river. A gray-haired couple in straw hats relaxed on lawn chairs. Baiting with worms, the woman said, "We're not catching any fish but we're feeding them a lot."

Since yesterday, the river had turned from olive brown to dirt brown. The Idaho Department of Health and Welfare's morose conclusion: "All beneficial uses of this reach are threatened."[2] The water carries a horrible load of bacteria, a horrible dose of pesticides, and a horrible lack of oxygen. In southwestern Idaho, 3,167 of 3,794 miles of streams are degraded by agriculture, but Gwen Burr of the department said, "We don't get complaints about the middle river. The expectation's just not there."

MIDDLE RIVER TRIBUTARIES

Eight miles below Homedale the river enters Oregon; the next 10 miles flow entirely within that state; for the following 200 miles, the river defines the state boundaries with Oregon on the west shore and Idaho on the east shore. The Owyhee River enters from the west though the flow was so low because of diversions that I couldn't see it. The Interior Department recommended national river designation of 178 miles of the upper Owyhee in 1975, and 112 miles were designated in 1984.

Credit is often given to Hoover Dam as the prototypical large dam—something new in 1935 that the engineers invented as they went along. But that's not really true. In 1928, the Bureau of Reclamation's 417-foot-high Owyhee Dam was the world's highest, a proving ground for construction theories that culminated in Hoover.[3] To store 1.1 million acre feet for irrigation, 50 miles of the Owyhee were flooded.

Like the Owyhee of Oregon, the Boise River, from the Idaho side of the Snake, is depleted so much for irrigation that I couldn't tell which thrombotic slough carried the average 2,007 cfs. The confluence is part of a 1,800-acre wildlife management area owned by Fish and Game, including the first impressive cottonwood bottomlands on this entire reach and the finest riparian habitat since Thousand Springs. I pitched my tent near the mouth of the phantom Boise.

Beginning in the Sawtooth Range, the Boise River is dammed to irrigate diverse crops of Canyon County. Fishermen and paddlers flock to whitewater of the South Fork between Anderson Ranch and Arrowrock dams; the Middle and North forks are threatened by the Twin Springs Dam proposal. Through the state capital, restoration has created one of the finer urban river parks in North America, with the refreshing touch that makes Boise one of the most attractive cities in the Rockies.

While a crop duster droned over nearby fields, I relaunched into the morning mist and drifted past the first complex of islands since the Fort Hall Bottoms. A sugar beet processing plant at Nyssa exuded the most remarkably rotten odor on the entire river. Where lime rose in a 20-foot embankment, I slogged up through the waste to photograph an industrial-scale desert. Beyond the Ontario bridge, the view from my camp showed a river and forest, but the sounds of trains and traffic cut through the night.

The Payette River and its paludal woodland of box elder and silver maple on the Idaho side invited me to stop. Unlike the Owyhee and Boise rivers, the Payette sent a noticeable flow into the Snake, though only a fraction of its average 3,183 cfs. I saw beaver trails and gadwall ducks, which are partial to sloughs. The Payette's South Fork—a gem of the Sawtooth Mountains, drops through wilderness, into green pools full of trout and over fabulous rapids for kayaking and canoeing. Below Lowman, the river thunders through a canyon of enormous drops, then ends in a rollicking rafting run to the main stem. The South Payette is one of few Snake tributaries with no dams or power plants; among the unprotected tributaries of the Snake River, none is more worthy of national river status than the South Fork Payette.

The North Fork fills the popular Cascade Reservoir and then roars through a canyon confined by Highway 55 and a railroad, the ultimate hydrotube where a screaming 1,700-foot drop in 15 miles offers some of the more challenging whitewater in America. J.R. Simplot's Western Power Company proposed to divert the North Fork's whitewater for 16 miles above Banks; the city of Tacoma could receive a third of the power.[4] The *Idaho Statesman* quoted Simplot, regarded as the wealthiest man in the Northwest, that it was time to "get the ecology kicks out of the road." But the South Fork, North Fork, and main stem above Black Canyon Dam were temporarily protected in Idaho's 1988 Rivers Planning and Protection Act, and longer term protection is likely. Both forks are now regarded as a success story in Idaho river conservation and as a sign of changing times.

I canoed past hundreds of ring-billed gulls—the largest rookery I've ever seen on a river. The Weiser River enters from the east, averaging 1,169 cfs but lifeless in the irrigation season. Fishermen spoke Spanish at the take-out in Weiser, famous for its fiddling festival. So far, the Snake River basin covered 69,200 square miles—larger than the state of Missouri—and the average flow was 18,490 cfs. Here at Weiser, the agricultural waterway has ended. In only a few miles, the current ceases behind the first of three massive hydroelectric dams.

THE HYDROPOWER COMPLEX

For 95 miles, from Brownlee Reservoir to Hells Canyon Dam, the river is given over entirely to electric generation by the Idaho Power Company. From the bypassed town of Huntington and its railroad yards, a gravel road angles north along the edge of the reservoir where water laps against steep slopes of sage. On gentler shorelines, people parked campers and fished from lawn chairs, but there was no riparian edge, no cottonwood or hackberry forest, no birdlife except for a few gulls.

Brownlee Dam, 295 feet high, impounds the river for 53 miles, followed by the 140-foot Oxbow Dam and the 318-foot Hells Canyon Dam. Brownlee was completed in 1958, Oxbow in 1961, and Hells Canyon in 1967, amassing 18,450 acres of flatwater, flooding 1,421 acres of riparian habitat.[5]

The dams barred salmon and steelhead from 368 miles of the Snake River (including the reach above Swan Falls Dam, which some fish had managed to climb). A total of 3,000 stream miles were blocked, among them the Weiser, Malheur, Payette, Boise, Owyhee, Bruneau, and Salmon Falls Creek—one-third of the anadromous habitat in the basin. The dams buried five of Hells Canyon's seven big rapids including Buck Creek and Kinney Creek. Martin Litton, who has been running rivers about as long as anybody, called the undammed Hells Canyon "very comparable to the Grand Canyon itself" in its rapids and wildness. Wildlife biologist Frank Craighead, who ran the canyon in the 1950s, said, "It was one of the outstanding big-water trips in the West, certainly the greatest in the Northwest."

Amos Burg, a little-known legend in river running, launched his canoe at Yellowstone National Park in 1925 and paddled or portaged to tidewater. He lost one canoe in the upper river and capsized at Buck Creek Rapid when a towline broke. On his final Hells Canyon trip in 1978, the seventy-seven-year-old Burg said, "Dams had destroyed one of nature's most magnificent masterpieces."[6]

With a lifetime of experience packing horses, trapping, ranching, and fishing, Freda Miller of Halfway, Oregon, recalled, "There was quite a lot of salmon fishing, but we mostly fished for steelhead. Elk and deer wintered on the slopes up above. People didn't like the dams, but nobody thought they could stop them."

Public and private utilities had scrambled for the permits to impound the river, and the Bureau of Reclamation proposed a towering structure below today's Hells Canyon Dam. Eisenhower administration policies favored private industry, and the Federal Power Commission (FPC) granted a license to the Idaho Power Company in 1955. The permit required passage for salmon, which company representatives promised could be done. Fish moving upstream would be trapped and trucked above the dams; a net was strung across Brownlee Reservoir to catch downstream migrants. This was plagued with problems, though an Oregon Fish Commis-

sion report stated that a quarter of the million smolts made it
through the turbines or over the spillway (accumulated mortality at
downstream dams was far worse).[7] Facing other problems at Oxbow Dam where a fish trap was intended to catch upstream migrants, Idaho Power abandoned the fishery.

The runs of salmon that had spawned as high as Shoshone Falls
abruptly ended in 1962. Compared with all the sites of regional
destruction, correctable mistakes, and unnecessary costs, this loss is
the greatest tragedy of the river. Furthermore, the dams created
excess nitrogen at the outflow of Hells Canyon Dam—lethal to fish
and detectable for 58 miles to the Salmon River—and caused erosion of beaches and riparian soils.

Brownlee produces an average of 272 megawatts, Oxbow 113,
and Hells Canyon Dam 223. The river's next largest hydroelectric
plant, for comparison, is Palisades at 119. (On the main stem, average megawatts total 2,387 from twenty dams; on tributaries,
Dworshak Dam is the major producer with 238 megawatts.)

At Hells Canyon Dam, Mark Briscoe of Idaho Power showed me
the generating plant—a bastion of cement and steel with gates and
penstocks 24 feet in diameter that can feed 10,000 cfs to each of
three turbines. He explained the network of dials, buttons, levers,
panels, gauges, and printouts in the humming control room. We
descended hundreds of steps into a dripping, black grotto within
the bowels of the dam. The river level downstream is raised or
lowered as much as 1 foot per hour—a limit imposed not by environmental concerns but by the federal license that anticipated construction of more power dams.

Since its first development in the Hagerman Valley early in this
century, Idaho Power has enjoyed such prominence that even
Governor Evans said that the state was named for the power company. It owns eleven dams on the Snake River, five projects on
tributaries, and a coal-burning plant in partnership with another
utility in Wyoming. Dams generate two-thirds of the company's
power in normal years (in the three northwestern states, hydropower accounts for three-quarters of the generating capacity).[8] Idaho Power funds three hatcheries operated by Idaho Fish and Game
and claims the Snake River fishery has been "relocated" to the
Salmon River, though that stream already had its own wild salmon
and steelhead of differing subspecies or "runs."

On a forty-year cycle, licenses for the dams are beginning to come up for renewal, and the Federal Energy Regulatory Commission (FERC) must consider new terms attached to the development of the public waterways. In a precedent-setting case, a federal court ruled that the FERC must consider environmental conditions when relicensing Kingsley Dam on the Platte River, where healthy flows are essential to whooping cranes.[9] "Every time there's a relicensing of a dam, we see more requirements for fish and wildlife," said Larry Taylor of Idaho Power. "The public wants low power rates but also protection of fish and wildlife. In 1980 we worked out a multimillion-dollar program over our obligation to mitigate fisheries losses. Our legal responsibility has been taken care of; the ratepayers are doing a lot for anadromous fish."

What is Idaho Power's vision for the Snake River? "It will continue to be a working river, and the company hopes to be a good steward of that, to enhance the recreational opportunities. We'll probably see greater efforts to improve fisheries around each facility. The company is in this for the long term. When our projects come up for relicensing, we want people to come in and say that we've done a good job."

Damming the Snake River is what makes power rates here the cheapest among all private utilities in North America; the residential rate of 4.5 cents a kilowatt-hour (kwh) is half the average. Irrigators pay 3.1 cents a kwh and industries pay 2.5 for power from the same sources. It follows that Idaho Power customers have the second highest consumption rate among 126 companies. Per capita use is four times that of New York.

What difference has cheap power made to Idaho? The high benches above the Snake River were opened for farming because water could be pumped inexpensively. Farmers were able to convert to sprinklers. And Idaho Power touts low rates in industrial promotion.

In the wake of the Pioneer power plant rejection, the Public Utilities Commission (PUC) mandated conservation programs and gained a reputation as one of the premier PUCs in the nation. Most directives were appealed by utilities, and some were rescinded by the legislature.[10] The reforms that survived and the economic recession in 1979 flattened demand, and Idaho Power scrapped plans for new dams on the Snake and South Payette. "There's no need for the next twenty years," Taylor said. "The power could be sold outside our service area, but that's not this company's orientation." Idaho Power will, however, expand its Twin Falls and Swan Falls plants. "They'll come up for relicensing, and if we don't make improvements, someone could come in and take those projects away from us."

If energy conservation were a priority, Idaho could extend its supplies even further. In Twin Falls, for example, houses built by Whitehead Home and Energy are one-third more energy-efficient than standard construction. "We support conservation," Taylor said, "but we've moved away from those programs. There's now more emphasis on marketing. We have a surplus of power, and our business has to show a profit to stockholders." Radio ads for electrically heated hot tubs offered 100 percent financing by the Idaho Power Company.

With 17 percent of the West's population, Oregon, Washington, and Idaho use 36 percent of the electricity. The Northwest Power Planning Council regarded conservation as the "premier new resource" for energy, capable of supplying new needs for twenty years at the growth rates of the mid-1980s. Revised building codes can save up to 600 megawatts over the next twenty years (Seattle uses about 1,000). Efficient water heaters, washing machines, and dishwashers can save 380 megawatts. Up to 2,900 megawatts could be available through conservation at 2.4 cents per kwh— enough to replace six large coal plants at half the cost.[11]

Hydroelectric entrepreneurs are a problem to Idaho Power because federal law requires utility companies to buy electricity at top prices from other power producers. Taylor said, "We don't need new dams, so we're not building them, and we don't think anyone else should either. Why suffer the environmental consequences of development before you have to?"

New hydroelectric dams proposed at eleven sites on the Snake River would flood 4,700 acres of riparian wetlands and 90 miles of river—18 percent of the free-flowing mileage that remains.[12] Below Hells Canyon, a dam was proposed at Asotin to flood 26 miles critical to salmon and recommended for national river designation. A bevy of small hydro dams are pushed on tributaries because of federal incentives to bolster domestic energy. In addition to the "avoided-cost" provision that requires Idaho Power to buy the electricity, a 21 percent tax credit and a five-year depreciation schedule stacked the deck formidably against free-flowing rivers.

Statewide, 234 FERC applications are "active." Over 360 miles of rivers and streams would be affected, the average diversion causing 1.6 miles of reduced streamflow with impacts on fisheries, water temperature, vegetation, wildlife, and recreation.[13] Fifty hydro projects have been built since 1980; sixty more are approved. Yet another possibility is that irrigators will apply for hydroelectric generators in canals, as some have done. Defending the right to sell power out of state, the Idaho Water Users Association in 1989 supported "free market sales of hydroelectric energy developed in Idaho without restriction upon the place of use." Some canal developments are benign, but most would increase diversions in the nonirrigation season and raise consumptive use because of the chronically leaking canals.

The Snake River mirrors other mountain-and-river regions nationwide. The American Rivers Council intervened in national forest planning and secured a temporary ban on dams on outstanding streams, followed by a commitment from Forest Service Chief Dale Robertson to add 200 waterways to the national wild and scenic rivers system by 1993.[14]

The hydroelectric plans with profits going to out-of-state firms through out-of-state sales stirred new interest in the protection of Idaho rivers. Sixty proposed hydro plants in the Salmon River basin drew nationwide opposition. "Ninety-eight percent of the hydroelectric proposals are detrimental to fish," said Al Van Vooren of the Idaho Department of Fish and Game, who regarded the export of power tantamount to the export of water. "New dam proposals are the greatest threat to the Snake River. Sites that were dropped could come up again in the next energy crisis. The Snake River is a workhorse, openly exploited, but you get to a point when you step back and say, 'We could lose this river completely.'"

While conservation groups with fish and wildlife agencies opposed the FERC for environmental reasons and the Idaho Power Company opposed it for economic reasons, the state of Idaho opposed the FERC for irrigation reasons. The Department of Water Resources intervened against the FERC guaranteeing flows to a Payette River hydro plant because the state wanted to protect opportunities for upstream diversions serving new irrigation. Keith

Higginson, director of the Idaho Department of Water Resources, said, "FERC would give hydropower developers the right to water and thereby put a cork in the river and limit upstream development, which is not in the interest of Idaho."

The Electric Consumers Protection Act of 1986 directed the FERC to consider fish, wildlife, recreation, and energy conservation equal to development, and the agency is inching toward change. FERC staff recommended instream flows for the Milner project, and the commission rejected a dam on Montana's Kootenay River.

A NEW APPROACH

Congress created the Northwest Power Planning Council in 1980 to plan for electrical needs, but fish and wildlife interests including Congressman John Dingell of Michigan seized an opportunity to restore natural resources that had been casualties of cheap power. The council is required to protect, mitigate, and enhance fish and wildlife affected by hydropower in the Columbia River basin. For the first time, fish and wildlife were to be treated not as leftovers but equals with hydropower.

The council adopted the goal of doubling the numbers of salmon and steelhead. The Bonneville Power Administration (BPA) alone spent $35 million a year on fish and wildlife; another $15 million per year is foregone because of water spilled for fisheries. The Army Corps has spent $550 million in the Columbia basin for fish and wildlife, much of it for hatcheries, and the Fish and Wildlife Service and state agencies invested additional millions. "With everyone spending that kind of money," said Beth Heinrich of the council, "it didn't make sense to allow more hydro projects that would only make things worse." Fish and wildlife agencies and the tribes urged protection of streams from new dams.

The council launched a "protected areas" program by reviewing 350,000 miles of waterways in the Columbia basin. With information prepared by state fish and game agencies and after an elaborate review process, the council recommended protection of 15 percent of the mileage having exceptional fisheries or wildlife habitat. The BPA agreed to block hydro proposals on the list by denying access to powerlines to the Southwest, and the FERC was obligated to consider the list in the permitting process. In Idaho, 12,441 miles recommended for protection included all remaining salmon and steelhead streams and most other valuable fisheries. The South Fork Payette, Henry's Fork, Salmon River, and all free-flowing reaches of the Snake in Idaho were included except Milner Gorge.[15]

After a history of destruction of fish and wildlife and after wholesale elimination of habitat through damming the Columbia, the Snake, and almost every large tributary, a compromise program was finally on the table to curb further damage: The protected areas would limit dams on only one-third of the stream miles in Idaho and preempt 27 percent of the energy of proposed hydro projects. The Northwest Power Planning Council argued that the designation made sense from a power development standpoint by identifying problem areas in advance and avoiding fish and wildlife losses that would ultimately cost money. The American Rivers Council called the action "one of the most exciting river protection proposals ever." In fact, no single action anywhere had the potential to save so many miles of excellent streams.

The Idaho Water Users Association called the list an "obstructionist agenda," though effects on irrigators were nil.[16] The Idaho House of Representatives opposed protection from the new dams because of "impact" on private property and on "multiple uses of public lands." The legislature maintained that Idaho "has adequate laws and processes."[17]

"The issue of state sovereignty was not important in any of the other states," Beth Heinrich said. "In Idaho, the irrigators and logging interests dominate." Pat Ford said, "Neither governors Evans nor Andrus made anadromous fish a priority, and as a result, the state agencies stumble along."

Seeing no need for the council's protection, Keith Higginson said, "We don't care how many permits a developer will get from the FERC; we won't give a water right if it's not in the public interest. They have to satisfy the Idaho Department of Water Resources." Records show that the department has turned down remarkably few applications because of fish and wildlife (two that might be counted were at Elk Creek Falls and Thousand Springs, denied because of related public interest reasons).[18] Furthermore, hydro developers typically ignore the state permitting process to an insulting degree until they have their FERC paperwork in hand as leverage. More important, the department's primary concern in the water rights process has not been for public interest but to assure that irrigators who come later retain the right to preempt water from hydro projects. The state doesn't even require hydro bypass flows that would keep token amounts of water in the stream; if this were done, then future upstream irrigators would implicitly have to comply as well. "The state screams about primacy and state's rights, but the state is a paper tiger acting on behalf of one group of users," a high state official told me.

Higginson objected to the council's plan for protection of fish. "Until we do our own plan, it's premature to lock up streams for a single purpose."

After the Department of Fish and Game's decision supporting the protected areas proposal emerged from the state bureaucracy in an unrecognizable form, the department sent its position directly to the Northwest Power Planning Council.

At a hearing in Boise, Idahoans testified overwhelmingly in favor of the protected areas. "The government hasn't yet changed very much," said William Platts of the Water Resource Board, "but the attitude of the people of Idaho has changed. More and more believe in quality of life." James Goller, Senator James McClure's former chief of staff and one of Idaho's two members on the council, argued that some hydro projects are beneficial to fish and wildlife and that the regulatory responsibility should remain entirely with the FERC, even though it's a federal agency. He voted against the protected areas, but he voted alone. In a remarkable victory for fish and wildlife, the council adopted the program in 1988.

Another approach to increase hydropower is to replace some of the flows that have been lost to irrigation. One acre foot of water consumed by irrigation above American Falls will produce 1,822 kilowatt-hours of electricity if it's allowed to go down river through the hydroelectric plants.[19] Each irrigated acre consumes about 2 acre feet of water, so an acre at American Falls consumes water that could provide 3,644 kwh of electricity (not counting the savings of electricity otherwise used in irrigation). Many of the acres are used for surplus crops and represent not a public benefit but a public cost in most years. Furthermore, the acreage yielding the most hydropower would be high in the basin where the growing season is the shortest, water losses through leaking canals and overapplications are greatest, and erosion problems are worst. But even if it pays, no one expects hydropower producers to buy land and water rights in order to receive the water (Idaho Power does lease water through the Water Bank).

A more realistic possibility: Hydropower revenues could be used to pay for irrigation efficiency improvements resulting in less diversion of water, making it more available at twenty hydroelectric plants on the Snake River (nine of them above Thousand Springs) and four plants on the lower Columbia. Likewise, higher flows would help with the gamut of instream flow problems. These and other issues may be relevant by the year 2000 as the licenses for the Idaho Power Company dams expire and when renewal will be based on public interest criteria.[20]

Seeking a break from the brown river at Weiser, I drove past the immoderately uninteresting shoreline of Brownlee Reservoir and to the meadow-and-forest town of Halfway, Oregon, where I was tempted to stay for years. For a week I roamed the forests, snowfields, and craggy peaks of the Wallowa Mountains, a 70-mile-square version of the Rockies, isolated in northeast Oregon. The Eagle Cap Wilderness is dressed in a mosaic of transparent lakes and topped with glaciated granite. At Enterprise, one man stated the view of many: "This is the best place on earth."

From the Wallowa and Blue mountains, the Grande Ronde River runs for 185 miles, and with its tributary, the Wallowa River, it offers excellent canoeing or rafting in canyons of grassland and pine. The Lostine's forks are mountain jewels. The Imnaha, a startling masterpiece of water, runs through logjams of fir, past ranches, and finally splits a stunning canyon of whitewater before entering the Snake River. An initiative in 1988 granted state protection to the Wallowa, and a national wild and scenic rivers act protected parts of forty Oregon rivers including the Imnaha, Grande Ronde, Lostine, North Fork Owyhee, West Little Owyhee, and Joseph Creek—all Snake tributaries.

East of the Wallowas, Idaho's Seven Devils Mountains are similarly isolated, and between these two ranges lies a canyon where I prepared for my wildest Snake River journey.

8

Hells Canyon

DAY 1

Water, foaming and full of life, boiled up under my raft. The river reached out in its welter of currents and licked a rock-armored shore that climbed without hesitation to gray cliffs and groves of pine, up onto benches hiding hanging canyons, then farther to summits beyond sight. We had entered the Snake River's greatest canyon, one of the greatest in North America.

The Snake River is both a national wild and scenic river and centerpiece to the Hells Canyon National Recreation Area, a congressional designation that came after one of the country's foremost struggles to save a river. More than just stopping dams, the protected status was intended to guard the canyon—Oregon on the west side and Idaho on the east—from other invasions and to manage recreation effectively.

This 104-mile, free-flowing reach is the second longest on the river. For eleven days Hugh Harper and I floated through big whitewater and the isolation of a river recessed into the earth about as deep as any recess anywhere, all of it unexplored by us. Harper, a wildlife biologist, had jumped at the chance to see the canyon. He had grown up on a Wisconsin farm where horses pulled the plows, then came west on a football scholarship that enabled him to study zoology at the University of Idaho. Six foot one, 215 pounds, he played tackle, though 48 years later I call his build that of a professional fullback. Though he has never been through this canyon, he has done other whitewater boating. In 1940 he and two friends who worked as lumberjacks lashed three logs into a raft, launched it on the Clearwater's North Fork, and survived the rapids now drowned by Dworshak Dam. Being three times wounded in the Marine Corps at Guadalcanal and Guam somehow left Harper with a desire to work with wildlife in Idaho. He started with the Department of Fish and Game and later transferred to the Bureau of Land Management as one of its first biologists. He primarily worked on the restoration of range land, and the reform—though not permanent—of grazing practices. In Lapwai and Boise he raised two sons and a daughter.

Trained on the Payette and Owyhee rivers and certified as a canoe and rafting guide, Hugh's the oldest licensed raft guide in Idaho, rowing commercial trips on the Salmon and its Middle Fork. At sixty-eight, his retirement hobbies are many. When a developer proposed expensive housing along the floodplain in Boise, he had to meet riverfront planning requirements and hired Harper to supervise restoration of native plantlife, erosion control, and wetlands rehabilitation. A plaque commemorates "Harper's Habitat" along 400 yards of the Boise River.

Expecting the heat for which this canyon could have been named, Hugh wore white pants and a white shirt, matching his hair. His eyes shine blue, squinted with intensity. Somewhat rigid in stance, he is solid and stable with the strength of years.

When I first met Hugh in Boise, he and his wife, Diane, hosted me to the sights of town. One afternoon we went canoeing on the Boise River. "How would you get over to that wave to surf on it?" Hugh asked as we paddled in separate boats. He thus became the only person I know with senior citizen discounts who has taken up whitewater surfing. With a squint in his eye, he now pointed his muscled old arm at a bench far up the slope of the canyon and said, "Six deer are browsing up there."

"Hold on," I advised as we danced over a train of waves, then into a depthless pool. While we spun on the eddy line, we gazed at the deer and audibly sighed at the perfection we had found on the Snake River, a river once again, reborn into a waterway of life and wonder, an adventurous passage through this monumental canyon shared by Idaho and Oregon.

Still spinning slowly on the eddy line, I thought, there's nothing like this anywhere. The beauty held a massive quality in rich blends of rock, grassland, conifers, and canyons within the canyon where tributaries carve through the great walls. A cross section of the landscape could be a graph of temperatures on Mars. From

6,895 feet above sea level on Bear Mountain in Oregon, the elevation plunges to 1,500 feet at the river and back to 9,393 on Idaho's He Devil Mountain, all in a horizontal distance of 8 miles. Cactus grow on the bottom, alpine meadows on top. If one considers the Seven Devils Mountains a part of the Rockies, then Hells Canyon, dropping to 800 feet, is the lowest place in the entire range.

Authors of just about every book or article on Hells Canyon claim that this is the deepest canyon in North America (some say in the world). But is it? Owens Valley between Mount Whitney in the Sierra and the Inyo Mountains is deeper, but it's a valley—10 miles wide—not a canyon. Lake Chelan in Washington may compete but only if depth is measured to the bed of the lake. The Grand Canyon, 5,500 feet from rim to floor in many places, is not as deep, though its inner gorge is the most extreme case of vertical walls lining both sides of a river for many miles, and it appears to be the deepest canyon because of its greater disport. The U.S. Geological Survey makes no judgment on the question of canyons; topographic maps are the only good source of information.

The highest point above Hells Canyon is He Devil Mountain, 7,900 feet above the water at a summit 6 miles from the river. The other side climbs only 5,400 feet to Bear Mountain. At the Kings River in the Sierra Nevada, Spanish Mountain rises 8,240 feet above the river and is only 4 miles away from it; the other side climbs 5,400 feet also. At several sections across the Middle and South forks of the Kings, the average canyon depth between peaks is 6,500 to 7,700 feet—unexcelled, to my knowledge, in North America. Topographic maps point to the Kings as the deepest canyon in the United States and Hells Canyon as the second deepest.

First or second, the scale is astounding. The enormity of the river, the breadth of the floor, the rise of the inner gorge, and the spaciousness of the wide scene are only vaguely realized until I imagine myself in the picture. I am nothing.

With that realization, the current gripped an oar, I pulled, and we popped out of the eddy and into the full flow of our river, remarkably the same river that ceases to exist at Milner Dam, that ponds into reservoirs for half its length, that runs filthy with irrigation return water. Finally, I thought, here is the river as it was, a waterway of power and wild exuberance. We were buoyed high on a wave and released downward again, one bend farther into the

canyon, separated, now, from Hells Canyon Dam and the powerlines that enmesh the American West. Ahead lay one of the longer
undeveloped reaches of river in North America. No bridge crosses
for 106 miles (ninety bridges span the river; other unbridged sections are 40-mile lengths at the headwaters and above Heise). The
Grand Canyon runs 278 miles, but few other American rivers outside Alaska rival this one for big whitewater in wilderness.

Back at the launching ramp, the river ranger had checked our
permit, required of people on nonmotorized trips. Sixty percent of
the permits go to private boaters, the rest to commercial companies.
Reservations fill early in the year. Lucky, I had received someone
else's canceled permit. While I rigged my raft, a Greyhound bus
idled for an hour waiting for clients riding on a jet boat.

Hugh took a turn rowing, and we arrived at Battle Creek where
after only an hour on the river, we beached. Because large rapids
lurk in the first 15 miles of the trip, I had arranged to row along
with the guides of Great River Journeys, a commercial company
owned by Martin Litton, but they wouldn't arrive for two days. We
didn't mind waiting. We carried gear to the hackberry shade.
Grunting, we pulled the craft up and, fearing an unpredictably
high flow because of hydroelectric releases upstream, I tied the
boat to rocks with two lines. At twilight we wandered downriver
and watched deer nibbling algae in a vernal pool. They also rel-
ished sweet clover at the upper edges of sandbars. The sunset
gleamed on canyon walls.

Hells Canyon seemed more like heaven than hell, or at least I
would be satisfied for heaven to be so. Other names were Box Canyon, Seven Devils Gorge, Grand Canyon of the Snake, and Snake
River Canyon, which appears on the 1955 Geological Survey map.
Not until Oregon Senator Richard Neuberger wrote articles in the
1950s about the "sinister splendor" of "Hells Canyon" did the current name gain wide usage.[1]

At dusk, while checking the lines holding the raft, I spotted a
large bear foraging on the slope above, so close it could have
kicked a rock on us. We repacked the food to minimize the scent,
and I settled near the boat. Stretching out in my bag, I smiled at the
soft music of riverflow under the stars of a sky squeezed thin by
canyon silhouettes.

DAY 2

After a day of hiking up Battle Creek, I said, "It's good to get to know this place before we rush on downriver."

Hugh nodded. "This is the right pace, half a mile a day."

DAY 3

We moved a mile downriver to Wild Sheep Rapid, the largest. Excited and curious, we studied all ways of running it and gazed, entranced, at fearsome boulders and at a mint-green curl of wave. The direct route terminated in a boat-sized hole.

We sat, we read, we napped, we talked. A group of rafters arrived, scouted, and their 16-foot raft—longer than mine—disappeared in the hole but resurfaced. "No problem," I said to Hugh, who looked at me and smiled.

A jet boat roared up the rapid, spun, powered down the rapid, whirled with engines gunning, and throttled up again.

When we walked up grassy slopes in the evening, Hugh said, "This is as good as the range gets. See this? Bluebunch wheatgrass. Not up on pedestals that remain when soil erodes around the roots after overgrazing, but thick, with solid stocks."

DAY 4

Great River Journeys' wooden boats showed an unmatched grace, the ends curving up past the waterline, the sides flaring out to bob on waves. Four guides spun their craft with a flick of an oar, while trainees rowed two rafts with the forgiving qualities of rubber. Each craft transported gear and two or three people. The whole mob now scouted the rapid. "Don't go into the Green Room," advised Lonnie Hutson, the chief guide, as he pointed to the curl of wave. "It hits you on the diagonal. It flips people."

He went. Then the others. From my boat, I couldn't see what fate awaited them in the hole. Entering left of a rock, I pulled right to the eddy below it, then pushed on the oars to regain momentum. "Power through the hole," I thought. Suddenly we were atop the vortex, a Niagara of noise. Breaking waves punched my blades as I pressed for power. We skidded sideways; at the last second I corrected the angle by pulling on one oar and pushing on the other. "Hang on," I yelled. Immediate now, the hole carved down in front of us to a pit of foam. Inevitably we would be buried in wash. It was not inevitable that we would emerge right-side-up. The front of the raft and my trusting friend dropped into the hole. As the center of the raft bottomed out, I replanted the oars and held rigidly as jets of water pounded the blades. I had braced my body so that the force on the oars would not lift me out of my seat, but it lifted me anyway. Water poured on my head. Now I was immersed in the hole, and as the front of the raft flushed out and tilted skyward, I lost the power to push because I was nearly falling into the back of the boat, but then water glittered from our bodies as if we had risen on wings from beneath a sea. Hugh cheered.

When we beached for lunch, Hugh shooed a rattlesnake from the rock where I needed to tie. We saw Indian pictographs and scouted the second big rapid, Granite. At 20,000 cfs it swells to one of the largest glassy green waves in North America, but at our lower level, it was just a good drop.

In another mile we camped, and the guides cooked chicken, rice, vegetables, and spice cake in a Dutch oven—a terrific meal. Men and women, age twenty-eight to sixty-eight, from New York, California, and Scotland sat on logs or in the sand and talked. We cleaned up, retrieving the tiniest shards of garbage. The outfitter leaves nothing behind; human waste is packed out in a portable toilet, odorless compared with the reeking outhouses found at popular campsites in the canyon.

DAY 5

The water dropped overnight, stranding our boats on rocks like worms when the sidewalk dries after a summer rain. "Every time the level changes," Lonnie said, "it reminds me of those dams upriver." For electricity, Idaho Power releases water in the afternoon and holds it back at night. Flows of 5,000 cfs can climb to 20,000, rising 4 feet. The river normally crests at 36,000 cfs and runs at 13,000 in August, but this was a dry year and Idaho Power received an exemption from an 8,000 cfs minimum. The river carries an average of 14 million acre feet a year at Hells Canyon Dam, about the same as the entire Colorado or Delaware river, and 26 million below the Salmon River.

The state of Washington requested 22,000 cfs at the boundary below the Snake confluence with the Clearwater, and minimum recommendations for fish and wildlife below Hells Canyon Dam were 12,000 cfs.[2] In spite of precedents such as Wyoming agreeing to let Idaho have 98 percent of its water in the Snake and the United States agreeing to a minimum flow in the Colorado River for Mexico, Idaho stone walled attempts by the state of Washington to establish a minimum flow in the Snake and even prevented a public hearing from being held on the question.[3] The Water Resource Board rubber-stamped federal requirements already set for Hells Canyon Dam: 13,000 cfs below the Salmon River for 92 percent of the time.[4]

The cycle from the peaking releases is a daily nuisance to us as we drag boats, and like Canada geese nesting below Palisades Dam, we must find sleeping sites that won't be flooded by a release. The more important effect, however, is shoreline erosion. Hells Canyon is the ultimate degrading riverbed. Silt is trapped in the dams, leaving "hungry" water to cause extraordinary erosion, aggravated by the peaking flush. The canyon used to be known for Rivieras of white sand. Less than 20 percent remains. "It eliminates wildlife, too," Hugh said. "Going straight from river to rockpile, there's not a lot to live on." This affects everything from the deer grazing at the sandbar's edge to the western toad, probably doomed here because it lays eggs in shallows, deepened or dried up depending on the power releases.

We enjoyed the beaches we found, not knowing how much better they used to be. Biologist Frank Craighead once reminisced about the empires of sand he found in 1950 and said, "A data bank on our rivers is important because there's a tendency for each generation to be satisfied, unaware of what has changed."

The problem exists below many western dams. Degradation is exacerbated by peaking releases fluctuating 13 vertical feet in the Grand Canyon, its famed beaches being lost not just through shoreline erosion but by mass wasting of banks caving in when the water is dropped on a daily basis. Even though impacts on Grand Canyon National Park are severe, the Bureau of Reclamation contented itself studying the issue for years. A lawsuit attempts to halt

the worst peaking flushes. About the Snake River, Larry Taylor of
Idaho Power has said, "Even if we had data, I don't know what we
could do." There's an inevitable doom with the dams; however,
less erratic peaking could spare some of the remaining sand.

Below Rush Creek Rapid we beached for lunch and then strag-
gled up to a cabin where Hugh explained the workings of farm
machinery abandoned long ago. Carefree rowing took us to Johnson Bar, the official head of a "navigation channel" maintained by
the Army Corps of Engineers from the ocean to this unlikely bend,
deep in the mountains. Above Lewiston, the corps does little more
than post mile markers.

We had seen about six jet boats a day, but below here we saw up
to thirty daily. While nonmotorized use has been tightly limited by
permits, jet boats are not restricted by permits at all. "We don't
begrudge them the use of the river," said Lonnie. "They paid up to
$45,000 for a boat and they want to use it. But this is a wild can-
yon, and now and then it's good to not hear motors. We have a lot
of people who say, 'Let's leave the rest of civilization behind—it's
so unavoidable everywhere else.' To them, the powerboats are an
annoyance. At one time there can be several hundred people moving down this canyon, and you're not aware of them because
they're in front or behind you. But two people in one jet boat go up
and back, encountering every other trip on the river. We believe jet
boaters should have permit restrictions the same as we do."

For sport, for fishing and hunting, and primarily as a tourist business, the boats motor up from Lewiston, the jet boat capital of
North America where seven companies manufacture the craft, or
from Pittsburgh Landing, in the middle of the canyon. "There's too
much traffic in Hells Canyon," said John Barker, a river outfitter
who used to pilot jet boats but now owns a rafting company. His
view is typical of many nonmotorized boaters: "Hells Canyon has
turned into a user circus."

Curtis Chang, manager of the outfitting company Great River
Journeys, was less fatalistic. "The canyon is unlike any place in the
world. We want to continue running trips and showing this place
to people. All we're asking for are reasonable limits on motorized
use."

The Forest Service had proposed to ban jet boats above Rush
Creek during summer to keep a 16-mile section free of motors.

From Rush Creek to Pittsburgh Landing, fifty powerboats would be allowed per week. This solution was "judged to have the least likelihood of causing further polarization between opposing groups."[5] Without giving any reasons, Assistant Secretary of Agriculture John Crowell ordered the agency to lift all powerboat restrictions.[6]

Jim Grothe, a jet boat builder in Lewiston, Idaho, and president of the Northwest Powerboaters Association, thinks that permits should not be required because most jet boaters don't camp. "There would have to be a tremendous increase before the number of boats would be a problem." Jet boat outfitter Myrna Beamer agreed, "It will never get so congested that we'll need limits." She and her husband operate the largest commercial business; their trade grew from 8,000 customers in 1987 to 9,000 a year later.

Nonmotorized floaters don't like the noise, wakes, and intrusion of the jet boats. Rafters tell stories about jet boaters who wait irritably for rafts coming slowly through the rapids. This is not a major difficulty for the motorized people only because the number of floaters has been limited by regulations since 1973. If floating use were allowed to grow as motorized use has, both sides—not just one—would have serious problems. Jet boats would be backed up at the base of rapids waiting for floaters backed up at the top of rapids.

In 1979, 4,320 float boaters and 8,134 powerboaters visited the canyon. Because of permit restrictions, floaters in 1986 still numbered 4,308 while powerboat use had climbed to 12,667, 88 percent of them commercial customers.

The Forest Service's compromise would have banned jet boats on only 15 percent of the miles above Lewiston. Beamer did not feel that most jet boaters should go above Rush Creek anyway because of the hazards. "There's a lot of aluminum in the bottom of the river up there." They restrict their own tours to a 190-mile round trip. "Ten hours is enough."

Area ranger Art Seamans said, "We're seeing a quantum increase in use by powerboaters. Tourist marketing is effective; I think Hells Canyon is about to be discovered." He admitted, "The present system *is* inequitable." Powerboat use increased by 30 percent in 1989, and the Forest Service, with hopes of consensus on a new

management plan, formed a committee and began holding
meetings.

The dories moved on downriver, but Hugh and I stayed behind.
We hiked to mountainsides where elk grazed. We climbed as far as
a grove of fir, 3,500 feet above the river, with plenty of rise to go.

DAY 7

At Kirkwood Ranch the Forest Service maintains historic buildings,
and Violet Shirley, who grew up in the canyon, showed us farming
tools and household items. Len Jordan lived here and was later
elected Idaho's governor and a U.S. senator. He wanted Nez Percé
Dam to be built. Grace Jordan wrote *Home Below Hells Canyon* as a
memoir of the family's years at the river.

Over 100 families lived in the canyon, but the weather and depressed stock prices drove 95 percent out by 1918. The impacts of
grazing were permanent; the Forest Service reported, "Many riparian zones and adjacent benches were very badly overgrazed and
trampled by early grazing operations, some totally denuded." In-
vader species still dominate many of the sites.[7]

We made camp on a sandbar, then crossed the river and walked
on a dirt road to Pittsburgh Landing, the only road since we embarked 31 miles upstream. We found a flat stone, smooth on one
side from Indians grinding seeds or roots. Nineteen of twenty pickups had trailers for hauling jet boats. Cans and paper lay accumulated in the sage.

Archaeologists digging square pits here found settlements 5,000
years old; Pittsburgh is the largest of 1,000 prehistoric sites in the
canyon.[8] The dig was "mitigation" for new development. The Forest Service will build a campground, with expansion possibilities,
for twenty-eight recreational vehicles, improve (but not pave) the
dirt road to Highway 95, and construct a new boat ramp. Plans for
a snack shop and boat dock were dropped, for now. The estimated
cost was $2.2 million, "But it's higher now," Seamans said.

Clearly a hotspot of jet boat activity, improved access to Pittsburgh will increase use as surely as more freeways carry more
commuters. "We're drawing a balance between developed and
nondeveloped opportunities," Seamans explained. The only sup-

port I could discern was from the chambers of commerce at Grangeville and Riggins—Idaho towns of 3,700 and 500 people at the other end of the road.

Jim Grothe of the Powerboaters Association said, "I can't figure out why we should have the improvements." Myrna Beamer was likewise uninterested in opening the canyon to more problems than it already has.

The Forest Service's environmental statement did not consider increases in use on the river. To control numbers of jet boats, the agency had unsuccessfully recommended regulations, and now the need for them will be exacerbated at great public expense by improved access. Studying Hells Canyon recreation, Stewart Allen of the University of Idaho said, "While we're looking at problems of overuse, the Forest Service is putting in facilities that will increase use. Development or the lack of it is a relatively painless management strategy; the alternative is regulation, regarded as an infringement on individual freedom." The Dug Bar road will be improved along with ten other roads, totaling 171 miles of reconstruction in the National Recreation Area, plus timber access roads, some of them for cutting in the basins of salmon spawning streams.

Martin Litton objected bitterly, "They're ruining Hells Canyon with Forest Service development, with logging along the tributaries, and with unregulated use of motorboats. It's supposed to be protected but it's not." Frustrated with the Forest Service, the Hells Canyon Preservation Council seeks to make this a national park, with hunting allowed.

Returning to our raft, we walked past pictographs where a parking lot and picnic area will be built.

DAY 8

Strong at the oars, Hugh picked his way through the rapids. Then I took the oars and Hugh caught a smallmouth bass. An eclectic fishery, Hells Canyon supports trout, catfish, sturgeon, steelhead, salmon, black crappie, suckers, squawfish, twenty-four species in all.[9] We camped at a cove above Five Pine Rapids, read books in the shade, then cooked dinner after the blistering sun dipped behind the rim.

DAY 9

We had traveled 45 miles in eight days, too fast. But in the next three days we had to cover 60 miles on a slow current against stiff headwinds of the lower canyon.

We arrived at Nez Percé Crossing where Chief Joseph and his band crossed the river in flood. Their Wallowa Mountain home had been recognized as theirs in an 1855 treaty defining a 6.5-million-acre reservation, but then miners discovered gold, so the government reduced the reservation to 768,000 acres (later reducing it further). Horses carried the entire band across the swollen river. Several days later, the legendary flight of the Nez Percé began, lasting 1,170 miles through the Northern Rockies until Joseph surrendered, 30 miles from the refuge of Canada.

The river was remarkably silent as I walked along the bank, trying to imagine the day when those people crossed in 1877. Having gone his own way, Hugh returned with two handfuls of trash; a dirt road slated for upgrading reaches the river from the Oregon side.

At the mouth of the Imnaha River we stopped to retrieve some gear. Three weeks before, while touring in the Wallowa Mountains, I had hiked the 5-mile wilderness trail down the Imnaha to the Snake. A skyline was pierced by pinnacles; a fantasy land of cliffs rose above whitewater that promised one of the finer canoe runs on earth. The problem was the shuttle—the little river ends in the heart of Hells Canyon, making it nearly impossible to get back to the van. Then I remembered my upcoming raft trip with Hugh. I paddled the Imnaha to the Snake, left the small canoe under a tree, and walked back to the van. Now I retrieved the canoe and tied it onto the raft.

We splashed through Imnaha Rapid and on quiet water drifted into a narrow canyon where I recognized a landmark of river conservation history—the High Mountain Sheep Dam site. I announced to Hugh, "This was the place."

Beginning in the early 1950s, private utilities and public power agencies vied for a Federal Power Commission (FPC) permit to impound the Snake River in lower Hells Canyon. They had many differences, but the one thing in common was a desire to dam one of the last great hydroelectric sites in the contiguous United States.

The Washington Public Power Supply System—a consortium of public companies—pressed for the 700-foot Nez Percé Dam below the mouth of the Salmon River, perhaps the worst dam proposal in American history. It would have eliminated salmon and steelhead from the entire Salmon River, flooded the lower end of that great stream, and buried all remaining miles of Hells Canyon. Private utilities organized as the Pacific Northwest Power Company proposed the High Mountain Sheep site just above the Salmon River. The fight that ensued was the first great conservation battle over the Snake River (earlier efforts such as at Grand Teton National Park dealt mainly with land protection).

Idaho Congresswoman Gracie Pfost and Boise lawyer Bruce Bowler opposed Nez Percé Dam. Bowler attended meetings, convinced politicians, and represented the Idaho Wildlife Federation, all for free. With an impish grin in 1988 he said, "I haven't been paid attorney's fees by a fish yet." An Idahoan since birth, Bowler explained that the proposal came at a time of changing attitudes in his state. "Idahoans were raised in an irrigation area. We didn't anticipate that we could save very much, so we pushed to move the Nez Percé site upstream to High Mountain Sheep." This 670-foot dam was even endorsed by the Department of Fish and Game. Preferring private development, the FPC in 1964 issued a license for High Mountain Sheep and its 58-mile-long reservoir to flood all of Hells Canyon and much of the Imnaha and Grande Ronde. To save not only the Salmon River but Hells Canyon as well, a new outlook with a sense of strength and outrage was needed.

Mixing business and pleasure, insurance salesman Floyd Harvey had been jet boating in Hells Canyon. "When it looked as though the dam was going in, I tried to work with them. I was a good chamber of commerce member, and everyone in Lewiston said this was going to be a great thing. I wanted a lodge on the lake. I approached the power company for a jet boat contract because their people needed to go back and forth, but after they gave all their business to another operator, I said, 'Okay, you screw up my playground, I'll screw up your dam.'" No one guessed what a formidable foe the insurance man would be. "I had heard about the Sierra Club from Martin Litton of Great Rivers Journeys. It was a way-out group as far as I was concerned, but I went to Seattle anyway and saw Brock Evans, the regional representative."

Word spread to eastern Idaho, where in 1967 people at the Idaho National Engineering Laboratory formed the Hells Canyon Preservation Council.[10] Attorney Bowler recalled, "It was easterners who came to us and said, 'Hey you idiots, are you going to let them *do* this to you?' Funny, you had to go clear across the state to find people willing to stick up for the protection of Idaho." Ted Trueblood wrote on the dam proposals, stirring interest.

The case of which developer should dam Hells Canyon reached the Supreme Court. Cecil Andrus recalled, "The only questions were who was going to build the dam and how high was it going to be." But to everyone's surprise, the court in 1967 decided that no dam should be built. In a historic case, Justice William O. Douglas wrote that the FPC's duty was not to decide simply on which dam should be built, but to consider if *any* dam should be built. "The test is whether the project will be in the public interest. And that determination can be made only after an exploration of all issues . . . including future power demand and supply, alternate sources of power, the public interest in preserving reaches of wild rivers and wilderness areas, the preservation of anadromous fish for commercial and recreational purposes and the protection of wildlife." The court required the commission to address "the need to destroy the river as a waterway, the desirability of its demise."[11] An appeal was filed against the next FPC ruling.

Floyd Harvey had started the fight against High Mountain Sheep Dam because he felt cheated out of business, but he became obsessed with stopping the dam builders. "At chamber of commerce meetings people called me 'selfish.' I wrote to a lot of people, including Arthur Godfrey, who came out and camped in the canyon. He wrote Interior Secretary Walter Hickel and leaked the letter to the press so that Hickel was under pressure to do something. So in 1970 *he* came out for a trip."

The secretary called the canyon "fantastically scenic" and told people that he not only supported a moratorium against new dams, but that "maybe we should even study which of the dams already built should be dismantled."[12]

The Preservation Council lobbied heavily, and Bob Packwood, Oregon's new senator, led the opposition to the dams. In 1970, Governor Andrus announced that the only dams in Hells Canyon would be built "over my dead body." Idaho Senator Frank Church reluctantly sponsored federal legislation to protect the river. Governors Andrus, Tom McCall of Oregon, and Dan Evans of Washington opposed the dam. Senator James McClure opposed protection of the river but later backed off. Idaho Congressman Steve Symms supported the dams.[13]

Senator Packwood and Representative John Saylor of Pennsylvania had introduced bills in 1970; an act was finally passed in 1975 creating a Hells Canyon Wilderness of 213,993 acres within a 652,468-acre National Recreation Area. Wild river designation was granted to 31.5 miles of the Snake from Hells Canyon Dam to Pittsburgh Landing, and scenic river status to 36 miles from Pittsburgh to the Washington border. Draining the Seven Devils, the Rapid River was also added to the national rivers system.

The dam fight was significant in the history of conservation because the Supreme Court precedent considered fish, wildlife, and recreation, and directed the FPC to deny dam permits when in the public interest. Most other protected rivers had been noncontroversial, but the Snake was saved against heavy odds.

Though isolated from other threats, the debate marked a turning point in the politics of the Snake River. Hydropower was defeated and the pendulum soon began to swing on other issues as well; the sacred cows of development would never be so sacred again. The Pioneer and Swan Falls debates followed. Protection in Hells Canyon represented a new view of the Snake River including recognition of natural wonders, respect for the community of life enriched by all creatures, and the possibility that future generations will know the earth better. In Snake River history, the Hells Canyon success best signified the new view of the river and of the human responsibilities toward it.

"The fight for our great natural assets used to be awfully lonely," Bruce Bowler recalled. "More people are supportive now, though we once had good leaders such as Frank Church. Today we have the worst delegation in the nation, the worst ever in Idaho. Symms and McClure are the worst enemies of the environment. In spite of that, you can see a renaissance in thought and values regarding flowing water. Len Jordan called this 'the working river' and said he wouldn't be satisfied until it ran dry. That attitude has changed."

Floyd Harvey quit piloting jet boats and took up rafting. His lodge at Pine Bar was burned by arsonists believed to be acting for people embittered by the dam fight. It took Harvey ten years to get the suspects to court where he won a $265,000 judgment, though collecting the money is another problem. He has done little additional conservation work. "My job was done on December 30, 1975, when the NRA [National Recreation Area] passed. I lost a lot of money and had to get back to making a living."

Is Harvey pleased with the outcome? "Certainly with stopping the dams. People don't want more dams now. But am I pleased? Back in those years, I'd be up there for days and not see anyone. There's too much pressure on the canyon now, pressure for logging and for more jet boats. We need limitations to keep the level of use reasonable."

A fiery light still gleamed in the eyes of this sixty-two-year-old man who had decided to beat the dam builders in a contest for the Snake River. "You get on the river, and the power of it gets in your blood, and you *feel* better. Most of the time you sit back and don't realize that encroachments are closing in, not until you've lost too much. I guess, up there at Pine Bar, I sat back and looked at that river and started thinking about what we could lose."

Hugh and I had drifted reverently to the mouth of the Salmon River where I pulled into an eddy. "It's a different world if you go that way," he said, looking up the great tributary that drains the largest wilderness in forty-nine states. I agreed, reflecting on a forty-two-day raft trip I had once enjoyed from the Salmon headwaters to Lewiston.

Below the next bend we camped on a sandbar; beaches are plentiful below the Salmon River, regulated by no dams. We saw driftwood for the first time on the trip. I burrowed in the shade of a boulder to read, but then stared only at the water, my mind empty, yet filled with new awareness of a larger river and a basin that now embraced the mountain heartland of Idaho. Waves washed in to me, each ribbed with the feathery texture of waves within a wave. Small eddies curled within the parent eddies; currents spun from the edges of larger currents. My canyon lay within other canyons, within the Wallowa and Seven Devils ranges, within the Columbia

Plateau and the Rocky Mountains, all of it laced together by the flow of water.

DAY 10

Through the quietest canyon the beauty was so rugged in quality that some people might not call it beautiful. Crumbling cliffs rose up and up and up. Then the valley opened to hills, and though we crossed the boundary of the wild and scenic river, it's all Hells Canyon—volcanic rock rising on mountains above the river. Beyond the anemically low Grande Ronde River, we came to a road and the Heller Bar ramp where most people end a 75-mile trip. We, however, would float as long as the Snake River flowed.

Hugh and I beached at Red Bird Creek where in 1953 he had personally turned loose the first chukar partridges stocked along the Snake River. This game bird is a native of overgrazed range in Afghanistan and one of few creatures that thrive on cheat grass seeds. "Under that mulberry tree is where we released them," he recalled. The flushing hydroelectric flows had eroded 4 feet around the mulberry, leaving a doomed tree on stilted roots. Ninety miles from the nearest dam, shorelines were still being ruined by Idaho Power releases.

Downstream, we passed beaches where teenagers sunbathed and mothers played with children in the water. The Interior Department studied the 33-mile reach from the National Recreation Area to Asotin and recommended national river status in 1979. Senator Packwood introduced legislation, but the Idaho senators categorically opposed designation, allowing four applicants to storm the Federal Energy Regulatory Commission (FERC) office with new plans for Asotin Dam. The last dam to be built—Lower Granite—caused near extinction of the anadromous fish, and now this additional structure would likely annihilate the wild salmon. Fishermen, outfitters, and jet boaters joined in opposition. As Jim Grothe said, "The one thing we all have in common is that we like being on the river." Part of Idaho's indignation was that the recipient of the FERC permit was owned by a firm in Connecticut. Senator McClure sponsored a bill in 1988 that rejected national river protection but banned new dams here and on the lower Salmon.

DAY 11

Ahead of the wind that begins by mid-morning, Hugh and I were floating at 6 A.M. A car winding up the canyon road stopped. As Hugh rowed through a rapid, Diane Harper stepped out to the riverbank and waved. "Hi honey," Hugh said as we touched the shore. With a clear sense of priorities, he went with his wife: "We'll see you at the ramp in Hells Gate State Park."

I stroked away from shore with a new feeling: just me, my boat, my river. The current pushed me around a bend where basalt columns climbed as volcanic rock has done since I entered the first canyon below Palisades Dam three months ago. Then, without warning, like a friend who suddenly dies in his youth, the current was gone. While eddies swirled to the sides, the river emptied into the pool of Lower Granite Dam. I didn't know it would come so soon, and I hadn't properly prepared. Every mile from here to tidewater would be blocked by dams.

To the Columbia

THE LAST DAMS

Pulled by an urge to see the rest of the river, I would finish my journey to the Columbia, then return to the headwaters. Not a river at all, the Snake's final 140 miles below Lewiston are in back-to-back reservoirs. Yet the efforts to replace the river's life-giving qualities are a fascinating study in natural science and political consensus, at once frustrating, tragic, and hopeful.

About as pleasant as an industrial town on a reservoir can be, Lewiston sports brick storefronts, shaded streets, and new development spilling onto benches once in orchards and wheat. With Clarkston, across the Snake in Washington, the urban area of 44,600 residents is the largest along the river.

The Clearwater is the largest tributary to the Snake, meeting it in Lewiston after being fed two of North America's preeminent wild and scenic rivers, the Selway and Lochsa, which form the Middle Fork of the Clearwater, all three protected in the original group of national wild and scenic rivers in 1968.

Lewis and Clark crossed Lolo Pass at the Lochsa headwaters and struggled on Bitterroot Mountain trails, the most strenuous leg of their journey. In October 1805, they built boats along the Clearwater, then paddled down the Snake to the Columbia. At one point they wrote that the Snake River was "full of furious water swirling round fragmented cliffs." They first named the Snake "Lewis's River,"[1] later calling it the Southeast Fork of the Columbia. On an 1814 map from the expedition journals, the Snake was called the North Fork of Lewis's River, and the Snake above the Salmon was called the South Fork of Lewis's River. Though three men ventured up Hells Canyon a short distance, Lewis and Clark never gained a true idea of the Snake River's extent and course.[2]

Lower Granite, 36 miles below Lewiston, was the last of four Army Corps of Engineers dams on the lower river. Fishermen opposed the plan, encountering open hostility from local businesses and employers. "Before Lower Granite went in, you could go out after work and catch at least one steelhead right in town," John Barker, a Lewiston outfitter, remembered. "The other dams had hurt the fishery, and we thought it would be nearly wiped out by Lower Granite, but everything was happening at once." Hells Canyon was being fought over, and Dworshak Dam was under way on the Clearwater's North Fork, but when the corps proposed a reregulating dam on the Clearwater, 600 people came to a meeting and told the corps to go back to their office in Walla Walla. The Clearwater Dam marked a turning point in local opinion, but it was too late to stop Lower Granite. "On an advisory ballot in Lewiston and Clarkston people voted against having slackwater in the towns, but we never had a chance," Baker recalled. "Because of the vote, we got a parks project along with the flatwater—the bike trails and beaches. Without that, we'll look like Pasco." Barker referred to a hot city of few amenities, divorced from its waterfront near the mouth of the Snake.

The main reason for Lower Granite Dam was to create the most inland seaport on the West Coast, 465 miles from the ocean, receiving barges 738 feet above sea level. The Columbia/Snake River Marketing Group confidently advertised that the lower Snake was "one of the most promising areas for industrial development in North America." Wheat accounts for 80 percent of the shipping, each barge the equivalent of 110 double tractor trailer rigs. Forest products weigh in second, mostly pulp and paper from the Potlatch mill in Lewiston, but also logs bound for Japan. Virtually all of the $200 million worth of goods go to foreign markets. The port accounts for a drop in the bucket of West Coast shipping. It is not barge revenues but property taxes that pay for 45 percent of the Lewiston Port budget, though director Dale Aldridge maintained that revenue nearly compensates for the taxes levied on Lewiston landowners. When barges began plying this 100 percent subsidized waterway, railroad traffic already covering the same route decreased.

Ice Harbor Dam was finished in 1962, Lower Monumental in 1970, Little Goose in 1970, and Lower Granite in 1975. Hydroelectric generators produce 1,305 average megawatts—enough for Seattle. Though navigation was the impetus for the project with power being incidental, hydroelectricity provides 96 percent of the benefits, navigation 2 percent. Construction of Lower Granite alone cost $370 million; annual operations require $14 million. No one has analyzed actual benefits and costs since the projects were built. "We don't sit around and worry about that anymore," said "Dug" Dugger, public affairs director for the Army Corps of Engineers in Walla Walla.

THE MITIGATION MYTH

Even though laws mandate mitigation for lost habitat, little has been done to replace the 140 miles of river, 14,400 acres, and forty-eight islands.[3] The Army Corps estimated losses of 1,800 deer, 120,800 upland game birds and animals, 13,400 fur bearers, and abundant waterfowl and nongame species.

A 1976 wildlife compensation plan led to development of 3,000 acres adjoining the reservoirs as "management areas" with irrigation systems for feed plots, rainwater catchment basins, constructed quail roosts, and fences for cattle, all costing $7 million plus a quarter million a year to maintain. The plan called for 8,400 acres of game bird habitat, 8,000 of it to be farmland with easements for hunting, but only a single 400-acre tract is under easement. Four hundred acres of riparian lands were to be bought, though 2,643 were lost.[4] Chukars were to be raised on 15,000 acres; none of it was acquired. To replace the 280 miles of shoreline, 750 acres were to be purchased for fishing access; 96 were bought.

"We've not had much success," concluded corps biologist Mike Passmore. "The farmers don't want to participate." County commissioners called the corps's plan "totally unacceptable" because of lost tax base. Under the best scenario, the rich, self-maintaining ecosystem of the riverway will be replaced by wildlife feed plots irrigated for hunters and by boat ramps. "Is that good wildlife management?" Passmore returned the question, "How *would* you replace riparian lands? All we can do is use the resources we have." Though supported by the corps at the region, $50 million for wildlife was cut from the budget in Washington, D.C.

The 1986 Water Resources Development Act requires mitigation at the time of development instead of later but does not require correction of old projects. Further losses occur in the disposal of a million cubic yards of silt that the corps dredges out of Lower Granite Reservoir, costing $4 million a year—another subsidy equal to four times the budget of the Lewiston Port. Only 10 to 20 percent of the corps's wildlife goals have been met, a common situation nationwide.

What could real mitigation entail? Private riparian lands that would otherwise be developed could be bought. Overgrazed riparian acreage could be acquired for wildlife. Obsolete dams could be removed. Flood-prone development could be cleared instead of using disaster relief funds to rebuild on the floodplain. Wetlands could be acquired and levees removed. Water rights could be bought for instream flows. The Army Corps of Engineers is barred by law from doing most of these things. Much *could* be done, but almost nothing *is* being done, not because biologists such as Passmore lack the will or competence, but because riparian values are not recognized in the political system.

THE SALMON AND THE STEELHEAD

Central to both modern economics and ancient spirituality, the salmon are the ultimate river travelers. These anadromous fish, living most of their lives in the ocean but swimming as far as 900 miles upriver to reproduce at their place of birth, are the subject of legends, prayers, songs, science, poetry, prose, and a fascination as deep and universal as the human reflection upon a fish can be. Still mystifying biologists, the salmon swim 10,000 miles in the sea, find their way from the Gulf of Alaska, pass hundreds of tributaries, and return to their birthplace.

At a riffle in the Salmon River, one summer evening in 1969, I had stood mesmerized by the play of light on the glassy surface and felt satisfied in the simple movement of the water, but suddenly it came alive with the fluttering, muscular body of a salmon, 3 feet long, powering through the current. The river truly had life.

The fish disappeared, but another appeared, and another, and though hidden, I knew that more lay beneath the mirrored surface. Part of the *mass* of the river was fish. Having been the whole way down and up the river, the salmon embodied the essence of river life.

The first white people described a paradisiac abundance of salmon. The Indians had been living off them since they got here. Commercial fishing in the 1800s began the decimation. In streams, unscreened irrigation ditches created death traps for up to 80 percent of the young smolts as they migrated downriver after living for a year in the headwaters. Ranchers are not required to screen their ditches, so the Fish and Game Department spends $407,000 a year doing this along the upper Salmon River alone. Some ranchers divert all the water from tributaries at low flows.

Indian and sport fishermen competed on the rivers with bloodshed between natives and state authorities in the 1970s. Treaties in 1855 had given the Indians rights to fish "at all usual and accustomed places." *U.S.* v. *Oregon* in 1969 granted Indians the rights to half the catch in the Columbia basin, a decision that sport anglers and the states fought. Recognizing that a "fair share" of almost nothing is almost nothing, the Indians sought comanagement of the fish, and Justice George Boldt's decision in *U.S.* v. *Washington* gave the tribes rights to participate in management.

Dams have been the primary cause of anadromous fishery decline since the building of Bonneville Dam in 1938. Runs of 10 to 16 million salmon and steelhead in the Columbia shrank to 2.5 million. The Snake River above Hells Canyon Dam accounts for the largest area in the United States blocked from historic runs.[5] Idaho once had 8,300 miles of habitat; now it has 5,400, only 2,400 of them undamaged.[6]

The run of fall chinook, once plentiful in the warm waters above Brownlee Dam, has nearly disappeared. The coho salmon, once strong in the Grande Ronde, was extinct in 1987. When Sunbeam Dam was breached on the upper Salmon River in 1934, sockeye salmon began to recover, but with Lower Granite Dam, the stocks faded toward extinction. Two fish were counted in 1989, perhaps the lonely last of their kind. Twenty-two unique types of salmon and steelhead could become extinct. No stocks can replace these because no others are adapted for the long migration.[7] In 1981,

1 million salmon of all kinds survived in the Columbia basin, and extinction was feared. Only the chinook had much chance of survival. The Northwest Power Planning Council estimated that 75 percent of the depletion was because of dams.

Though anyone can gaze through fascinating windows at the Army Corps's visitor centers and see the salmon swimming up fish ladders, the problems of upstream migration are not solved. "People now tend to disregard the upriver trip," said Ted Bjornn, assistant leader of the Fish and Wildlife Research Unit at the University of Idaho, "but there are still a lot of losses." Migration of steelhead is halted when the water reaches 75 degrees as a result of depleted flows. Mortality of fish migrating upriver is 37 to 61 percent.[8]

Trying to compensate, the corps built the world's largest steelhead hatchery on the Clearwater. Total releases from Idaho hatcheries were 17 million salmon and 11 million steelhead in 1988, an ingenious success of a sort as fish became one more crop of the Snake River basin. Hatcheries eliminate natural hazards that can claim 90 percent of wild salmon eggs, but a majority of the young fish can die from diseases in the feedlot industry of the hatcheries. At the Clearwater facility, 98 percent of the eggs and fry were lost in 1983; average losses to diseases are 30 percent.[9] Hatchery salmon require frequent inoculations against bacterial kidney disease. Wild salmon eggs are taken to supply the hatcheries. Even worse, wild fish could be irrevocably weakened by outplanting of hatchery stocks whose genetic strains are inferior.[10] Some believe that without wild salmon for breeding stocks, the health of the hatchery fish will decline and ultimately be economically unsustainable.

Leading to an even greater dependency on hatcheries, management plans called for dozens of new hatcheries at sites including the Middle Fork of the Salmon—the pristine stronghold of wild fish. The Shoshone and Bannock oppose the downriver Indian tribes because of the plan's emphasis on harvest rather than stewardship. "If the wild salmon are not saved," said attorney Howard Funke, "the upper river runs are destined for extinction."

The wild salmon are the fish that endure as they have for thousands of years, laying eggs in the river, surviving predators, floods, and drought, then overcoming repeated hazards of the civilized river. Only wild fish hold religious importance to the Shoshone and Bannock. Only wild fish carry the genes of the native fishery.

Losing the wild salmon would be like losing the grizzly bear or the bald eagle. The wild salmon are a symbol of the natural river, the spirit of the place. "Our mission is to keep those remaining runs from being on the endangered species list," said Roy Heberger of the Fish and Wildlife Service. "The hatcheries are theoretically there to replenish the wild stocks, not to serve as the main source of salmon. Unless we can improve conditions for smolts going back to sea, we may lose the wild salmon."

Conceived in mid-century, the hatcheries have been regarded as a panacea to fisheries problems, not only for anadromous runs but also for resident trout. Much like the bias toward new dams rather than conservation of water, hatcheries involve building rather than managing something and are favored. Biologists estimate that half the Salmon River run is now hatchery fish; the Bonneville Power Administration (BPA) reported that hatcheries produce 80 percent of the returning salmon and steelhead in the Columbia basin.[11] Three to five chinook return for every 1,000 stocked. The hatcheries have increased numbers of fish by dumping more fish into the system but do nothing to eliminate the causes of migratory deaths.

Downstream migration is more troublesome than upstream passage. Following the current, smolts are attracted to powerhouse intakes leading to turbines; 15 percent of the migrants may be killed at each dam. Counting all fatalities, up to 95 percent of the fish fail to reach the ocean.[12]

The corps installed deflector screens at turbine intakes on Lower Granite and Little Goose dams, allowing 70 percent of the fish to avoid turbines, but no screens were installed at Lower Monumental, Ice Harbor, or The Dalles, and modifications to bypass facilities are needed at five other dams. The Northwest Power Planning Council reported that each unscreened dam kills 10 to 30 percent of the juvenile fish; cumulative turbine mortality kills 55 percent of the migrants. The council called for outfitting all dams with screens to cut losses in half,[13] improvements that will cost $160 million throughout the Columbia system.

The Army Corps supported some improvements, but Colonel James Royce said, "We don't see the economic benefits at all the dams." The Office of Management and Budget called passage facilities a "new start" as if they were a new dam and not the correction of errors in old dams, thus requiring cost sharing from nonfederal sponsors. Once stopping environmentally destructive projects of the corps, the cost-sharing argument ironically was used to oppose fisheries' improvements.

Even if the fish bypass the turbines, the flatwater of eight reservoirs and depleted flows resulting from storage dams on the Snake River extend a downriver journey of twenty-two days before the dams were built to one or two months—often longer than the fishes' transformation from freshwater to saltwater allows. To bypass the dams and reservoirs, the corps installed screens to collect fish at Lower Granite, Little Goose, and McNary where smolts are piped onto barges, then motored through the reservoirs and released four days later in the tailwaters of the lowest dam—Bonneville. Steelhead do well but many of the salmon die. Until ordered otherwise by Congress, the corps spent money intended for bypass improvements to fund the barging program. In 1988, a record 20 million fish were transported on the Columbia system (9 million from the Snake River), up from 5.4 million in the similar low-water year of 1977. The Army Corps estimated that up to twenty times more fish survive in the transport program than by swimming to sea.

Even if barging were effective for salmon and even if bypass facilities were built at every dam, catastrophic numbers of fish are stranded by low flows in the reservoir above Lower Granite Dam—15 million in 1988. "We must get an adequate flow coming down the Snake River to flush the smolts past the dams and to offer attraction flows for adults coming upriver," said Bert Bowler of Idaho Fish and Game. Ted Bjornn added, "In low-water years we have a lot of fish above Lower Granite waiting to die because there isn't enough water going past the dam." For further improvement of the anadromous fish, and especially the salmon, much will depend on restoring some of the natural springtime flows of the Snake River.

It's not a coincidence but a matter of evolution that the outgoing salmon need high flows when the river flooded from snowmelt, but those flows are now detained to fill irrigation reservoirs and they're diverted into fields. "Restoring healthy mainstem flows is *the* anadromous issue," said Ed Chaney, a resource consultant who has worked on the problem for two decades.

Fishery agencies cooperating in a Fish Passage Center implemented a "water budget" aimed at increasing Snake River flows when the fish need them. The target is a minimum of 85,000 cfs at Lower Granite. Augmented flows would wash 80 percent of the smolts through the reservoirs and past the dams in April and May (140,000 cfs is considered optimum). The Northwest Power Planning Council estimated that survival rates can double with improved passage facilities and water budget flows. However, the only Snake River water that the Fish Passage Center could obtain in 1988 was 300,000 acre feet from Dworshak Dam and Brownlee (the Idaho Power Company was reimbursed for the water with electricity from the BPA). The Snake River's target for the budget is 1.2 million acre feet. A separate water budget for the Columbia yields 3.5 million acre feet, some of it released to compensate for inadequate Snake River flows in the lower Columbia. Frustrated with budget deliveries, the National Marine Fisheries Service reported, "There has been very little progress toward achieving the equitable balance and coequal treatment for fish and wildlife that the fishery agencies and tribes had hoped for."[14]

Idaho would be the chief beneficiary of improved Snake River flows, primarily aiding fish in the Clearwater and Salmon rivers, but Keith Higginson said, "We oppose the use of Snake River storage for anadromous fish. That water is needed for the growth of Idaho. To dump that water in the river and flush it downstream doesn't seem to be a wise use of stored water. The problem is the federal dams; they should solve the problem."

As with other issues regarding the Snake River, it's difficult to tell where the outlooks of the state, the irrigation establishment, and the Bureau of Reclamation each begin and each leave off. Sherl Chapman of the Water Users Association said, "Some of the federal agencies say that our water should be available for fish flows. They have a lack of understanding about how the Snake River operates. It is two rivers breaking at Milner. Until they understand that, we won't accomplish much." Bob Riley of the Bureau of Reclamation said, "There is talk about squeezing the irrigators for water, but scrutiny has to be applied to maintain a balance regarding the water budget."

Balance? Now that fisheries agencies talk about searching for some fraction of the river's natural flow to flush salmon downriver for one month a year and are successful in meeting minimum targets on one day in 1988, the irrigators and their agencies are worried about balance?

Ed Chaney called the state's view self-destructive. "The impediments are institutional, not hydrologic. With a businesslike approach, there can be enough water for everybody." Pat Ford added, "The institutions aren't serving the present or the future. They're serving the past."

The irrigation establishment poses a curious argument that it's "impractical" to move water from upriver dams to lower dams. This would be true if the water were released all at once, but dozens of dams can allow flexibility. Even Governor Andrus wrote, "Idaho's capacity to allocate water to the Water Budget is less dependent on availability of water than on coordination of management."[15]

The proposed Galloway Dam on the Weiser River could increase flows for salmon. In 1989 the Army Corps withdrew, leaving the project to the state or other interests.

The Shoshone and Bannock seek upper Snake River water under the Winters Doctrine and plan to sell it for budget releases for the salmon (see Chapter 2). If they are successful, a major source of water could breathe new life into the beleaguered runs of salmon and steelhead. If they're not successful or if the water they secure isn't enough, the Indians could take court action.

The Northwest Power Planning Council is central to the attempts to rebuild stocks of fish and wildlife and recognizes its work as "quite possibly, the most ambitious effort in the world to save a biological resource."[16] Unlike impacts on wildlife, riparian lands, and resident fisheries, the loss of salmon and steelhead enraged many more people and led to the political consensus of an entire region. The council credits a new era of cooperation in launching the restoration program, and even the Army Corps of Engineers touted "balanced development" as its mission. "The whole nation has changed," James Royce said. "The corps is now looking at resources and saying 'Let's preserve some of what's left.' There are very few reasons to build more dams."

The council's interim goal is to double anadromous runs to 5 million fish. With receipts from ratepayers, the BPA funds 80 percent of the council's fish and wildlife program, which represents a 4 percent share of the electric bills, with the logic that people who benefit from the cheapest power in the nation should help pay for damage caused by the dams.

Efforts are paying off in some respects with agencies touting a "new era." In the low-water year of 1987, 37,677 chinook appeared at Lower Granite Dam compared with 26,644 as a ten-year average. All salmonids at Lower Granite totaled 107,857 in 1987 and 98,479 as a ten-year average.[17] The council credited weather and runoff, hatcheries, an ocean harvest treaty, and downriver passage. The restoration hype of the 1980s ignored the decline of minor runs and the extinction of stocks such as the brilliant sockeye of Redfish Lake. Concern for Snake River stocks grew in 1989. "It's too early to say we've turned a corner," cautioned Ted Bjornn. "Though it looks good for the steelhead, the minor stocks of salmon are in danger." (In 1990, the Shoshone and Bannock Tribes petitioned to have the Snake River sockeye listed as an endangered species, intensifying the debate about river management.)

The problems of salmon and steelhead symbolize the Snake River's accumulation of error in dams, diversions, water quality, and riparian habitat. The anadromous fish also represent the essence of the natural river itself. Being dependent on the stream from tributary headwaters to the sea, these fish have drawn many interests together and forced people to look holistically at a large part of the river.

MARMES MAN

After seeing the barge for transporting salmon, my lower river travels consisted of doggedly driving from one dam to the next. On a rocky road I rattled to a reservoir, and walking toward the water, edged by dank mud and debris, I searched for the Marmes Rockshelter, occupied for 10,000 to 11,000 years.[18] Skeletal remains of "Marmes Man" are among North America's oldest. Because the site was be flooded by Lower Monumental Dam, the Army Corps of Engineers pushed up a levee against the rising reservoir, but it flooded the shelter anyway (the corps's dams buried 300 known archaeological sites).

I spotted the dark amphitheater where the basalt wall had eroded to the shape of a bowl on edge, facing the river. Because the reservoir was lower than normal, a portion of the shelter's floor was exposed. Catfish darted from my path when I walked into the water. Slowly, cautiously, I swam toward the shelter's opening.

Before the floodwaters had arrived, archaeologists piled sand on the shelter's floor to protect the original surface, and on that floor I now waded from the brown reservoir. Spiders crawled on the arch. Because it was hot and dry, I watched for rattlesnakes near the water. Tracks of a great blue heron patterned the floor along with those of a bobcat that had arrived from a steep, brush-choked hillside. My barefoot tracks were added, probably the first in some time. I sat on the sand in the shade of that nurturing rock. Then I lay back and watched the glimmering, sunlit reflection of water that enlightened the half-dome of the ceiling.

In the arms of that shelter—what remained of it—my mind rolled back to so much else that had been lost along the Snake River. Yet something of value endured. Quiet and still, I sat for an hour and said nothing, did nothing. Then I swam away.

THE END OF THE RIVER

I had seen Lower Granite Dam below Lewiston, Little Goose Dam, Lower Monumental Dam, and Ice Harbor Dam. They are all about 100 feet high; they all look about the same. One stop remained on my downriver journey: the confluence, the end of the river. This reach was boated by Lewis and Clark on October 16, 1805, when they ran one rapid, then drifted for 6 miles to the confluence.

Where the two waterways meet, the Columbia has run 1,214 miles, only 158 longer than the Snake. By the time the Columbia reaches the ocean, it has run 1,450 miles and is the fourth largest river in North America. The basin of 259,000 square miles is larger than France, 42 percent of it in the Snake River watershed.

Only fifty of the Columbia's 745 miles in the United States remain free-flowing, and those pass through the restricted Hanford nuclear reservation. Even in Canada, 80 percent of the Columbia is dammed. Though heavily developed, the Snake River presents a preservation opportunity in contrast to the Columbia, and in contrast to all the great interior rivers of the West except the Yellowstone.

I turned from Highway 12 at a Chevron tank farm and drove beneath a monumental set of powerlines. Just before the cranes and trucking depot of the Port of Pasco, I veered left to a park named for every explorer's heroine, Sacajawea.

McNary Dam flooded the confluence, but I was perversely determined to visit the site anyway. I carried my canoe to the water. In Sacajawea's time, the waters had probably met as gentle but powerful currents. Now, the Snake River's flow—a 50,000 cfs average yielding 36 million acre feet a year—was imperceptible. The sun set; the day's 107 degrees began to fade. I splashed water on my arms and face. Carp darted with submarine wakes from my bow. In the white, yellow, and blue tones of twilight I paddled toward the center of water where I pictured the two rivers still meeting in free-flowing splendor beneath dark fathoms of the reservoir.

A diesel-powered riverboat pushed eight barges up the Columbia into the Snake. The pilot would not notice me in my canoe at night. I avoided him, bobbed on the surf-sized wake, then stroked into the path he had taken.

Two men with fishing gear motored downriver. Their wake passed; I sat alone in stillness. Was this the end of the Snake River? Not yet. I paddled on, far from both shores. A hot wind gusted upriver, spiced with cooler evening air that licked the water's surface. The distances, then, seemed right. As near as I could tell, this was where Lewis and Clark had left the Snake River and entered the Columbia. I stared into the water, navy blue, streaked with black.

I imagined camping there on an ancient sandbar. The swish of the river rubs against the shore. A heron wades and spears a fish. Indians have built fires and dried salmon here for 10,000 years, ever since the first Americans arrived from what is now Alberta and British Columbia. I walk upstream from the confluence and then wade far into the Snake River. Beyond a shallow sandbar, I lie back and let the water pour over me, and then I float with my face in the evening sun and let the river take me away. The current carries me over sand and stone toward the eddy where the Columbia picks up this water of Yellowstone, of the Tetons, and of the enriching cottonwood forests. The Columbia picks up the cool spring flows of the Fort Hall Bottoms and the rampage of undiverted gorge flows below Milner. An unpiped Thousand Springs wells beneath me. Sturgeon-filled for hundreds of miles, the middle river washes up around me; I am pushed also by the powerful forces of Hells Canyon—an undammed canyon of 200 miles from Weiser to Lewiston. Here I am buoyed by the incomparable Salmon and Clearwater with chinook and sockeye and coho so plentiful that a civilization was based on them. Here, too, is the lower river where salmon and steelhead swam in hordes resembling a solid mass and where grizzly bears and eagles gorged themselves until they could eat no more. I swim on and join the Columbia. I swim on. . . .

The breeze slowly spun my canoe. A train crossed the Snake River bridge, and the quiet returned. One star pierced the horizon, then another, and soon hundreds populated the night, and more arrived each moment, seemingly unlimited in their numbers and their promise to light the sky. Slowly, with time to glide almost to a stop between each stroke of my paddle, I began my return, with starlight reflected in the water by my side.

The Tetons and the Mountain River

YELLOWSTONE TO GRAND TETON NATIONAL PARK

From the Columbia, I drove east into Montana and then south as I returned toward the upper river in Wyoming. Through a zone of crackling forest fires, latent volcanism, seismic potential and tourist realities, I crossed Yellowstone National Park, the greatest recreation attraction of the Rockies and the headwaters of the Snake River. I felt at home, with the sight of pellucid streams, healthy sandbars, beavers, moose, and eagles. The river rocks were not sharp as in the lower canyons, but round. Plants were not thorny but thriving in a soft sweetness of green.

The Yellowstone geography is what remains after one of the world's largest volcanic explosions, 10,000 times that of Mt. St. Helens. Rock and ash blown sky-high left an empty space, and the surface settled into a caldera—a collapsed cake of earth, 25 miles wide and 39 miles long. The southwest portion drains into the Lewis River, uppermost of the major Snake tributaries, with hot springs and two glacial lakes, Shoshone and Lewis.

The caldera is the most recent in a series found to the southwest at the Henry's Fork headwaters and on across the Snake River plain, each caldera older than the one to its northeast. All this exists because radioactivity in the earth generates heat venting upward as a "hot spot," which remains stationary while the North American plate moves slowly to the southwest. The result is something like passing a sheet of plastic over a blowtorch.

From Swan Falls up to the Henry's Fork, the Snake River follows the "path" of the hot spot, but then the path curves up that tribu-

231

tary. Only a low divide, 255 feet above Yellowstone Lake, prevents it from flowing southwest to the Henry's Fork rather than the Missouri River system. At one time, the lake was 600 feet higher and drained south to the Snake River. Seeking the same result, Idaho irrigators in the 1930s planned to divert the lake, but the protection of national park status proved to be too much.

Outside the south entrance to Yellowstone I parked the van above the Snake River. My plan was to canoe the uppermost boatable section of the river—9 miles to Jackson Reservoir.

A lime green pool emptied into a scratching shallow riffle, then a gorge. Rock-studded rapids came quickly where rafters thrill to eight-foot waves during high water.

The Flagg Ranch bridge and resort of motels, a gas station, and store are the only man-made things along the upper 55 miles of the river. Park Service plans call for relocation of the buildings farther from the Snake, but for awhile, the concessionaire refused to move. At the same time that the Park Service demands restoration of some natural values, it allows destruction of others, encouraging expansion of Flagg Ranch development though the site is "situation 1" grizzly habitat—the most important for the endangered bears. Why would the Park Service add facilities here while it's trying to remove them in other bear habitat such as at Yellowstone's Fishing Bridge?

"This is the edge of Yellowstone," said Jack Stark, superintendent of Grand Teton National Park. "The public needs to stay somewhere. Rather than add facilities in the parks, it can be done at Flagg Ranch if the need exists." This interpark corridor—the John D. Rockefeller, Jr., Parkway—is a national park in everything but name, and just 15 miles to the south, beyond the grizzly's shrunken domain, the Colter Bay recreation metropolis is already one of the most developed in the entire national park system.

I drifted into a riverine wildness that looped around meadows rimmed by cottonwoods holding osprey nests. Marshlands sprawled to my left—a beaver, moose, and duck district exceeding all others from here up to the headwaters. It looked good from the water, but the clank, smash, and clatter of a quarry cut through the air. Contractors digging up the wetlands for new roads in Yellowstone have converted 66 acres into a biological ghetto. "It's an atrocity," said Pete Hayden, Grand Teton's biologist, who grew up in Jackson Hole. "It's the biggest impact in the entire river corridor in many ways. If it were up to me, we would have closed it yesterday." The mining will continue for five years or more but will broaden no farther into the salad of moose feed.

On shore, I tracked mink and moose. After hundreds of miles of degraded river on the lower Snake, I no longer took the sandbars and willow thickets for granted. I beached and walked to the top of a riffle, waded into the pebbly river, and floated flat on my back downstream, the way I had imagined at the Columbia confluence. When I paddled around another bend, the visually magnetic Tetons rose into the sky.

THE SHINING MOUNTAINS

The Tetons are younger than any subranges of the Rockies, their uplift beginning 9 million years ago compared with 50 million for other mountains. Unfinished, the Tetons are still growing higher. Perhaps the most photographed mountain image in North America, they form a celestial background to the Snake River and are the most dramatic in a whole cast of extraordinary geologic features bordering the upper river.

"The Snake is the most interesting river for geologic processes," said David Love, Wyoming's eminent geologist. "There are so many faults of so many types, and volcanism and glaciation. Why does the river wrap around the way it does? The Yellowstone, Colorado, and Rio Grande don't do that. The river is delicately responsive to the tilting of the earth's surface, and in the Snake drainage we have many tilts in many directions."

The geology of the mountains and hydrology of the river intertwine as one system of cause and effect. Beyond the river's route, plotted by faults, lava, and ice, geological flourishes accent the waterway. The quartzite cobbles in the Snake, for example, were brought eastward by an ancient river to the north. During glacial melt, the Snake had a volume that eroded a broad swath through Jackson Hole; several levels of terraces mark riverbeds that migrated back and forth (a scene comparable with the ice age Snake can now be seen on the Alsek River of Alaska). In the Gros Ventre River, a landslide formed a dam that burst in 1927, releasing the highest known flood on the upper Snake, dumping 6 feet of water on the village of Wilson. Continuous faulting now pushes the Snake toward the west side of Jackson Hole.

"When I came here, the mountains were the first attraction," said Frank Craighead, the renowned wildlife biologist who settled at Moose in 1946, "but the river is what grew in my interest." While 10,000 people a year hike in the world-class backcountry, over 60,000 raft on the river.

Enjoying the Teton views, I paddled through a dreamland of scenery, but then the character of the river began to warp. Fresh silt buried the banks. Mud zones oozed like spilled oil across the valley. I knew I had entered the backwaters of Jackson Dam when I saw cottonwood stumps on flats covered with Canadian thistle. To reconstruct the dam, the Bureau of Reclamation had drawn the reservoir down from a normal 847,000 acre feet to one-third that volume and half its surface area, equaling roughly the glacial lake that existed prior to the dam. Meandering for miles, the river channel had not been so exposed since the dam was built in 1916. Melissa Conner, a Park Service archaeologist excavating sites in the drawn-down reservoir, said that this had been "one of the most densely populated places in the Yellowstone–Teton area."

Mountain views were some of the most spectacular from any river in North America, but only above the foreground's wasteland of dead cottonwoods and dried mud. After canoeing through gooseneck loops, I entered the reservoir, pulled the paddles across a grain of waves, and in the twilight of purple peaks, crunched ashore at Leeks Marina.

A RESERVOIR, NOT A LAKE

In 1876 Gustavus Doane canoed through the glacial lake and wrote, "Hundreds of otter seen. . . . there are marshes and Beaver swamps of great extent." A photo by William Henry Jackson in 1878 shows an archipelago of islands with peninsulas.[1] The Fish and Wildlife Service reported that 12,750 acres of riparian woodlands, mostly cottonwoods, were flooded by Jackson Dam—one-quarter of all riparian woodland losses on the Snake.

After small dams had been washed out, construction by the Bureau of Reclamation was considered a patriotic effort. Boss Frank Crowe gained legendary status on the Yellowstone and here, later supervising construction of Hoover Dam. Crowe's attitude about rivers was representative of many; when Shasta Dam on the Sacramento River backed water into its reservoir, he said, "That meant we had the river licked. Pinned down, shoulders right on the mat. Hell, that's what we came up here for."[2]

Visiting Jackson Dam, author Owen Wister wrote, "That disgusting dam has destroyed the august serenity of the lake's outlet forever; and has defaced and degraded the shores of the lake where once the pines grew green and dark."[3] Wister told fishing guide Curtin Winsor about the natural Jackson Lake of 1904 where he caught five-pound cutthroat trout and gave them to hungry Indians camped along the shore. "The damming of Jackson Lake was an act of environmental desecration second only to the inundation of Yosemite's Hetch Hetchy Valley," wrote Robert Righter, historian of Grand Teton National Park. The National Parks and Conservation Association called the reservoir "nationally depreciated desolation."[4]

Being the uppermost Snake River reservoir, Jackson is the last to be drawn down, which irrigators have rarely had to do very much. Because the full impoundment lacks the drained-bathtub mud line, many people are unaware that this is a man-made reservoir and not a natural lake.

After the Teton Dam failure, the Bureau of Reclamation found Jackson Dam to be alarmingly unsafe. The largest earthquake expected at the Teton fault is 7.5 on the Richter Scale—far more powerful than the San Francisco disaster of 1989. In building the dam, Crowe had simply dumped fill on snow and waited for the snow to melt, no longer an approved practice. The underlying soil, 635 feet deep, is unconsolidated glacial till. When wet, this was described by David Love as having the consistency of jelly. Dam reconstruction included a new 1,800-foot embankment, "densified" by thumping a 30-ton weight to compact soil, a technique never before tried in North America.[5] "I view the project rather dimly," Love said. "I would have rather have seen the reservoir left at the old lake level."

Producing a document that never saw much light of day, the hydrologic firm Bio/West analyzed reconstruction alternatives under a Bureau of Reclamation contract. During the driest year since Palisades Dam was built, 521,410 acre feet were drawn from Jackson Reservoir, leaving a pool about the same as the old glacial lake. With minor improvements, a 393,000–acre foot reservoir would have been safe and resulted in a worst-year deficit of only 128,410 acre feet—a drop in the Snake River bucket. The smaller reservoir would have met demands in all but the three driest years since Palisades. Bio/West concluded, "Water conservation measures on several Minidoka Project canal systems are a feasible method of reducing irrigation water requirements from Jackson Lake. . . . Many of these measures resulted in costs less than or comparable to the anticipated cost of modifying Jackson Lake Dam at little or no environmental cost." The firm called for "further consideration" of alternatives to rebuilding the dam.[6] The bureau did not do this. "Every acre foot of storage space in Jackson Lake is sold to irrigators," explained regional director John Keys.

Jackson Dam raised a nationally important question that has never been adequately addressed: Are the recipients of federal benefits from dams entitled to them in perpetuity regardless of public costs and shifting priorities, or only so long as the current contracts, facilities, and perceived public interest last? Rather than consider efficient use of water by the irrigators, the Bureau of Reclamation plotted an alternate dam site to flood the Snake's famed Oxbow Bend, one of the richest riparian areas in the Rocky Mountains. Other dam sites were listed for the Buffalo, Gros Ventre, Hoback, and Greys rivers, for the Snake River in Alpine Canyon, and at the Lynn Crandall site—a lineup of environmental horrors.

National Park officials did not want reconstruction. Chief ranger–naturalist Patrick Smith said, "To have a major dam within our boundaries is counter to the purposes of the parks." Superintendent Jack Stark said, "To eliminate the dam was our first choice. We suggested that the bureau buy the water rights to the reservoir."

Interior officials under Secretary James Watt ordered the Park Service to support the bureau on an environmental statement. "Initially the Park Service was appalled at that," said biologist Pete Hayden. "Just about everybody saw this as a good opportunity to get rid of the dam. The Park Service went to bed with the bureau because the secretary's office told us to." Assistant Superintendent

Marshall Gingery added, "We were told that we would not look for alternatives to the dam."

"The bureau's strategy was effective," recalled Len Carlman of the Jackson Hole Alliance for Responsible Planning. "Nobody wanted a dam at the Oxbow, and people in Jackson didn't want the old dam to fail during an earthquake."

The timing was not quite right for a campaign to return one of the Rocky Mountains' greatest riparian ecosystems to the way it was. But not long after the bureau proceeded with reconstruction of this dam, impounding the largest reservoir in the national park system, Interior Secretary Donald Hodel recommended the removal of a perfectly safe dam—O'Shaughnessy on the Tuolumne River—because it lay within Yosemite National Park. Unlike Jackson Dam, O'Shaughnessy annually serves real needs. The difference was that Jackson Dam was owned by Hodel's own Bureau of Reclamation while the Yosemite dam belonged to the city of San Francisco.

GRAND TETON NATIONAL PARK

Clearly a star in the national park system, Grand Teton is one of the finest parks for seeing mountain scenery and large animals. Much wildlife that summers in Yellowstone migrates to Jackson Hole for the winter. The Tetons are "long regarded as the center of United States alpinism," wrote the climbers' historian, Chris Jones. In 1987, 2.4 million visitors made Grand Teton one of the more popular national parks. The Snake River is floated more than any other river in the park system. (The New River, Chattahoochee River, and Ozark Riverways are administered by the Park Service and have greater use but are not national parks.)

Even before Grand Teton's designation, the Park Service fought proposals by the Wyoming state engineer to dam Jenny and Leigh lakes in 1919. Private companies secured water rights to Emma Matilda and Two Ocean lakes and planned major diversions; wooden headgates were not removed until 1950.[7] Support grew to extend park protection south from Yellowstone in the 1920s. Lowlands of the Snake River Valley were proposed for protection of winter range for elk that used Jackson Hole and crossed here on their way to the Green River, but the idea of protecting parks for wildlife was not yet accepted. Instead, designation in 1929 exemplified "rock and ice conservation." Geologist Fritiof Fryxell called Grand Teton "the park of Matterhorns."

Seeing the beauty of Jackson Hole and foreseeing subdivisions and the resulting ban on public access, John D. Rockefeller, Jr., launched one of the larger private efforts ever to protect scenic land and expand a park, quietly buying up 35,310 acres from ranchers north of Jackson with the intent to give the land to the Park Service.

Once ranchers and businesspeople discovered his motive, they resolved to thwart the "Eastern plot." In 1943 President Franklin Roosevelt unilaterally designated public lands in the northern part of the valley a national monument—essentially a park that bypasses congressional process. Western governors called this an "autocratic act of meddling bureaucracy." Wyoming congressmen introduced bills to rescind monument status; one passed in 1944 but Roosevelt vetoed it. In 1949 Rockefeller deeded the lands he had bought for $1.5 million to the government, including Snake River frontage as a frame and foreground of the Tetons. President Truman signed legislation to expand the park in 1950.

Park status has prevented dams, logging, gas drilling, and private development. Management has protected this stunning landscape immeasurably better than would have resulted without park status. Protection, however, did not come without compromises, nor does management continue without them.

"This is the most compromised park in the system," said Assistant Superintendent Marshall Gingery. "Dams, roads, hunting, grazing, irrigation—other parks have one or two of those intrusions—we have them all." One compromise by Congress allows grazing in the park until thirty-three permit-holding ranchers and their children die. About 5,000 acres and 80 percent of the original ditches are now retired, but many miles remain, irrigating 1,500 acres. Ranchers own seventy-five water rights and take up to 160 cfs from the Gros Ventre River, 30 cfs from Spread Creek, and 120 cfs from the Snake River. Ditch Creek is dewatered, severing that riparian artery that links the Mt. Leidy Highlands to the Snake River and Blacktail Butte. Late in summer, irrigators take flows of 350 cfs from the park's waterways. "That's a lot during months of low flow," said Pete Hayden. The privilege extends to Elk Ranch Dam maintained by the Park Service for ranchers and costing the taxpayer tens of thousands of dollars in some years. "The ranchers pay about one-tenth the cost of maintaining the system," Hayden said. Superintendent Stark explained, "The ranchers had grazed cattle in the potholes area—an elk calving ground. Maintaining the irrigation system was something we did to get the ranchers to move the cattle."

Even along the Snake River, cows preempt wildlife in early summer before ranchers move them back to irrigated pasture. Beneficiaries of the park's irrigation network include former U.S. Senator Clifford Hansen, who draws water from the Gros Ventre River, a tributary to the Snake. In one ditch, irrigators hold rights to 28 cfs but withdraw up to 165. Though the excessive withdrawal impacts the park, officials believe they have no standing to protect instream flows. "Wyoming Game and Fish raised the issue once and got squashed," Hayden recalled. As if this weren't enough, the irrigators want 21,000 feet of new ditch that would cross national wildlife refuge and park lands, and they want the government to help pay for it.[8]

Hansen is one of the men who in 1943 carried rifles and drove cattle across the newly protected national monument to demonstrate that ranchers would do whatever they wanted.[9] But in 1988 he said, "There's no doubt in my mind that the destiny of the valley was to be the national park."

The Gros Ventre River lies in dusty desolation at the Highway 89 bridge in late summer of dry years because ranchers divert all the water. Furthermore, the Gros Ventre water is ditched south and dumped into Flat Creek where it carried choking quantities of silt and decimated one of the region's finest trout streams; fishing guide Bob Carmichael called Flat Creek's demise one of the greater losses in Jackson Hole fishing. The diversion also reduced numbers of ducks and rare trumpeter swans. Irrigation for pasture thus ruins the lower Gros Ventre, from which the water comes, it degraded Flat Creek, to which the water goes, and in between it depletes the Snake River.

Going from the "park of Matterhorns" to the "park of compromises," Grand Teton is the only national park with a major commercial airport. Approved for temporary use while an airport board looked for a better site to land jets, traffic increased and commercial jets now approach at frequent intervals over the Snake River. In 1988 air traffic was up 47 percent over 1987, much of it because of Jackson Hole Ski Corporation's booming business. The runway and adjacent development block an important wildlife migration route between the park and a wildlife refuge. Interior Secretary Cecil Andrus had announced that the airport lease would be terminated at its expiration date in 1995, a move heartily recommended by the Park Service. Replacing Andrus, James Watt extended the lease for fifty years, stating that the commercial airport was essential to federal agencies. After his dismissal as secretary of the Department of the Interior, Watt moved to a home near Jackson, from which he flies frequently on commercial airlines.

Watt's decision on the airport epitomized conditions criticized in 1987 by Howard Chapman, an outgoing regional director of the Park Service. "If we're going to succeed in preserving the greatness of our national parks, they must be held inviolate. If we're going to whittle away at them, we must realize that it's cumulative and the end result will be mediocrity; greatness will be gone."[10]

HOPE FOR THE FUTURE

At the Oxbow of the Snake River, I joined Roger Smith and a group of eighth graders attending the Teton Science School. Smith cautioned the students to walk quietly and stay close to the trail. "We don't want to bother nesting birds." (To avoid disturbing wildlife, the school later discontinued the use of the Oxbow except for research.) The willows and cottonwoods were thick, the grasses, matted and spongy. White pelicans floated on placid water.

"Look!" a boy said. "It's a hawk. No, its an osprey! No! It's an eagle! An eagle! Look guys, it's an eagle!"

We visited Jackson Dam, where reconstruction produced a scene of strip mining in front of the Tetons. A Bureau of Reclamation engineer explained densification and the need for the reservoir. The kids asked a lot of questions.

Returning to the vans, Smith said, "Not one student leaves with the same impression of a river that he or she arrived with. We've talked about flow, food chains, cottonwoods, beavers, and fish. But more than that, we talk about the connections. Life is a process and doesn't end when the individual dies. These kids won't take rivers for granted anymore. Just crossing a bridge, they might see more than they used to see. And when they *see* more clearly, they're going to *think* about what we're doing. Once you start thinking, you start feeling responsible. The abuse of the earth might stop if enough people take responsibility for what we're doing."

ON THE RIVER

Below Jackson Dam, I slipped my canoe into the water for my eighth Snake River trip and my final overnight boating journey. Camping along the river is not allowed in the park or on private lands below it, so I planned to paddle on to a Bureau of Land Management island.

As the fourth longest free-flowing section of the river, this 69-mile reach has no North American rival combining wildlife and mountain scenery. The riparian corridor may have no equal for wildlife in the Rockies. Veteran river guide Verne Huser said, "With the Yellowstone rivers being off-limits to boating, the Snake in Grand Teton is the best wildlife river this side of Alaska." I launched late in the morning to avoid feeding hours, but eagles were still perched on limbs over the river. A muskrat scurried from land to water; a mink, adept at broken-field running and swimming, scrambled down the shoreline—the Snake River zoo. Head down, a Canada goose with adolescents ducked under the cover of an overhanging bank. In May, when the downy goslings are not fully bonded to the parent, one might swim toward a boat and follow it, becoming separated from its mother in the process. This happened while I was canoeing, and I couldn't get the chick to go back; baby birds are one reason to wait until summer to go paddling. I edged into the Oxbow, then backed out. The bottom produced a thick carpet of water milfoil, lunch for moose. Below Pacific Creek, 3 miles from a put-in, the river began to riffle. Deceptive, the current can dangerously push boats toward fallen logs, which are plentiful.

More than a third of the river through the park lies impounded behind Jackson Dam, but below it, these 27 miles remain a show-case. Fly fishermen waded in the shallows. The Tetons burst into view, a point-blank rise of 7,000 feet to rock and snow on moun-tains as pointed as those drawn by first graders.

Beyond the access area at Deadman's Bar I stayed to the right until I threaded through a skinny slot and thought the hazards of "the Maze" were past. Confronted with three channels, I picked the middle one. Water sieved left and right, it soaked into the cob-bles, and I was soon facing a tangle of fallen spruce. The current pushed me toward the snags—the worst hazard because water runs not around but through them. I drew to shore, jumped into shallow water, and dragged the canoe onto the rocks. Unable to carry it over the debris, I tugged the boat back upriver and floated down the far right slough.

Above the Park Service community of Moose, I pulled over to let three commercial rafts drift by. In 1987, river outfitters guided 69,000 people in the national park. Though fishermen had been guided down the river since the 1930s, scenic trips began with the Grand Teton Lodge Company in 1956. Today, this is one of the most run rivers in the West.

Superintendent Jack Stark said, "Bumper to bumper, you can find more wilderness in Kansas." The park's plan, however, allows commercial boating to increase another 30 percent to 98,000.[11] Commercial use climbed from 1964 to 1978, then declined slightly. Noncommercial use increased steadily to 32,000. The outfitters of-fer natural history dialogue by trained guides. "We require it," said park naturalist Patrick Smith, "and some of the outfitters have a record as leaders in this kind of interpretation."

River outfitter Dick Barker entered the business as a fishing guide in 1956. "Now and then people said, 'We want to float down the river, but do we have to fish?' We guides would wink or nudge each other, but then we saw an opportunity." Barker started busi-ness with a $35 raft, later combing the country for more craft, find-ing one in Florida, one in Philadelphia. In 1967 he pooled equipment with Frank Ewing and created Barker–Ewing float trips, one of the older river outfitters in the West.

"Verne Huser was our first guide," Barker recalled, "and set a pattern for knowledge of natural history. There's something about wildlife—people are more thrilled to see a bald eagle than Niagara

Falls. If we can give people a greater appreciation of the river, we'll all be better off."

John Turner, another commercial raft operator, received a master's degree in wildlife ecology and returned home to manage the family's dude ranch. In 1988 he was president of the Wyoming Senate. A month after my canoe trip, I joined Turner and his clients as he enriched a frosty morning raft trip with narratives on biology and politics. "We're now trying to increase the minimum flow from the dam to carry this fishery over the winter. . . . There were stonefly hatches that would cover you like snow; you don't see that anymore and nobody knows why. . . . Except for Jackson Lake Dam and the loss of the timber wolves, this area is relatively intact. I believe that Jackson Hole up through Yellowstone is one of the most outstanding wildlife complexes in the world." Turner became the director of the U.S. Fish and Wildlife Service in 1989.

Canoeing through the park, I noticed eagles' nests in cottonwoods. Part of a team of biologists studying the national bird, Al Bath said, "The Snake River is the best area for eagles in the Yellowstone ecosystem." Eagles would be affected little by the raft trips if boaters avoided early morning and late evening feeding hours, which they don't. Bird behavior is strongly affected when people stop or fish. "The main problem, however, is a loss of nesting and foraging areas because of land development downstream from the park." The fate of the eagle is tied to that of the Snake River; not only do the birds nest in cottonwoods, but 90 percent of their summertime diet is fish.

WATER FOR FISH

The upper river is a coldwater stream, ideal for the Snake River cutthroat, the primary sporting fish above Palisades. The river is also home to whitefish, two kinds of sculpins, five minnows, and three suckers. The June sucker, a 20-pound bottom dweller, has not been seen since 1927; its extinction is blamed on Jackson Dam.

Jackson Hole has been popular for anglers since President Chester Arthur rode 300 miles on horseback to fish in 1882, though the river was never in the same league as the Henry's Fork or Silver Creek. "The alkalinity is lower, the temperature colder, and the cutthroat doesn't have the longevity and size of the brown trout and some rainbows," said Jon Erickson, fisheries biologist for the Wyoming Game and Fish Department.

A University of Wyoming study found that anglers drop $11 million a year into the Jackson Hole economy; 403,000 user days were reported. Over 30 percent of all visiting parties fished. An economic study for the Jackson Hole Alliance reported that $10 million to $20 million a year were generated by fishing, not counting real estate sales. Additionally, eleven rafting outfitters in the park and thirteen in the canyon below Jackson host over 140,000 floaters a year and pump $7 million into the economy. Water-based activities count for 15 to 20 percent of recreational expenditures.[12]

Everyone agrees that the Snake River fishery isn't what it used to be. In a *Trout* magazine article, Curtin Winsor blamed the early decline on Jackson Dam, which blocked spawning habitat, and blamed the decline since then on irrigation diversions and siltation, low flows from the dam, levees below the park, and fishing pressure, especially from anglers in boats, "lashing the river into constant foam." Frank Craighead has seen a marked decline in the park's fishery since the 1940s. Between 1,000 and 2,000 guided fishing trips occur each year in the park, but Jack Dennis of Jackson's prestigious fly fishing shop said, "We don't get the expert fly fisherman anymore."

The critical problem is at Jackson Dam in winter when water is held back for the irrigation season. The Bureau of Reclamation cut winter releases to 100 cfs in the dry year of 1987. With low flows repeated in 1988, trout populations were down 71 percent, with larger trout hit the hardest.[13] In the similar low-water year of 1977, 43 percent of the beavers along the river in the park died because of depleted winter flows. Wyoming law established no minimum flow for the river, though the Department of Game and Fish recommended at least 280 cfs below the dam and an optimum of 400 (winter inflow to the reservoir is about 500). Erickson said, "Invertebrates are lost when the river drops below 280, which is devastating to the sculpin population and to trout that eat the sculpins."

The Bureau of Reclamation repeated that the wishes of Idaho irrigators must be met before anyone else's. Committee of Nine chair Lester Saunders wrote, "There is no legal right for anyone (including federal agencies) to demand the release of water from

Jackson Lake without the permission of the owners of the water."[14] (The irrigators don't "own" the water. See Chapter 4.)

An easy solution is available for part of the problem. The Wyoming Compact in 1949 granted Idaho users the right to all but 4 percent of the river's flow originating in Wyoming's 5,139 square miles, accounting for 3.8 million acre feet or 73 percent of the basin's water above Milner Dam. With mystifying rationale, the compact required that half of this 4 percent go to Wyoming only if it builds storage dams to accommodate one-sixth of the 4 percent or pays for an equivalent share of Palisades Dam construction costs. Ranchers use some of the available 2 percent in Jackson Hole; the rest is unavailable because the water is stored in Palisades Reservoir down where Wyoming can't withdraw it. What did the headwaters state get in return for giving away 98 percent of its largest river? Nothing that is apparent.

Clifford Hansen, a Jackson Hole rancher, former county commissioner, governor, and U.S. senator, was on the board that negotiated the compact. In 1988 he said, "We can irrigate all the irrigable land in Teton County without using anywhere near the amount reserved for us." Apparently no one thought about instream flow problems. In the future, the public trust doctrine could affect compacts the same way it promises to affect water rights based on outdated criteria (see Chapter 1).

The obvious solution is to trade the Palisades storage space, usable only by Idahoans, for Jackson storage space. To do this, Wyoming must pay a one-time construction reimbursement to the Bureau of Reclamation of $18 an acre foot. Then Wyoming could order releases of 33,000 acre feet as instream flow from Jackson Dam. This is only half of what's needed in dry years, according to Erickson. "For the rest, Wyoming may have to buy water rights."

All of this ignores questions of the bureau's responsibilities to the health of the river. Because irrigators own rights to storage space in the federal reservoir, do they have the right to destroy the fishery in the river below the dam? That fishery is in a national park, seriously damaged in low-water years by a dam that's also in the national park, where 85 percent of reconstruction was funded by the taxpayers. The endangered bald eagle depends on this river. Why isn't the bureau required to consider the formidable body of federal law dealing with wildlife and the environment when it manages the reservoir? The bureau has elected to do this in a very limited way or not at all, and no one has pursued the issue in the courts. "Even so, we have a better situation now than in the fifties," said Hayden. "The river is no longer seen as just a conduit between a dam and a bunch of potato fields."

Tougher questions deal with the hydrologic effects of the dam's artificial flows. Floods are infrequent, and high floods are nearly eliminated, doubtless affecting the river's braiding pattern, sandbars, floodplains, and riparian forest. Outfitter Dick Barker notices fewer channels and believes that spruce are invading the cottonwood forest because of fewer floods. Spruce naturally succeed cottonwood, but the balancing process of cottonwoods' seeding on new sandbars occurs far less frequently without floods that cut new channels and without deposition of silt now trapped in the dam. Pete Hayden said, "The stabilized flow may be harmful to wildlife because the river is not moving back and forth as much, which constantly renews riparian vegetation needed by moose, beaver, and other animals."

On my many trips down the river, I found virtually no major sandbars below Jackson Dam, yet I saw them on the river above the reservoir. Bank erosion is common. Though cobblestones prevent rapid downcutting of the channel, the Snake River in Grand Teton National Park may show the symptoms of a degrading riverbed caused by an upstream reservoir.

Among all rivers flowing below dams in the national park system, the Snake may be the most critical for riparian, wildlife, and recreational values. The Grand Canyon is likewise important, though unlike the Snake, the Colorado's riparian corridor was comparatively threadbare to begin with.

"Interesting studies could be done on the Snake River," said hydrologist Luna Leopold, "but agencies seem uninterested in the dam's effects on the park." The reluctance may be a presumption of defeat. Without some hope for change, why study the dam's effects? If studies showed that bureau operation *is* degrading the park—obvious in regard to winter flows—there would be pressure for the Park Service and bureau to cooperate not only in easy times of high flow when water is released for rafting, but during low flows as well. The bureau has historically won most inner-departmental conflicts at the Department of the Interior.

"We could study effects of the dam, but we couldn't expect anything to happen," said Marshall Gingery. "If you think that Park
Service decisions are based on biology, you're wrong." A ray of
optimism: A University of Wyoming hydrologist, under a park contract, will consider geomorphology below the dam. "We have a
long way to go," Gingery said, "but a new generation of managers
will be able to use scientific data. I think the American people want
to take better care of the parks."

After discussing minimum flows from Jackson Dam to Hells
Canyon, I wondered, why *minimum*? Even in their most ambitious
moments, fish and wildlife interests talk about the lowest amount
of water to sustain some twitching semblance of life. I'd not heard
the Idaho Power Company pressing for enough water to turn their
smallest turbine. I'd not heard irrigators talking about the 2 acre
feet that the crops actually consume. All water users tolerate low
flows from time to time, but no one would be in business if they
settled for truly minimum flows. What about *optimum* flows for
fish and wildlife? Especially in a national park. Especially when the
problem is caused by a dam that's also in the national park. Maybe
the fish and wildlife target should be halfway between minimum
and optimum. But the legal and economic system is so stacked
against a healthy river that to achieve even a minimum flow is a
gruesome political challenge.

IF NOT HERE, THEN WHERE?

I paddled on toward Moose and stopped to walk along the shore.
From a wooded bank I stared into the water, and, suddenly, like an
apparition, a beaver appeared, 2 feet under water. It swam into the
current. It later returned with a cottonwood branch and entered a
hole in the bank beneath me.

Even with low winter flows below the dam, even with jets ap-
proaching the airport, the Snake River at the Tetons remains one of
the finest large mountain rivers in North America. Four sections of
the Snake remain relatively natural: the headwaters to Jackson Reservoir, this section, Palisades Dam to the Henry's Fork, and Hells
Canyon. Only four. Where is the positive view of a whole river?
Among agencies, I found that only the Fish and Wildlife Service

was inclined to address the Snake beyond a limited reach. The
Park Service, however, displays a photo of the river in the visitor
center with this caption: "After leaving the protection of the park,
the Snake River faces many ecological threats. As it meanders
westward toward the Pacific, every effort should be made to protect its remaining wild stretches, particularly those that are essential to endangered and threatened species."

That's not an elaborate vision, but it's something. Along with the
Shoshone and Bannock's lyrical view of river wholeness, Idaho's
new river planning program, the Northwest Power Planning
Council's obligation to restore salmon, the Bureau of Reclamation's
optimization study, and the Fish and Wildlife Service's push to
protect riparian habitat, maybe there's a way. Perhaps there's a
means to care for this river so that the qualities found in Yellowstone and Grand Teton national parks are not rare but expected of
a civilization that's wealthy, technologically armed, and educated.

Jackson Hole

A CIVILIZATION IN PARADISE

Beyond the park, the Snake River flows on down, rolling glacial cobbles, flushing in the floods of May and receding in the dam-induced drought of winter, winding back and forth, but not winding much, because the current collides with levees.

Pierced by the river, Jackson Hole is a 48-by-8-mile valley guarded on the west by the Tetons and on the east by the Washakie Range, Mt. Leidy Highlands, and Gros Ventre Range. The Forest Service called this "one of the largest enclosed valleys in the Rocky Mountains."[1] The northern two-thirds lies in Grand Teton National Park; the southern third is mostly private land. The place is not what "hole" connotes—not a graben lowered on all sides, but a valley with substantial gradient from north to south. The list of deceptive names grows: Jackson Lake is no longer a lake but a reservoir; the South Fork of the Snake River is not a fork but the main stem; there are dams and not falls at Idaho Falls and American Falls; Hells Canyon is in many ways more like heaven, perhaps; and the Snake River is probably not named for a serpent but for an error in translating "Shoshone" from sign language.

The town of Jackson, elevation 6,244 feet, lies 4 miles east of the river and is a melting pot of tourists, cowboys, dilettantes on trust accounts, residual rednecks, construction workers, ski bums, mountain lovers, resource workers, merchants, artists, anglers, and climbers. Many people are family folk, with livelihoods and lives like elsewhere in the West. Unlike most Rocky Mountain towns, the place is tolerant and culturally safe for a person born in California or New York.

"I've been here six years, longer than I thought I'd be."

"This is an adventure place."

"The pay is notoriously low."

"Housing's the problem; no place for workers to live."

"Winter lasts six months; in March I *have* to get out."

"The best skiing in the country."

"The last and best of the old West." This oft-repeated one-liner is false—Jackson is not the old West but the new West.

"There are more people, more motor homes, more climbers, more everything, just like the rest of the world."

"A tourist trap, too tacky."

"Businessmen run this place." "Realtors run this place." "Developers run this place." Let them argue; I'll agree with the winner. Yet, planning is stronger in Jackson than in almost any mountain town or rural county, and it has a staunch environmental community, with the Jackson Hole Alliance for Responsible Planning being the area's largest membership organization.

The pressures for growth are intense. Some would say the opportunities for wealth are extreme. In 1950 there were 2,600 people in Teton County, 11,000 in 1988. In 1970 there were 1,995 housing units, 5,356 in 1986.[2] That 6.4 percent annual growth is a runaway rate more typically found in southern California.

Much touted by advocates of private land rights is the following statistic: 96 percent of the county is owned by the public. The other 4 percent contains 75,400 acres and almost half the valley floor. Outside Jackson city limits, there are already as many approved but empty lots as developed lots. Multiply existing cement, asphalt, lumber, and lawns by two and you have the future that "planning" has already approved. Current zoning—without increases in density that are all but inevitable—allows three times the existing number of dwellings for a population of 26,700—larger than Twin Falls.

Is Twin Falls the future of Jackson Hole? A highway master plan ostensibly written by thinking people as recently as 1984 had the county growing to 100,000 people with a six-lane road down the middle. A key element in this vision of paved grandiosity challenging the Tetons was a new Snake River bridge linking the airport to the Teton Village ski area and its choice real estate. The crossing, at the mouth of the Gros Ventre River, may be the most environmentally sensitive private acreage in Jackson Hole. A scaled-back plan in 1989 foresaw a population of 40,000, 5.6 times that of Cody, Wyoming.

Tourism is the economic backbone—85 percent of the jobs are based on it. My own impression is that people come to see mountains and wildlife, not the condominiums and golden arches that new growth has delivered, but the city council changed specifications for zoning to allow a K-Mart with cosmetic qualifications and moved toward annexation plans to allow a Wal-Mart (the competing discount vendor later dropped out). Editors of the *Jackson Hole Guide* wrote, "Jackson is not some small oil town down on its luck. . . . The valley has a beautiful tourist economy and time and again, tourists say they come here to get away from the type of urban living now being discussed for Jackson."[3]

A plan in 1978 established open space and agricultural zones that are politically unlikely in most rural counties—three acres per house in undeveloped areas—but still resulting in a mowed-lawn, matchbox patchwork hardly fitting the splendor of this world-class gem. The wetlands of South Park, bordered by cottonwoods and the Snake River, are home to bald eagles and elk in winter, but the pressure to grid that idyllic mountain foreground into homesites is coming as inevitably as K-Mart followed McDonald's.

It didn't have to be this way. In 1977 a bill was introduced to designate a Jackson Hole National Scenic Area with federal funds to buy open space, but Wyoming's delegation moved the bill nowhere. From the ashes, however, two organizations grew: the Jackson Hole Alliance and the Jackson Hole Land Trust. The alliance pushes for planning on private lands and better management of public lands; the trust has accepted 6,026 acres of open space easements and seeks "conservation buyers" who will invest in additional lands and then leave most of their tract the way it is.

Not the least of concerns are the awesome hazards of the mountains themselves. "Mountain sides are prone to sliding but are developed anyway," said county planner John Bradley. "The whole valley is like a cracked eggshell with faults. Major earthquakes are expected. The levee could easily fail some day. But you stand up at a public meeting with those facts and people say, 'Get that guy *out* of here. I *own* it. I have to be able to *sell* it.'" Will it all be developed?

"I think so," said rancher Earl Hardeman. "I don't know of an outfit that won't sell for development. The thing about ranching is, you never see any money. We're sitting on our money—this land. We get the money only if we sell. It doesn't make sense to sit on a $10,000 acre of ground with a $400 calf." After a massive fund-raising effort, the Land Trust bought part of the Hardeman property, but the choice scenery was not included.

THE OSTRICH RESPONSE

Before the levee was built, the Snake River flowed in broad meanders across Jackson Hole. "It used to be a mass of channels," biologist Pete Hayden said. "Now it's a sea of cobbles. There's no tree cover, so no shade, and the shallow waters heat up. Fisheries productivity is way down."

From my canoe, I saw that the river whips back and forth as it did in the national park, but only until it hits the levee, often head on, where the timeless power of the water scours deep, then turns upon the opposite bank. Cottonwoods grow behind the levees where land is not overgrazed, mowed for hay, or leveled for homesites, but even those forests are severed from the river, and many of the cottonwoods are likely to disappear. Wyoming Game and Fish biologist Jon Erickson explained that increased velocity of water makes the riverbed unstable and impossible for spawning, and up to 15 miles of side channels and spring creeks that were once excellent are also divorced from the river. Having lost those spawning beds, Game and Fish buys gravel from commercial quarries and dumps it in tributaries, which, of course, was never counted as a cost of the flood control project.

Instead of a 1,000-foot width, Hayden believes that the levees, if built, should have been 3,000 or more feet apart. "All you can say about the effect on the river is that it's negative. That levee is the worst environmental sacrilege in Jackson Hole." Unpublished reports at the Game and Fish Department predicted "nearly complete destruction of the existing river ecosystem" and "the pending ecological disaster associated with the levee system." The river could become a hatchery-dependent fishery within fifty years; habitat for bald eagles, peregrine falcons, cranes, trumpeter swans, beaver, and otter will degrade.[4]

Levees were first built by cattlemen. "This was beautiful pasture and the ranchers didn't want the river gouging it out," Earl Hardeman remembered. Private levees on the west bank caused heightened flooding on the east bank, so those ranchers pushed up levees of their own. Expelled flood waters were a cannon aimed at downriver landowners, so they extended homemade levees southward, most of them simply piles of gravel subject to frequent failure.

To involve the Army Corps of Engineers in an expensive job protecting nothing but pasture required political clout. In charge of the Walla Walla District, which includes Jackson Hole, Colonel James Royce said, "Today we would not recommend building that levee at all. Whoever was there at the time had enough clout to get it through." Some people pointed to Senator Clifford Hansen, whose family's land is protected by the levee. Denying credit, or at least sharing it, Hansen said, "Everybody in Jackson Hole was for the levee." Some people attribute the decision to the Resor family, which in 1943 had built a private levee to protect their extensive holdings. Stanley Resor founded the world's largest advertising firm, J. Walter Thompson Co., and his son, Stanley R., was secretary of the army under President Lyndon Johnson, but that was after the army had been baited into the project.

The Flood Control Act of 1950 required the Army Corps of Engineers to build the Jackson Hole levee, reconstructed from 1957 to 1964 for $2.2 million, all of it from the federal treasury.[5] The Park Service objected to a 2-mile section in the park but to no avail. Today, 24 miles are "federal" levee and 7.4 were built by private or county earthmovers.

Aside from the ecological damage, the short-range problem— one of them—is that medium-to-high flows can rupture the levee; erosion chewing on it is extreme. Luna Leopold, perhaps America's best-known hydrologist and the author of a text and other books on hydrology, compiled the essays written by his father, Aldo, that constitute *A Sand County Almanac* and has been involved in questions of river management going back to the proposals to dam Echo Park on the Green River in the 1950s. Hired by Teton County to study the levee, Luna Leopold concluded that it was not designed for flows hitting at 90 degrees and will likely fail, not by overtopping but by lateral erosion during even a mediocre flood. The fill material is also the wrong size. The corps admitted that the levee may not hold. It will certainly fail if maintenance is anything but dependable, effective, and vigilant.

The long-range problem—one of them—is that the west side of the valley is tilting downward. David Love reported that it is dropping one foot in 300 to 400 years, hardly enough to concern realtors, but this has already been going on for some time, and Fish Creek at Wilson is currently 15 feet *below* the elevation of the perched Snake River, 2 miles east.[6] Will the levees be damaged by earthquakes? "Sure," Love said; "I think it's inevitable. All you have to do is break the levee, and the west bank will flood." Is it alarmist to fear a failure? "No, I don't think so," said the most respected geologist in Wyoming history.

Uncompromising faith in the works of man persists. As novelist John Steinbeck wrote, a triumph of the human is that he can know something and still not believe it. One west bank landowner said, "Those levees could last 100,000 years." But John Bradley cautioned, "I consider the levee an artificial control; it could open with one minor shift in the earth's surface. The county sheriff wanted alarm devices installed in each house to warn people when the levee goes out. The Planning Commission *knows* the levee can fail, but people would rather live there anyway. They're confident that engineering will protect them." All three county commissioners and three of five Planning Commission members lived on the west bank. "There's a tendency to think something is less of a hazard if you live with it. It will take a disaster to change people's minds."

The river has come within a rockpile of rupturing the levee a number of times. In 1986, failure was prevented only by spending $2.4 million, more than the original cost of the whole levee.

"There's no record of failures," said Don Barney, the county's official flood fighter. During flood watches, he assigns employees to look for weak spots. They radio back, and within an hour or so truckloads of rock are dumped onto eroding faces, provided rock can be found. The county recently had to blast at a quarry while a flood was going on. "When we're about out of money, we call the corps, and they relieve us. If we run out before the corps gets here, I go to the commissioners for an emergency appropriation." Barney said he had to hold up emergency patching in 1986 until the commissioners got together and approved more work.

Under federal law, the corps builds levees but local governments are to maintain them. The Mississippi River is an exception, at a scale beyond local capabilities, but hundreds of other levees follow the formula of local maintenance. Otherwise, Congress would have seen local flood control as an inimitable drain on the taxpayer, and the levees would never have been built. The problem here is that Teton County would rather not pay for maintenance. Several decades ago, annual costs were supposed to be $35,000 a year, an estimate on which the county still stands as if it were a wedding vow. In fact, the cost averages $400,000 a year according to the corps. As for "emergency" flood fighting, the U.S. Army has maintained, improved, and reconstructed the levee by spending $10 million between 1964 and 1987, adjusted to 1986 dollars. Bob Gifford of the corps said, "We're spending money every other year or so to fix that levee, and it's not supposed to be that way; that money's supposed to be for an *emergency*." Colonel Royce said, "In Jackson we have nonfederal levees in the wrong places built to substandard conditions. To maintain those is like throwing dollars down the drain. Should we build new levees? There we have the cost problem; we are structured by law to show a positive benefit cost ratio." Another corps engineer flatly stated, "If any project in the history of the Walla Walla District fits the definition of pork barrel, this is the one. What I mean is, if there was any project where the district engineer was told, 'You're going to build this and don't bother with economic justification,' you're looking at it."

The Wyoming delegation updated the antieconomic, antiprocess approach that corps officials blamed on their involvement in the first place by directing the corps to maintain and reconstruct the levee no matter what. The 1986 federal Water Resources Development Act called for the corps to perform all work exceeding $35,000 a year. As if the levee were not the idea of local politicians, Wyoming Senator Alan Simpson warned that the corps was "not going to get off the hook. They're not going to come this far in twenty years and leave part of the river without operation and maintenance money."[7] Why should Jackson Hole enjoy this subsidy when other communities don't? "We can't afford it," said Commissioner Leslie Petersen, who has fine conservation credentials but reflects the development line on this question. "We already have the real estate development. We don't see any way out. We can't quit now."

Politicians push to have the Army Corps of Engineers "comply" with the 1986 forget-economics provision that was once a hallmark to corps activities but embarrasses the agency today. "Our first reaction," said Bob Gifford, "was to fix the levee. It's a long story, but you can't *do* that. We're spending $25,000 this summer just on a geologist looking for a quarry site, and I'm not sure we'll find one." The question of maintenance involves not only levee repair and reconstruction, but plans to clear the river of 3,100 dead trees and dredge gravel, opposed by fisheries groups who fear many miles of channelized ditch.

Not stopping at federal maintenance, county representatives want the levee extended upriver and down. Don Barney said, "We support expansion, you bet." Upriver extension would protect more of the Hansen ranchland near the national park. Downriver expansion would render a paradise of wetlands in South Park prime for subdivision. Bradley said, "The same people who don't want the government involved in 'anything' want the government to build the levee for them."

Colonel Royce concluded, "I'm loathe to put more levees in. It's not cost-effective to build them. That thing is a *river*. It's going to do what it wants to do. We can spend the money to protect those mansions, but it will cost millions."

The fate of the corps' beachhead on economic priorities was unclear when Richard Cheney—the Wyoming congressman who sponsored legislation directing the army to maintain the levees—became secretary of defense. It was not long until a new corps report concluded that the federal government should assume operation and maintenance of the federal and local levees. While money for fish and wildlife is legally available, it was not recommended even though the corps admitted, "The levees impact upon the area's natural ecology, and impacts associated with secondary development . . . continue to degrade natural resources."[8] The environmental statement claimed that the levee would provide "continued flood protection for riparian vegetation"—a contradiction of terms—and would cause "the potential disturbance of up to five bald eagle nests." The Fish and Wildlife Service issued a 148-page response documenting myriad environmental problems and called for a wide range of solutions.[9] John Turner, director of the

Fish and Wildlife Service, called for the corps to accept "full responsibility of managing this ecosystem of national importance."

Who benefits from the $10 million spent so far by the federal
government and the many millions more to come?—owners of
low-lying west bank property and the developers of flood-prone
open space. Normally poor people live on the flood plain—the
"other" side of the tracks—but not in Jackson Hole. In the inevitable path of the Snake River, multimillion dollar homes and resorts
with festive flags at their entrances are growing as at Palm Springs.
Assessed value of these properties was $24 million (8 percent of
market value) in 1988.[10] This levee-dependent real estate brought
in $1.6 million a year in tax revenue from the wealthiest, newest
landowners in the county and from the corporations with golf
courses, condos, and designer layouts, and the amount escalated
sharply in the following years. Has the county considered assessing
those who directly benefit for some of the cost of the levee? "No,"
Don Barney said. In some other areas of the nation, flood control
districts pay for their own protection.

Is there any way out of the levee imbroglio? "Decisions are based
on the development of land," Pete Hayden said. "I see a long
downward spiral for the river." Jon Erickson said, "In the 1960s we
recommended that if the levee were breached, the river should be
allowed to establish new channels with meanders. There's so much
development now, no one would consider that feasible." With as
much political perspective as anybody, Clifford Hansen said, "The
dikes will be extended, if for no other reason than there are valuable homes being built."

People speak of the west bank as if it's an urban area. It isn't.
Thousands of undeveloped acres lie next to the levee. More than
75 percent of the development is along a 6-mile section on one side
of the river, and even that has no resemblence to an urban area.
Most of the vulnerable acreage grows hay or cottonwoods. Could
the levees be relocated farther from the river in open space areas
and consolidated as ring levees around existing high-density development? This would be a considerable undertaking, but perhaps
only a fraction as formidable as the long-term maintenance that is
currently destroying the river. The corps has succeeded elsewhere
in projects far more ambitious. "It's not inconceivable that you

could undo the problem," Colonel Royce agreed, "but that's expensive land with influential landowners."

Everyone stands quite comfortably with their heads in the sand. The Army Corps of Engineers has considered neither the impending ecological ruin nor taxpayers' ultimate costs, though the National Environmental Policy Act (1969) requires such study. Squinting through the political blizzard, the Fish and Wildlife Service recommended the corps's incorporation of "a program to maintain and restore to the greatest extent possible, the long-term productivity of this ecosystem." Acquisition of open space easements was recommended. The most productive stand for river conservationists is to insist that the corps fix levee damage as a prerequisite to further work, and there may be no better forum for this than to resurrect a proposal to designate the Snake as a national recreation river through Jackson Hole.

Given the infinite and nearly hopeless nature of the problem, it would be nice to say that some of the subsidy used on the sinkhole of levee maintenance—destined to be billions in this chic resort community—could be used to buy private lands in levee-failure zones and thereby be rid of the problem. But because of existing and potential development, a hammerlock has been placed on even the study of alternate solutions. Perhaps the only thing to do is avoid exacerbating the ruin by limiting future growth in flood areas, a relatively painless though partial solution.

AN UNCALCULATED DISASTER

The west bank bottoms used to be zoned for floods, but the ruling was overturned when challenged by developers in 1984 in spite of eloquent advice from Luna Leopold. Flood zones no longer apply to lands historically flooded outside the levee, nor to lands that will flood when the levee fails. In 1988, Teton County approved an exclusive twenty-three-lot subdivision on the floodplain behind the levee, as it will continue to do. The Federal Emergency Management Agency (FEMA) subsidizes flood insurance at a high rate provided the county zones the floodplain to minimize future losses. However, FEMA concurred with the county's decision. Is the implicit safety of the levee a real security or just an ingenious fiction of engineers hired to do numbers for the developers? Is the levee safe?

"No," said Luna Leopold, hired by the county to answer the question. "The lowlands behind the levee are not protected from the 100-year flood." Bob Twiss, an eminent land use planner, advised that the area remain zoned as floodplain. If the county had not rescinded the restrictions, developers would surely have sued. Instead, new landowners will likely sue when their approved homesites are flooded, but that's for someone in the future to worry about and not a part of politics today. John Bradley believes that development densities on the floodplain will increase as water and sewer systems are added on the west bank. Classy development sitting by its own sewage is the current reason flood-prone development isn't denser.

Furthermore, the county "assisted" ranchers in the South Park area—not protected by the federal levee—who are seeking fewer restrictions. FEMA, however, retained a residual backbone and did not cave in on the South Park hazard rating. That's one reason politicians push for the corps to extend the levees.

Zoning requiring open space having been rescinded, the undeveloped land on the west bank skyrocketed in market value and ripened for subdivision. The county then contributed half a million dollars to the Jackson Hole Land Trust's campaign to buy the Hardeman's west bank ranch for open space. The county at once seeks levee improvements to make development possible while spending great sums to stop the development once it's proposed. Bradley clarified that the county is only spending money for scenic views from the highway—not for wildlife or reduction of flood hazards.

"We need open space," said chamber of commerce director Suzanne Young, "and we have to figure out some way of paying for it. It's no coincidence that our brochures are full of wildlife photos. We don't need to worry about accommodating the tourist; we need to accommodate the natural base of our economy." Her goal is visionary for a chamber of commerce; I've never heard better. Yet Jackson wants it all. The community has supported levees, roads, an airport, improved services, and an empire-building fund for tourist promotion, and now that the infrastructure is in place that makes development inevitable, people say, "We need money to prevent development."

Another card in Jackson Hole's deck has not been turned. Up to 30 percent of the private land may meet the legal definition of wetlands, determined by water near the surface and by hydric soils with riparian plants.[11] Federal law requires the corps to manage wetlands under section 404 of the federal Clean Water Act (1972); the Environmental Protection Agency can veto a corps permit. After two centuries of draining and filling that left token remnants of waterfowl and riparian habitat, the government adopted a policy of zero net wetland loss. Instead of one dwelling on 3 acres—typical of residential/agricultural zones—the county's requirement for wetlands is one unit per 20 acres, and federal rules could halt some development altogether, but thus far the corps has ineffectively applied the section 404 program. While the wetlands initiative appears to pack some legal leverage, it's difficult to imagine that the development forces will fail in circumvention.

Remoteness and climate once stifled development in Jackson Hole, but they don't anymore. Zoning and floodplain regulations are stronger here than in most rural counties, but they only delay or curb the worst changes. Bradley said, "When county zoning was passed ten years ago, it was a compromise. Now it's difficult to upgrade requirements for less development; you're just feeding lawyers when you try." Worse, evidence shows that zoning inexorably becomes a less-limiting process in which requirements that were not restrictive to begin with are whittled down until only shavings remain. The Jackson Hole Land Trust has protected important tracts, but it can't buy it all. Wetlands regulations may dent the onslaught of draining and building, but only if someone with unforeseen fortitude pushes for action.

Progress could be made by selling government land in areas without as much environmental sensitivity and by buying riparian acreage in Jackson Hole and along other waterways. This approach has served remarkably well at Lake Tahoe in the Sierra Nevada (see Chapter 1) and could work on the Snake River where transfer of federal or state lands to private hands near desert towns or in mining areas could satisfy antigovernment dispositions while protecting the environment in riparian areas. Also, the Wyoming delegation could use its considerable influence to appropriate money to buy lands critical to the future of Jackson Hole and Wyoming's economy. But that does not seem to be a part of the ideology or interest of Wyoming politicians.

Apart from the levees, the river through Jackson Hole was a paddler's dream of quick current and mountain scenery where bald eagles still soared. Then the river narrowed with steep banks. In my canoe, I passed the confluence with the Hoback River, a cutthroat fishery that tumbles in Class II rapids. The Snake braided through a floodplain without levees, and on a rare site untrampled by cows, I beached for the night.

Downstream, a canyon enclosed the river; conifers blanketed the slopes. Cliffs dropped to water and alpine meadows soared to wind-pummeled ridges. Whitewater begins with a whisper and grows as gradient steepens. This canyon is one of many Snake River canyons, yet different. Here is the most popular whitewater in the Rocky Mountain West. I had finally arrived at the dreamland of the kayaker, the rafter, and the rapid-hungry canoeist.

THE WHITEWATER OF ALPINE CANYON

In early September, just below Jackson Hole, the river served up a heart-thumping, eye-widening, paddle-gripping, mind-settling rush of water. An adrenaline boost is one thing, raw fear another, and so far I had kept on the exultant side of that thin but consequential line.

This is it, I thought, the Snake River I've been looking for. I had already found others: the cottonwood river, the spring-fed river, the desert river, the monolithic canyon. But here, finally, I bathed and basked in resplendent water, embraced by mountains scented with spruce. Rocks perforated some rapids and other rapids obscured their rocks. Here was a river more mature than most mountain waterways but still youthful.

The sky glittered when spray washed my face, my canoe glistened in the foam of white-on-green, and I laughed out loud because I had survived and it had been so much fun. I planted my paddle in the eddy at the base of Cottonwood Rapid, leaned upstream, and spun like a toy into the slackwater.

The rapid had started with a panting swiftness, swept chaotically left and then right, and completed the S curve with a conclusion—like so much of life—unseen from the beginning. I get on it and go and hope that my skills and foresight will serve me well. The complications of life are reduced to getting through the rapid; the rest of the world ceases to exist. If I make it through this one, I can run another. To do this is a mixture of negotiating for my future and simply following the pull of the river while fending off hazards as they come. Being in a canoe in Cottonwood is a matter of accepting this river for what it is. To run the rapid is to join the river, to become a part of it. In his kayak, Len Carlman angled into the eddy and smiled.

"When you die, may I have those stickers on the end of your canoe?" He spoke of my Friends of the River logo.

"You can have the whole boat, Len."

"When you die there won't *be* a whole boat."

In 1811 the Hunt expedition looked at the river near here and a member wrote, "Waters swept off through the valley in one impetuous stream." They trekked overland to the Henry's Fork. Farther downstream, a voyager named the Snake the La Maudite Rivière Enragée—the accursed mad river. In 1872, as a southern contingent of the Hayden expedition, several men walked through the canyon,[12] and in December 1876, Gustavus Doane attempted to boat here. He would not be my choice for a paddling partner: "I desired to get the boat through if we had to risk everything in order to do so."[13] The craft wrecked on a rock.

In Jackson, this 10-mile reach is called the "Snake River Canyon." But there are seven Snake River canyons: the headwaters in Yellowstone, this reach below Jackson Hole, the foothills above Heise, the Milner–Hagerman complex, Bliss, Birds of Prey, and Hells Canyon. Some people call this reach above Palisades the Grand Canyon of the Snake River, but it is not—Hells Canyon is deeper, longer, and grander. And besides, that name mimics the Colorado's Grand Canyon. Other people, especially in Idaho, call this Alpine Canyon, after the community where the river enters Palisades Reservoir. I can see up to the alpine zone of meadows, and the river's elevation at 5,000 feet rates quite high for a popular whitewater run, most being in foothills and drier country. This is truly a Rocky Mountain river; the Snake River Range rises to the right; the Wyoming Range to my left.

With air bags in my canoe for flotation, I had come prepared for the descent. Rapids are more frequent than in any other reach except the Milner. Alpine Canyon is the whitewater highlight of the river, the festive playground where rafters, kayakers, and canoeists practice their arts to distraction. On the water below the East Table put-in, I paddled on green pools, in accelerating riffles, and over ledges outlined in the black and white of rock and foam.

Though kayaking was new to Len, the river was not; before his job with the Jackson Hole Alliance, he had guided rafts commercially. Now we glided from one rapid to another, then entered green water, backed up by the ledge forming Kahuna rapid, the big one. Len ran it down the middle, and I hugged the safe right side. Below the ledge we played on waves and in holes of substanceless foam. With a whole river in which to dart about, my course on a surfing wave converged broadside upon Len, I struck him like an icebreaker, and my friend was instantly eliminated from the scene. He rolled up with new respect for my mass if not my control. "Sorry Len, I didn't mean to do it."

"Why don't you pick on *those* guys?" A raft now approached like a floating amusement park. We scattered to secondary currents while the slinky boat caterpillared through the center hole.

Below Kahuna is Lunch Counter, a deluge at high water but hydraulically intricate at the low flow. I drew right and caught an eddy at a rock wall. Facing upriver, I buried the front of my boat in a hole and rode a wave's crest so that gravity pulled me upstream as fast as rushing water pushed me downstream. In unlikely equilibrium, I surfed while the Snake River jetted beneath my boat. My favorite rapid, "Rope," is a smorgasbord of breakers, eddies, and rocks beneath a great cliff.

Whitewater canoeing requires thinking and doing, but I don't like to think too much. A wave rose ahead of me, so I tilted the facing gunnel high. Buoyed to the summit, I shifted my weight to the other knee to raise the opposite gunnel and sideslip down the back side of the wave. Then a rock wanted me in the worst way. I C-stroked frenziedly to push away from the crunching chunk of lava. Immediately I was sucked into a hole. When in doubt, paddle!

I powered forward and bottomed out in a very wet space but leaned downriver and flushed through by momentum. With each crisis, I had shipped a bucket of water, except for the hole, which delivered the contents of a four-legged bathtub. At a gravel bar I struggled my Titanic aground and drained the sea that sloshed between gunnels.

At Champagne, named for billions of bubbles, nature's whimsical alignment of waves and holes allowed me a rare opportunity: After running the rapid, I turned upriver, pulled to a hole in the center, stairstepped into a higher hole, then climbed to the shoreline eddy and tugged triumphantly back to the top of the rapid. I had defied gravity for a short time. I dropped through again, rested in the carbonated outwash and looked up. A screaming bald eagle and an osprey spiraled through the sky in an aerial dogfight, more like ballet.

It is an understatement to say that Len and I shared the river with other boaters. Forest Service data show that 90,454 people ran this section of the Snake River in 1987. In the West, only California's South Fork American hosts more whitewater use, and that's on two separate reaches (several rivers without whitewater see more use). Weekends in Alpine Canyon fill with the destiny of a river offering rapids, few dangerous hazards, easy access, summerlong flows, and a half-day digression for road-weary travelers from the national park.

Eight companies carried 65,200 people through the canyon and 1,900 on the gentler reach above. Each outfitter has a Forest Service permit allowing a specified number of boats, totaling thirty-two, which may be used as often as possible. River guides as efficiency engineers squeeze in four trips daily. At twelve people per boat, up to 1,536 customers can cruise the canyon in a day. No restrictions govern private boaters; 24,700 ran the canyon and 5,000 floated the 16-mile reach from South Park to East Table.

While the raft trip in Grand Teton Park has a reputation for scenery and wildlife, the canyon is billed for thrills. "Most people haven't been rafting before and look for excitement," said outfitter Frank Ewing, "but we hire guides with more than whitewater skills. A competent boatman will know a lot about natural history and western rivers." One of the earlier outfitters, Ewing guided for the Grand Teton Lodge Company in 1957 and began canyon trips in 1972.

From his guiding days, Len recalled, "The people showed up, we threw them a life jacket, and we put them on the boat. They didn't know what to expect, but they ended up having the best experience of their vacation. It's only when we enjoy these things that we become motivated to save them."

"This is a commercial river," said Breck O'Neil, owner of Mad River, the busiest outfitter company. "Trips are sold like T-shirts in storefronts on the town square. People come for an amusement-park-sort-of ride, and we put out the fun image."

Floaters didn't complain about crowding (of course, boaters who disagree were not surveyed because they were boating someplace else). The preferences of bald eagles raise harder questions. With five nests, the reach just above the canyon is called "the best eagle habitat in the Yellowstone ecosystem" by Floyd Gordon, Bridger–Teton National Forest biologist. "In the park, the eagles are better protected, but down here, the river's more productive and the weather is moderate." Biologist Mike Whitfield reported that this endangered species is distracted by heavy use, especially by people who stop, and that the birds must fly farther to forage, leaving their nests vulnerable.

When an eagle moved to a tree 250 yards from O'Neil's commercial campsite in the national forest just above the canyon, the Forest Service required the outfitter to move. "The eagle didn't seem to be bothered by us," he said. "The guides controlled the customers. Now other people go in there and bother the eagles." (The Forest Service has not posted the site against trespassing, as the Park Service did to its nesting sites upstream.) O'Neil hired a lawyer and fought the Forest Service, in charge of recreation, and the Fish and Wildlife Service, in charge of eagles. Caught between the outfitter and the Endangered Species Act (1973), the Forest Service wanted to let the outfitter remain. If necessary, O'Neil said he will sue to reclaim the campsite.

A FINAL THREAT

Len and I neared Sheep Gulch take-out, where the Forest Service paved a large boat ramp and parking lot. A hydroelectric dam was proposed here in the 1970s and would have flooded 25 miles of the canyon up to Jackson Hole. An alternate proposal would have wiped out 2.4 of the finest canyon miles; yet another would have raised Palisades Dam 50 feet, obliterating 4 miles of the canyon.

Temporarily banning the dams, Congress called for national wild and scenic river study from Grand Teton Park to Palisades. The Department of Game and Fish and the Park Service supported protection of the entire 50 miles; outfitters and conservation groups supported at least the canyon reach. Using the letterhead of the Idaho Department of Water Resources, the irrigators' Committee of Nine opposed designation and favored "harnessing" the river.[14] In written responses to the Forest Service's study, seventy-five people supported wild and scenic status for the entire 50 miles. Twenty-four letters supported no designation. Opposed by ranchers who feared for their diversions and levees, the Jackson Hole reach was "worthy of protection" but was recommended for state or county action. Well-crafted designation, however, could accommodate existing uses and also provide the needed emphasis for the Army Corps to add fish and wildlife restoration into its maintenance of the levees.

Substantially compromised, the Forest Service in 1979 recommended 26 miles that met standards "at a very high level." To prevent development of 2,600 acres, $5 million was recommended for scenic easements so that owners could remain but be paid for development potential. Under Reagan administration directives the recommendation was cut to 13 miles to exclude all private lands. Bridger–Teton supervisor Brian Stout had worked as a political liaison with Capitol Hill and recalled, "We tried to interest Senators Wallop and Simpson, but nobody saw wild and scenic river designation as important." The canyon remains vulnerable to the dam proposals.

A NEARLY COMPLETED CYCLE

With Palisades Reservoir drawn down in September, I later snatched a rare opportunity to run the Narrows, the canyon's longest rapids, culminating in the narrowest place on the Snake below Flagg Ranch. The river rips through a 30-foot slot, terrorizing at high flows. Pesky dangers can also be found at low levels.

After an approach of wave and rock, I glided left and was battered over a ledge. I rock-picked a long alley before threading the Narrows itself—simply a glorious flush at that level.

The Snake riffled on down through a riverscape normally darkened by the dam. The ring of mud grew and the bed was buried in sand laid down when the reservoir had been full. Near the mud-cracked take-out, the Greys River spilled into the reservoir after tumbling through an array of glimmering pools and boulder stops, running an average of 671 cfs. The Salt River's 819 cfs also enters the reservoir nearby. In the slack water, I had nearly completed a cycle begun in May when I launched at Palisades Dam and paddled to Idaho Falls. One piece, however, was missing—the source.

In Jackson, I stopped at Len Carlman's office. "It was good seeing the canyon," he said. "That's the lower end of the land we work on at the Alliance. It helps to know the whole thing."

"What about the other end? How would you like to hike to the source? Come along."

"All right," Len said. "Yes, let's go. In October before the snow falls. Or after the snow falls. Sure, let's go."

12

To the Source

A PILGRIMAGE

Somewhere up on the roof of the continent the river begins, and I wanted to stand there and let my eyes reach out over the land and down the canyons where the water starts to flow, to see as far as I could across the Snake River's Rocky Mountain source. After spending six months trying to see the river and its landscape for what it is, what it was, and what it might be, I just wanted to look, with no more goals, out across the mountains where the water rises.

Len Carlman and I swung packs onto our backs at Pacific Creek, a tributary that enters the Snake River below Jackson Dam in Grand Teton National Park. The creek rose gently eastward toward the wetlands of Two Ocean Pass, a source shared with Atlantic Creek. We departed for the high country with a thoughtful awareness of the pecking order in the wilderness of the Northern Rockies. The Snake River headwaters are favored territory of the Yellowstone grizzly, including some who've been trapped, drugged, and helicoptered here after offending humans near the roads. Wild grizzlies are one thing but humanized *Ursus arctos horribilis* is another—much more frightening. Our response to the threat of being eaten was to counterbalance our food in trees, make noise when walking in brush, and avoid carrion that's appetizing to bears. We took all precautions short of the best one, which is to hike in a group.

"Hope I'm in shape for this," Len said.

"What? You're twenty-eight. What could be the problem?" Five-feet-eight, Len was trim and strong, which I attribute to youth and good genes more than moribund days behind his desk at the Alliance. He does, however, get out for ample wood splitting and weekend hiking and skiing. His hair is red; his complexion requires a hat if ozone depletion is as bad as they say it is. "Want any of this sunscreen?" I hinted. Articulate, relaxed, Carlman seems older than his age and is an impressive spokesman for the environmental movement of the Northern Rockies, handling casual and formal situations with ease.

On the winding trail through dog-hair thickets of lodgepole, it was prudent to warn grizzlies of our coming. This is done by talking. And I was curious anyway. "How'd you get here, Len?"

"The Teton Science School—I took a high school summer ecology course. The instructor told the class, 'Scientists and biologists alone can't win conservation battles. It takes lawyers and politicians as well.' I decided to study both forestry and political science. Utah State University had an internship program, and I ended up in Senator Malcolm Wallop's office."

This, I knew, would be a chemistry experiment requiring goggles. "Yes?"

"First I worked on raising Buffalo Bill Dam on the Shoshone River. I didn't think I should be ruining two more blue ribbon trout streams and said, 'Take me off this.'"

"You weren't much help to Malcolm, were you?"

"Next I was asked to work on renewing approval for compound 1080 to poison coyotes and predators. I asked, 'What are the moral implications of this?' Someone led me aside and said, 'Look Lenny, moral implications are not a part of the job.' What did I know? At that point I said, 'Just give me errands to do.'"

Carlman retreated to where he really wanted to be and worked for free at the Jackson Hole Alliance. One of few environmental pros working exclusively on the Snake River basin, Carlman eventually became director of the group.

Oppressively heavy, our packs contained gear for a cold snap and 2 feet of snow. I dropped the thudding burden at a ford where we lounged on a gravel bar. A moose entertained us at close range. I leaned against the lumpy comfort of my grounded load and took a nap.

We had entered a psychic womb of sorts—the Bridger–Teton Wilderness, which includes 7 miles of the Snake River but excludes the upper limits of the basin, which are in Yellowstone. The river flows past only one other wilderness—Hells Canyon, its wildness muted by jet boats' roar. Likewise, the only section protected in the wild and scenic rivers system is Hells Canyon's 67.5 miles. Park status in Yellowstone and Grand Teton protects 33 and 27 miles, respectively, bringing the total safeguarded mileage to 134.5, only 12.7 percent of the river's length. Wild and scenic river studies were completed for 33 miles below Hells Canyon and 50 miles below Grand Teton; 46 miles were recommended. Another 83 miles below Palisades, Milner, and Lower Salmon Falls dams were identified for national river study by the Bureau of Land Management. If by some political miracle all this were protected, it would be only 28 percent of the river.

On frozen ground, on day two, we hiked up Mink Creek valley and entered the famed Yellowstone Plateau (the uppermost reach of the Snake River is southeast of the plateau in the Washakie Range). At noon, we approached a tent village and corral—Harold Turner's hunting camp for out-of-state clients who pay a lot of money to shoot an elk, deer, or moose in Wyoming. The foreman, rough-cut and soft-spoken, invited us to lunch. Beyond Turner's camp we saw elk tracks as we approached Yellowstone.

ELK, WILDNESS, AND THE BEAR

The Jackson Hole elk herd mixes with the northern Yellowstone herd in summer; combined, they are the largest group of elk in North America. While summer food is plentiful, winter range at lower elevations is short because of ranching, dams, development, and roads. A national wildlife refuge encompassing one-quarter of the herd's traditional range was established at the upper limits of Jackson Hole and became more important as urbanization usurped wintering ground and as ranches, roads, and subdivisions continued to block migration routes. The refuge is fenced to stop the elk's downhill wanderings; up to 11,500 are fed alfalfa pellets to compensate for lost range. Others migrate to South Park—once a choice wintering ground but now the residual of ranching where elk are herded by wardens on snowmobiles though fences and down roads to a tract near the river, something like the salmon and steelhead being barged around the dams. Even in our largest eco-

systems—Greater Yellowstone and the Snake River—wildlife and
fisheries are dependent on intensive and artificial management.

Len and I strode to a windswept ridge and looked down to the
river beneath the continental divide. Entering meadows strung out
for miles, we talked loudly because willows were thick and the
wind buffeted against us. We scrambled up the bank and claimed a
level place to pitch the tent.

In the evening, we strolled to Fox Park, a mile and a half long
and a mile wide, the largest meadow along the river. The Turners
call Fox Creek, which enters from the south, the Snake River. An
early survey map likewise called today's Fox Creek the Snake, but
the Geological Survey disagrees; a northern fork is larger and longer. Going back to 1872, the Hayden expedition—one of the last
explorations of unknown North America—called Wolverine Creek
the Snake River, though Wolverine is a tributary 10 miles above
Flagg Ranch. Hayden's men were likely fooled by the creek's broad
valley, contrasting to the river's inconspicuous gap just below the
confluence.

After dinner I sat bundled in my down parka, thinking, of
course, about the Snake River. Finally, this was real wilderness, but
it felt troublingly tame. I had enough gear to be comfortable no
matter what. Also, the Turner's were packing hunters through daily. And unlike most of my backcountry trips, I had company. Right
now was the first I was alone all day, the first I stared into that
wonderfully infinite sky and that sadly finite washboard of the
Rockies and thought about just them and me. I pictured myself
from high in the sky, a solitary figure huddled on a log surrounded
by mountains in this mountainous heart of the West. The uppermost 40 miles of the Snake River are the longest reach without
roads (runner-up is 31 miles in Hells Canyon). The southeast
Yellowstone region is one of only five I could locate in forty-eight
states where I can get more than 10 miles from a road (others are
northeast Yellowstone, Montana's Anaconda–Pintlar Wilderness,
northern Yosemite, and the Kings–Kern divide in the Sierra). The
upper Snake is in the largest wild country of all; the nearby Thorofare basin is called the remotest place from a road in the contiguous
states.

With the aerial view now in mind, everything seemed wilder, a
real wilderness. Amazing—the entire Snake was this wild only 150

years ago. For awhile I thought about the riddles of the river's future, and then I just watched stars popping out. Drafting down the valley, nighttime air was the whispering wind of winter on my face. The river, babbling over stones, made the only noise.

A branch snapped in the willows. Then another. Right away I knew that I shared this place with someone besides Leonard Carlman. I stood. I heard not the impact of paws, but hooves, and felt relieved. Something large, however, was slapping through the brush, coming my way. Now the hooves clattered on stones—whatever it was, it crossed the river. Now the hooves climbed the bank. What *is* it? Staring into the dark, I saw an animal grow larger as it cleared the riverbank and ascended the slope. Black, enormous, it had to be a moose, but what kind of moose would walk straight into camp?

"Hey buddy," said a voice from atop the moose. It was one of the hunting guides on horseback. Unaccustomed to campers, he came to check us out. The faceless dark inhibited our conversation, and Wyoming outfitters aren't the chatty type anyway, rather given to three-word phrases.

I sleep lightly, and the grunts, barks, and shrill announcements of moose wakened me in between the talk and laughter of coyotes. Bagged in goose down through twelve hours of darkness, I got up at first light, put on all my clothes to fight the frost, lowered the food bags, and boiled water for tea.

In the rising sun, a bull moose clumped into the meadow, browsing on willow in the nutrient-rich riparian zone. He strode upriver ahead of a cow, which apparently lost this year's calf; a yearling tagged along behind. The moose is the largest member of the deer family, largest animal in the Rockies, and largest antlered beast that ever lived. They browsed so close I could see the separate hairs on their glossy backs.

This was the big day; Len and I set out to baptize ourselves in the source of the Snake River. Though William Sublette and other trappers crossed the headwaters to Yellowstone Lake as early as 1827, and though outfitters have ridden nearby hundreds of times, and though Ned Fritz of Boise visited a headwaters spring while clearing trails in the 1950s, Paul Lawrence and Joe Shellenberger's hike in 1970 may have been the first time somebody deliberately sought the beginning of the river, and they were probably the first to write about their trip. Lawrence reported that the source was a spring bursting from a mountain side south of Yellowstone Park. The Geological Survey's Two Ocean Pass quadrangle showed the river extending above that site and beginning half a mile north of the park boundary. (The 1989 Badger Creek quadrangle shows the source at the spring.) Len and I simply followed the largest flow of water upward to see where it would lead.

Our unmapped path crossed the river, one-step wide, where we examined bear scat. "I'd like to see a grizzly," Len said, "on that ridge up there." While the Shoshone sculpin and Bliss Rapid snail may be as rare as the grizzly, this animal and the bald eagle have attracted more attention as endangered species than any others along the river. The Yellowstone ecosystem is one of two in forty-nine states with populous grizzlies, though as few as 200 may remain here. In the ecosystem, 83 percent of the grizzlies die unnatural deaths, over half killed illegally by hunters, ranchers, or landowners, and 20 percent by official "management control."[1] Chris Servheen, of the Interagency Grizzly Bear Committee, reported in 1989 that the population is climbing again.[2] No one knows, however, if the extinction threat is really past. If the population is strong, why wouldn't the bears wander south through the Bridger–Teton Wilderness? One reason may be that, unlike the La-mar Valley of northern Yellowstone where the bears have a low elevation base, the corresponding area of the Snake basin is flooded by Jackson Dam.

Writing about the grizzly, Frank Craighead could have been writing about the Snake River: "Alive, the grizzly is a symbol of freedom and understanding—a sign that man *can* learn to conserve what is left of the earth. Extinct, it will be another fading testimony to things man could have learned more about but was too preoccupied with himself to notice. In its beleaguered condition, it is above all a symbol of what man is doing to the entire planet."[3]

Most of the Snake River headwaters in Yellowstone are under a bear closure; people may not stray from the trails during most months of the year. One of my reactions was that the Park Service allows gross abuse of bear territory at the Fishing Bridge recreation metropolis where more bears get into trouble than anywhere else in the park. Worse, concessionaires built the Grant "village" in grizzly habitat even after the Park Service knew better. While the commercialization of grizzly space is sanctioned and subsidized, I was banned from walking lightly across a remote mountaintop. Rangers admitted that the upper basin is closed because few people want to go there. If a pro-bear decision were made where entrepreneurial trade flourishes, the concessionaire could get the Wyoming delegation to retaliate with threats about firing people and cutting budgets. This brand of politics is entrenched, and so Fishing Bridge continues to boom with visitors who unknowingly ruin what they've come to see and grizzlies are killed by park rangers.

I didn't mind the backcountry restriction. I liked it. I liked the idea of a sanctuary for animals whose habitat once covered western America but is now small. At the height of this 1,056-mile-long river, a clear priority is given not to people but to wild creatures. That seemed right to me, the perfect way for a journey to end, the perfect way for a river to begin.

However, it did present a problem to my pilgrimage. Len and I will follow the river to the base of an unnamed mountain and then climb to its summit on the continental divide at 10,022 feet, just south of Yellowstone, clearly the height of land towering over the headwaters of the Snake River. Any portion of the river flowing in Yellowstone's refuge for bears will be admired from a distance.

ONE ECOSYSTEM

Because bears roam widely, they symbolized the need to protect the entire ecosystem, not only the 25 percent that lies in national parks. At the Teton Science School in 1983, people formed the Greater Yellowstone Coalition, dedicated to management of the 13 million–acre ecosystem running south from the Yellowstone River near Livingston to the Snake River as far as the Henry's Fork, a region one-third again the size of Switzerland. Included are 224 miles of the Snake, which is more than twice the Yellowstone River's mileage in the ecosystem. The Park Service calls this "the largest essentially intact natural area in the temperate zone of the earth." Sixty percent of the land is open for oil and gas leasing, and logging is scheduled to increase by 20 percent, though all seven national forests lose public money on timber sales.[4]

"Rivers are a symbol of the ecosystem," said the coalition's

Louisa Wilcox. "Rivers stand for life more than anything else. The Snake River is difficult. We've let things slip away, but it remains one of the most crucial areas—swans, eagles, and other wildlife are dependent on the river."

The coalition is our foremost example of awareness that the parks are not enough. Biologist William Newmark considered the survival of fifty individuals of each terrestrial species and reported that seven of North America's largest parks have biotic boundaries 1.2 to 9.6 times larger than the parks' legal boundaries.[5] In other words, the parks are not nearly big enough for the animals. Here at the top of the continent, Wilcox and others are setting a pace for protection elsewhere—the Everglades, Glacier, Olympic, Yosemite—all have similar needs, not to mention the preeminent river-and-wilderness heartland of central Idaho.

As with Yellowstone, agencies have not seen the Snake River basin as a whole system but one of isolations. Addressing the need for a larger view, a Pacific Northwest Basins Commission was formed in 1967 but abolished by the U.S. Water Resources Council just before the council was abolished by Interior Secretary James Watt. Teton County Commissioner Leslie Petersen said, "People do not have a basin view. For Wyomingites, the Snake River ends at the Idaho state line." The Bureau of Reclamation, irrigators, the Idaho Power Company, and the Army Corps of Engineers have sliced the river into fragments, and wealth is systematically squeezed from the separate domains. During Swan Falls negotiations, the agencies considered the question, "What steps are available to operate the Snake River system as a whole to mutually satisfy anadromous fish, resident fish, and wildlife?" The federal agencies voted to address the question; the state of Idaho and the Idaho Power Company voted against it.[6] The narrow view insulates single-use exploiters whose effects appear minimized when the small view is taken. If the river "ends" at Milner Dam, then nobody is responsible for what happens there.

Even at a local scale, the river is seldom seen as a part of the communities. Most towns with river frontage are in fact on reservoir frontage, and those that are along the free-flowing river tend to ignore it. The strength of the communities is credited to the exploitation of the river, and that is understandable in a traditional economic view. Missing, however, is community strength through acceptance of the river as an artery, as a part of the town, as a force not to be expended but as a remarkable entity bringing life to the valleys and canyons. Would the city of Twin Falls appear any different if people who go to the acclaimed falls saw a falls rather than the trickle of green scum? A minimum flow could be reinstated and life returned to Shoshone Falls—a veritable Niagara in waiting. A community's adoption of a living river doesn't have to be ambitious; a picnic area or bicycle trail does much to reintroduce the waterway to the people.

Conservation groups are effective in the basin, but none addresses the river as a whole system. The Northwest Power Planning Council integrates fish and wildlife issues but only in regard to hydropower. The Fish and Wildlife Service comes close to a river-length view with its interest in riparian habitat but has limited responsibilities and even less political support. The isolated caretaking of conservationists served well in stopping dams in Hells Canyon, protecting the last of the Thousand Springs, and expanding Grand Teton National Park, but single-issue protection encounters limits with the more complex problems. Efforts to restore salmon and steelhead have led to a broader view but stop short of the complete outlook needed for instream flows, riparian habitat, wildlife, and recreation.

The holistic view is lacking, yet the Snake River may offer better opportunities for a basinwide awareness than any other large western river because it begins in the well-known national parks, it crosses Idaho where the water's economic importance is obvious, and it ends in the Northwest where a consensus has formed to restore salmon and steelhead. This is a waterway of the Rockies and of the Northwest, one system no matter what is said about the tourniquet knotted around the river at Milner Dam.

Almost at the source, I looked out to mountains and to where the water flows. Clouds streaked across from Idaho, and I felt the winds that wash the land in shadows, rain, and snow. I thought, yes, this is one place, "a unique and unitary ecosystem," as the Shoshone and Bannock said.

Len and I tramped upriver and the frost melted in Indian summer's sun. We spotted a confluence below the trail, metered the cfs in our minds, and judged the southern fork to run one pint per second larger. The topo map agreed. Then the river, 3 feet wide, tumbled from a rugged gorge. We climbed to a ridge, and the river disappeared beneath cliffs. When we descended a mile farther, the streambed was dry, but its water-scoured stones wound through the meadow exactly as streams do. Like a Japanese gardener's symbol for a waterway, the Snake River was a meandering of rocks. Water clearly flows here during part of the year, proven by the streambed and the erosion of the valley. A mountain side rose to the height of land south of Yellowstone. It was time to climb.

AN END AND A BEGINNING

Precisely where the river begins has little consequence; there are several choices. My judgment was that the river begins at the highest sign of a watercourse—earth washed by a channel of runoff— whether or not water was running when I happened to be there.

Len and I panted at the mountaintop, its ridge curving north and down to a saddle at the head of the Snake River basin where two swales converge into a channel that carries water during its runoff season. That streambed of the Snake River lay below the headwall of the continental divide in Yellowstone National Park.

Len wanted to ramble east and peer into the canyon of the Thorofare River. "Go ahead, I'll be over here." Behind a whitebark pine, I took shelter from the wind. Southeast rose the Wind River Mountains, directly south lay the Mt. Leidy Highlands and Gros Ventres, west was the Teton skyline, north were the Gallatin and Beartooth ranges beyond Yellowstone Lake, luminous in afternoon sun. Finally sitting at the top of the river, I felt a great happiness, but one that already slipped off into other emotions.

Like living a lifetime, I had followed the river to its end and its beginning, and like it, I had changed. Youth and discovery can never be seen again as they're seen for the first time, and now— humbler and fuller—an edge of happiness was gone but knowledge had taken its place. I had seen heartbreaking losses, the momentum of destruction, qualities that remain, the promise of preservation, the potential for restoration, and a coming era of awareness and reform. The times are inevitably changing. Some wish this were true but doubt it and are timid. Some fear the change or see it as the meddling of misinformed outsiders. Some know it's true but grasp an older way with fierce possession because they fear the loss of a good life. Some see change as inevitable and will adjust. Some have grasped the vision of a better place and are ready to pursue that vision with the vigor and promise that has drawn people to endeavors that might be described as the building of a better world.

In the pursuit of one American dream, another was nearly killed. But with tenacity that is a hallmark of western settlement, people are working to reinstill the dream of nature's garden, of the cottonwood's summer shade, of the salmon's return, of wildness beyond the fields, of water's endless flow to sea. People are working to integrate the nearly forgotten dream of a living river with the powerfully successful dream of individual strength and material wealth. While the grossest damage to the earth might be averted with laws, the river's return to health will not be possible until more people believe that this should happen. Otherwise, each advance will be marked by the need to defend that advance or by backsliding in some other way.

The most troubling fact was that I had found little sense of vision among people professionally involved with the Snake River. The "working river" was mentioned the most. We've developed hydropower and irrigation to the exclusion of the more basic vision of a river as life, both real and symbolic, yet there's no reason this river can't be flowing as well as working. I'm searching for a vision that includes compassion for all that the river supports and hope for a future when people grant importance to life of all forms, large and small, domestic and wild—a vision that includes life, in the many forms that were given to us, as a thing of reverence.

From people in charge of government agencies, from most elected officials, and from organizations that control the fate of the river, I found little vision that the future can be better than what we now have. What are the chances of turning the river's fate into a brilliant opportunity? The democratic system, at its best, requires that people take responsibility at the same time they assert their rights and that the interests of others be recognized while fulfilling individual needs. Pride in American government and in what we've done is fine, but what are we doing to *extend* democracy to its real ideals and not just in clichés that defend the right to destroy a river because you "own" the water? Doesn't patriotism mean to love your country enough to take care of it?

My goal in following the river to its beginning and its end was far simpler than the route of management and stewardship for this waterway, and that, of course, is no surprise. Can we begin with the simple principle that we should not destroy the qualities of the earth that made life for all creatures possible? There are many myths to overcome, the leading one being that economic vitality and the current way of life will end if we compromise development with river protection. But at the Snake River, the Northern Rockies, and the Pacific Northwest, there is enough of the earth's wealth for everyone if we use restraint and foresight. The future can be sustainable, positive, desirable—a fresh vision of the American dream. Cooperation, not radical individualism, won the West. Even Idaho's Committee of Nine was formed to foster cooperation among farmers. Can a larger committee represent all uses of the river? Can we make decisions on behalf of the future rather than the past?

People who look at the twenty-five Snake River dams, the diversions including Milner, and the Hells Canyon hydroelectric plants as they eliminate the salmon would say that balance is needed. If we restore only half the life that this river once supported, it would be a sign to the world that people in fact have the ability to care for the earth, to survive.

Veteran conservationist Ernie Day said, "The stakes are higher today because less remains, but one thing is clear with the new generation of conservationists: *Nothing* is going to be lost by default."

"Progress will occur through steady, unremitting discussion and negotiation," said the younger veteran, Pat Ford. "The enduring answer is to build grass-roots support. We have to build a unified vision that's shared by many people."

"I'm an optimist, and my reason is that I believe in young people," said the eighty-six-year-old conservationist Mardy Murie, unequivocally a woman of the West at her log cabin along the upper Snake River.

Len returned from his stroll on this wildest American mileage of the continental divide. "Good country."

"Let's go find the river."

We scrambled down to the dry path of the Snake and walked

through a meadow. An elk wallow was the first sign of water. We entered the gorge we had bypassed on our hike upstream. A trickle appeared—the first flowing water in the riverbed—but it vanished in gravel. We stepped over rocks and fallen trees, and when we stopped, we heard water. Len and I strode faster down the riverbed.

A stream, 3 feet wide, suddenly plunged through the gorge. From a 2-foot slot in the rock, padded by moss and saxifrage, the Snake River's water flowed from the ground, clear and cold, brilliant, perfect.

Len knelt in the riverbed, eyes level with the spring. He reached out with his hands to let the water pour over them. He leaned forward so the water could flow onto his face. Then he took handfuls of runoff and splashed his head and threw water in the air where drops glinted like jewels in the sun and quickly rejoined to begin their long journey. To me it was a scene of birth and beginnings, but Len had leaped a lifetime ahead of me, and said, "This is what I want to think about when I'm old and dying."

He sat back on a rock and smiled. I stepped slowly across this highest pathway of the Snake River, wanting to touch the spring, yet wanting to wait. Finally, I cupped my hands where the water spilled from the earth, and I drank from the river.

Notes, Other Sources, and Interviews

For each chapter, I have given notes for controversial facts, for data where conflicting figures may exist, for some of the government documents, and for items readers may want to pursue further. Other sources of data follow the notes. Sources are largely conservative, primarily by government agencies. A list of people I interviewed follows the sources. Some information was given "off the record," and I respected people's concerns.

Most of the figures for acre feet of water came from the Idaho State Water Plan of 1988 or the Bureau of Reclamation; cfs figures came from the U.S. Geological Survey.

In addition to the listed sources, I also used newspapers, periodicals, and agency files. Especially helpful newspapers were the *Idaho Statesman* (Boise), *Post–Register* (Idaho Falls), *Times–News* (Twin Falls, Idaho), *Lewiston Tribune* (Idaho), *Jackson Hole News* (Wyoming), *Jackson Hole Guide* (Wyoming), *Casper Star Tribune* (Idaho), the *Washington Post*, and *High Country News* (Paonia, Colo.).

I also consulted many state and national magazines, as well as newsletters of conservation, fishing, irrigation, and agriculture groups.

INTRODUCTION

Notes

1. The 1,056 figure is derived from an Army Corps of Engineers river log and from U.S. Geological Survey maps for the section above Jackson Lake Dam.
2. *Information Please Almanac* (Boston: Houghton Mifflin Co., 1987).
3. Marshall Sprague, *The Mountain States* (New York: Time–Life, 1967), 53.
4. Diane Ronayne, "Enchanted Circle," *Northern Lights* (Missoula, Mont.), Nov.–Dec. 1987.

5. Orrin H. Bonney and Lorraine Bonney, *Battle Drums and Geysers* (Chicago: Swallow Press, 1970).

CHAPTER 1

Notes

1. U.S. Dept. of the Interior, Bureau of Reclamation, *Palisades Project* (Boise, Jan. 1983), pamphlet.
2. Bernard DeVoto, *Across the Wide Missouri* (New York: Houghton Mifflin Co., 1947), 50.
3. U.S. Dept. of the Interior, Bureau of Land Management, *Medicine Lodge Environmental Impact Statement* (Idaho Falls, n.d.).
4. J. W. Thomas, C. Maser, and J. E. Rodiek, *Wildlife Habitats in Managed Forests* (Washington, D.C.: U.S. Dept. of Agriculture, Forest Service, 1979).
5. Signe Sather-Blair, "Western Riparian Wetland Losses and Degradation: Status and Trends" (U.S. Dept. of the Interior, Fish and Wildlife Service, 1988), 232, unpublished report.
6. Dyan Zaslowsky, *These American Lands* (New York: Henry Holt and Co., 1986), 232.
7. Cheryl E. Bradley, "Modifications by Dams of River Regimes in North America," paper to joint conference on water management, University of Lethbridge, Alberta, Canada, Nov. 1988.
8. Constance Hunt, *Down by the River* (Washington, D.C.: Island Press, 1988).
9. U.S. Dept. of the Interior, Fish and Wildlife Service, *Waterfowl for the Future* (Washington, D.C., Dec. 1987).
10. M. M. Brinson, *Riparian Ecosystems: Their Ecology and Status* (Washington, D.C.: U.S. Dept. of the Interior, Fish and Wildlife Service, 1981), 155.
11. Sather-Blair, "Western Riparian Wetland," 17.
12. Gordon Robinson, *The Forest and the Trees* (Washington, D.C.: Island Press, 1988).
13. Cheryl E. Bradley and D. G. Smith, "Plains Cottonwood Recruitment and Survival on a Prairie Meandering River Floodplain, Milk River, Southern Alberta and Northern Montana," *Canadian Journal of Botany* 64 (1986):1442.
14. Bradley, "Modifications by Dams," 8.
15. Jeffrey Brune, "Spring Break for Sandhill Cranes," *Science World*, March 10, 1989, 11.
16. U.S. Dept. of the Interior, Bureau of Land Management, *Riparian Area Management* (Washington, D.C.: U.S. Government Printing Office, 1987), 19, brochure.

17. "Can the South Fork Recover?" *Greater Yellowstone Report,* Summer 1989, 1.
18. Idaho Dept. of Water Resources, *Draft State Water Plan* (Boise, 1976), pt. 2, 87.
19. U.S. Water Resources Council, *The Nation's Water Resources* (Washington, D.C., Dec. 1978), 59.
20. G. P. Williams and M. G. Wolman, "Effects of Dams and Reservoirs on Surface-Water Hydrology—Changes in Rivers Downstream from Dams," *National Water Summary, 1985* (Washington, D.C.: U.S. Geological Survey, 1985).
21. U.S. Dept. of the Interior, Bureau of Reclamation, *Critical Water Problems Facing the Eleven Western States* (Washington, D.C., 1975), 65 (commonly called the *Westwide* study).
22. Supreme Court of Idaho, "Kootenai Environmental Alliance vs. Panhandle Yacht Club," *Idaho Reports,* Nov. 2, 1983; and "Shokel vs. A. Kenneth Dunn," *Idaho Reports,* Sept. 24, 1985.
23. Scott W. Reed, "The Public Trust Doctrine in Idaho," *Environmental Law* (Northwestern School of Law of Lewis and Clark College, Portland, Oreg.) 19 (1989).
24. Ibid., 23.
25. Felix E. Smith, "Water Development and Management in the Central Valley of California and the Public Trust" (Sacramento: U.S. Dept. of the Interior, Fish and Wildlife Service, June 1987), 7, unpublished paper.
26. "What's So Special About the Henry's Fork?" *Idaho Conservation League News* (Boise), Dec. 1986.
27. U.S. Dept. of Energy, *Geohydrologic Story of the Eastern Snake River Plain and the Idaho National Engineering Laboratory* (Washington, D.C., 1986), 15.
28. Tim Palmer, *Endangered Rivers and the Conservation Movement* (Berkeley: University of California Press, 1986), 113.
29. Dwight William Jensen, *Discovering Idaho* (Caldwell, Idaho: Caxton, 1977).

Other Sources

U.S. Dept. of the Interior, Fish and Wildlife Service. "Upper Snake River Optimization Study, Fish and Wildlife Problems and Needs" (1988), unpublished paper.
J. H. Sather and R. D. Smith, "An Overview of Major Wetland Functions and Values" (Washington, D.C.: U.S. Dept. of the Interior, Fish and Wildlife Service, 1984), unpublished paper.

Interviews

Betsy Buffington, The Wilderness Society, Boise, Idaho
John Butz, Bureau of Land Management, Idaho Falls, Idaho
Ron Carlson, District 1 Water Master, Idaho Falls, Idaho
Sherl Chapman, executive director, Water Users Association, Boise, Idaho
Craig Contour, fisheries biologist, Idaho State University, Pocatello
Jeff Fereday, attorney, Boise, Idaho
Ruth Gale, biologist, Dept. of Fish and Game, Idaho Falls, Idaho
Jack Griffith, fisheries biologist, Idaho State University, Pocatello
Jerry Hansen, resident, upper Snake River
Keith Higginson, executive director, Dept. of Water Resources, Boise, Idaho
Mark Hill, fisheries biologist, consultant, Boise, Idaho
Marv Hoyt, Trout Unlimited, Idaho Falls, Idaho
Steve Johnson, Defenders of Wildlife, Tucson, Ariz.
John Keys, regional director, Bureau of Reclamation, Boise, Idaho
Mary Maj, Targhee National Forest, Driggs, Idaho
Tom Martens, League to Save Lake Tahoe, South Lake Tahoe, Calif.
M. R. "Mick" Mickelson, president, Henry's Fork Foundation, Pocatello, Idaho
Reed Oldham, Committee of Nine, Boise, Idaho
William Platts, riparian consultant, Boise, Idaho
Scott Reed, attorney, Coeur d'Alene, Idaho
Bob Riley, Bureau of Reclamation, Boise, Idaho
Signe Sather-Blair, Fish and Wildlife Service, Boise, Idaho
Dick Schwarz, president, South Fork Coalition, Idaho Falls, Idaho
Steve Serr, Bonneville County planner, Idaho Falls, Idaho
Rhey Solomon, hydrologist, U.S. Forest Service, Washington, D.C.
Max Van Den Berg, director, Minidoka Project, Bureau of Reclamation, Burley, Idaho
Al Van Vooren, Dept. of Fish and Game, Boise, Idaho
Mike Whitfield, Montana State University, Bozeman
Jim Wood, Army Corps of Engineers, Walla Walla, Wash.
Ron Wright, Targhee National Forest, Driggs, Idaho

CHAPTER 2

Notes

1. Gerard F. Lindholm, *Snake River Plain Regional Aquifer System, Phase II Study* (Boise: U.S. Dept. of the Interior, Geological Survey, 1988), 10.
2. John A. Shimer, *Fieldguide to Landforms in the United States* (New York: Macmillan, 1972).

3. U.S. Dept. of Energy, *Geohydrologic Story of the Eastern Snake River Plain and the Idaho National Engineering Laboratory* (Washington, D.C., Nov. 1986), booklet.
4. Idaho Dept. of Health and Welfare, *Idaho Environmental Quality Profile* (Boise, April 1987), 24.
5. F. Ross Peterson, *A Bicentennial History of Idaho* (New York: Norton, 1976).
6. Glenn Oakley, "Snake River Anthology," *Focus* (Boise State University), Summer 1989, 23.
7. Diane Ronayne, "Enchanted Circle," *Northern Lights* (Missoula, Mont.), Nov.–Dec. 1987, 32.
8. Don Snow, "The Unfinished Weapon," *Northern Lights* (Missoula, Mont.), Sept.–Oct. 1987, 10.
9. Idaho Dept. of Water Resources, *Draft State Water Plan* (Boise, 1976).
10. Shoshone–Bannock Tribes, "Presentation of Claims to Instream Flows and Water Quality for the Fort Hall Indian Reservation in Idaho" (May 19, 1987), 29, 36, unpublished paper.
11. U.S. Dept. of Energy, *Geohydrologic Story of the Eastern Snake River Plain and the Idaho National Engineering Laboratory,* (Washington, D.C., 1986), 8, booklet.
12. Shoshone–Bannock Tribes, "Presentation of Claims," 2.
13. David Lavender, *The Rockies* (Lincoln: University of Nebraska Press, 1968), 42.
14. Shoshone–Bannock Tribes, "Presentation of Claims," 6.
15. Ibid.
16. U.S. Dept. of the Interior, Bureau of Reclamation, *Critical Water Problems Facing the Eleven Western States* (Washington, D.C., 1975), 3 (commonly called the *Westwide* study).
17. Howard Funke and Charles Pace, "Indian Water Marketing: Opposition or Opportunity" (1988), 7, unpublished paper.
18. Donald Johnson and James Kent, *The Source of American Falls Reservoir Pollutants* (Moscow: Idaho Water Resource Research Institute, 1978).
19. Irvin E. Rockwell, *The Saga of American Falls Dam* (New York: Hobson Book Press, 1947).

Other Sources

Maley, Terry. *Exploring Idaho Geology.* Boise: Mineral Land Publications, 1987.
Schneider, Keith. "Idaho Says No." *New York Times Magazine,* March 11, 1990 (regarding Idaho National Engineering Laboratory).
Shoshone–Bannock Tribes. *Draft: the Fort Hall Indian Reservation Comprehensive Land Use Plan.* Fort Hall, Dec. 1985.

"The Winters Doctrine." *Wilderness* (Washington, D.C.), Fall 1987.

Interviews

Stan Allen, Dept. of Fish and Game, Boise, Idaho
Arnold Appenay, tribal councilman, Shoshone and Bannock tribes, Fort Hall, Idaho
Janice Berndt, staff member, Snake River Alliance, Boise, Idaho
Sue Broderick, biologist, Shoshone and Bannock tribes, Fort Hall, Idaho
Linda Burke, Idaho Conservation League, Pocatello
Sherl Chapman, executive director, Water Users Association, Boise, Idaho
Kristin Fletcher, resident, Hailey, Idaho
Pat Ford, journalist, Boise, Idaho
Howard Funke, attorney, Shoshone and Bannock tribes, Fort Hall, Idaho
Jack Griffith, fisheries biologist, Idaho State University, Pocatello
Steve Harrison, city hydroelectricity manager, Idaho Falls, Idaho
Steve Hill, Dept. of Health and Welfare, Boise, Idaho
Glenn Oakley, journalist, Boise, Idaho
Reed Oldham, Committee of Nine, Idaho Falls, Idaho
Claire Ormond, city councilmember, Shelley, Idaho
Tom Ore, geologist, Idaho State University, Pocatello
Charles Pace, economist, Pocatello, Idaho
Liz Paul, staff member, Snake River Alliance, Ketchum, Idaho
William Platts, riparian consultant, Boise, Idaho
Bob Riley, Bureau of Reclamation, Boise, Idaho
Robert Smith, geolophysicist, University of Utah
Bob Sutter, staff, Dept. of Water Resources, Boise, Idaho
Kenneth Timbanna, planner, Shoshone and Bannock tribes, Fort Hall, Idaho
Max Van Den Berg, director, Minidoka Project, Bureau of Reclamation, Burley, Idaho
Ron Watters, outdoor program director, Idaho State University, Pocatello

CHAPTER 3

Notes

1. Idaho Dept. of Water Resources, inventory of dams; U.S. Dept. of the Interior, Geological Survey, maps, ca. 1980.
2. Floyd R. Barber and Dan W. Martin, *Idaho in the Pacific Northwest* (Caldwell, Idaho: Caxton, 1956), 264.
3. U.S. Dept. of the Interior, Geological Survey, *National Water Summary* (Washington, D.C., 1985), 207, 212.

4. F. Ross Peterson, *A Bicentennial History of Idaho* (New York: Norton, 1976).
5. Richard D. Lamb and Michael McCarthy, *The Angry West* (Boston: Houghton Mifflin Co., 1982).
6. Donald Worster, *Rivers of Empire* (New York: Pantheon Books, 1985), 157.
7. Richard L. Berkman and W. Kip Viscusi, *Damming the West* (New York: Grossman, 1973).
8. Lamb and McCarthy, *Angry West*, 195.
9. U.S. Dept. of the Interior, Bureau of Reclamation, "Water Systems Operation and Maintenance Cost Index" (1987), unpublished paper.
10. Signe Sather-Blair, "Western Riparian Wetland Losses and Degradation: Status and Trends" (U.S. Dept. of the Interior, Fish and Wildlife Service, 1988), 41, unpublished report.
11. Ibid.
12. Bruce Brown, *Mountain in the Clouds* (New York: Simon & Schuster, 1982), 84.
13. Idaho Power Company, *Hydro Era* (Boise, n.d.); and correspondence with Steve Waid, Bureau of Reclamation, Boise, 1989.
14. Correspondence with Steve Waid, Bureau of Reclamation, Boise, 1989.
15. Scott Reed, "The Other Uses for Water," *Idaho Yesterdays* (Boise) Spring 1986.
16. National Association of Conservation Districts, *Dam Safety: Who Is Responsible?* (Washington, D.C., ca. 1982), brochure.
17. U.S. Dept. of the Interior, Bureau of Reclamation, correspondence from Wayne Merchant, Assistant Secretary for Water and Science, to Congressman George Miller, Feb. 1988.
18. Ibid.
19. Wallace Stegner, *Beyond the Hundredth Meridian* (Lincoln: University of Nebraska Press, 1953), 222.
20. Donald Worster, "An End to Ecstasy," *Wilderness* (Washington, D.C.), Feb. 1987, 21.
21. Frank Welsh, *How to Create a Water Crisis* (Boulder: Johnson Books, 1985), 73.
22. U.S. Dept. of the Interior, Bureau of Reclamation, *Critical Water Problems Facing the Eleven Western States* (Washington, D.C., 1975), 32 (commonly called the *Westwide* study).
23. Sather-Blair, "Western Riparian Wetland," 21.
24. Richard A. Bartlett, *Nature's Yellowstone* (Albuquerque: University of New Mexico Press, 1974), 89.
25. U.S. Dept. of the Interior, Bureau of Reclamation, *Critical Water Problems*, 29, 49.
26. Ibid., 83.

27. Tim Palmer, *Endangered Rivers and the Conservation Movement* (Berkeley: University of California Press, 1986), 200.
28. U.S. Dept. of the Interior, Office of the Solicitor, "Renewal of Friant Unit Contracts," memo to Assistant Secretary for Water and Science, Nov. 1988, 15.
29. Daniel P. Sheer, "Managing Water Supplies to Insure Water Availability," *National Water Summary* (Washington, D.C.: U.S. Dept. of the Interior, Geological Survey, 1985), 101.
30. Idaho Dept. of Water Resources, *Draft State Water Plan* (Boise, 1976), 69.
31. U.S. Dept. of Agriculture, Forest Service, *Snake River, Wyoming, a Potential Wild and Scenic River, Final Statement and Report*, appendix, letter from Lester Saunders to the Forest Service (Jackson, Wyo., 1979).
32. Katherine Collins, "Congressional Candidates Declare Support for Dams," *Casper Star Tribune* (Idaho), Oct. 25, 1988, A1.

Other Sources

Paul, Elliot. *Desperate Scenery*. New York: Random House, 1954.
U.S. Dept. of the Interior, Bureau of Reclamation. *Bureau of Reclamation Projects*. Boise, 1983.

Interviews

Robert Banks, Bureau of Reclamation, Boise, Idaho
Michael Beus, Bureau of Reclamation, Burley, Idaho
Brent Blackwelder, Environmental Policy Institute, Washington, D.C.
Arvin Budge, Dept. of Agriculture, Washington, D.C.
Bob Burks, past president and board member, Water Users Association, Wendell, Idaho
Ron Carlson, District 1 Water Master, Idaho Falls, Idaho
Sherl Chapman, executive director, Water Users Association, Boise, Idaho
Earl Corliss, Bureau of Reclamation, Burley, Idaho
Jim Doty, Bureau of Reclamation, Boise, Idaho
Ralph Flager, Bureau of Reclamation, Boise, Idaho
Howard Funke, attorney, Shoshone and Bannock tribes, Fort Hall, Idaho
Ruth Gale, biologist, Dept. of Fish and Game, Idaho Falls, Idaho
Karen Garrison, Natural Resources Defense Council, San Francisco, Calif.
Reed Hansen, farmer and legislator, Idaho Falls, Idaho
Bob Harper, U.S. Geological Survey, Boise, Idaho
Pete Hayden, biologist, Grand Teton National Park, Wyo.
Keith Higginson, executive director, Dept. of Water Resources, Boise, Idaho
David Hollingshed, Dept. of Water Resources, Boise, Idaho
John Keys, regional director, Bureau of Reclamation, Boise, Idaho

Luna Leopold, hydrologist, University of California, Berkeley
Bob Miller, U.S. Dept. of Agriculture, Washington, D.C.
Reed Oldham, Committee of Nine, Idaho Falls, Idaho
Scott Reed, attorney, Coeur d'Alene, Idaho
Bob Riley, Bureau of Reclamation, Boise, Idaho
Max Van Den Berg, director, Minidoka Project, Bureau of Reclamation, Burley, Idaho
Steve Waid, Bureau of Reclamation, Boise, Idaho

CHAPTER 4

Notes

1. Idaho Dept. of Water Resources, data printouts, 1988.
2. U.S. Dept. of Agriculture, Soil Conservation Service, *Snake River Basin Cooperative Study, Upper Snake Main Report* (Boise, 1979).
3. Idaho Cooperative Extension Service, *Agricultural Data* (Moscow, 1986).
4. U.S. Dept. of the Interior, Bureau of Reclamation, *Summary Statistics*, Vol. 1: *Water, Land, and Related Data* (Boise, 1986).
5. "1987 Summary, U.S. Irrigated Acreage," *Irrigation Journal* (Van Nuys, Calif.), Jan. 1988.
6. Frank Welsh, *How to Create a Water Crisis* (Boulder: Johnson Books, 1985), 46.
7. Idaho Dept. of Agriculture, *1987 Idaho Agricultural Statistics* (Boise, 1988).
8. Ed Chaney, *The Desert Land and Carey Acts in Idaho, Agricultural Lands Project Summary Report* (Boise: Idaho Conservation League, 1977).
9. U.S. Army Corps of Engineers, *Columbia Basin Water Withdrawal, Environmental Review* (Portland, Oreg., n.d.), Appendix B, pt. 1, 3.
10. "Idaho Farmers Continue Efforts to Stop Bacon Siphon," *Idaho Potato Grower*, May 1979, 9.
11. U.S. Dept. of Agriculture, Agricultural Stabilization and Conservation Service (Boise, 1988), unpublished paper.
12. U.S. Dept. of the Interior, Bureau of Reclamation, *Idaho Bureau of Reclamation Projects* (Boise, 1983).
13. Helen M. Newell, *Idaho's Place in the Sun* (Boise: Syms–York, 1975), 138.
14. Idaho Dept. of Water Resources, *Draft State Water Plan* (Boise, 1976), 29.
15. Idaho Dept. of Water Resources and the Dept. of Health and Welfare, *A Survey of Public Attitudes and Opinions* (Boise, 1975).
16. Idaho Water Resource Board, *State Water Plan* (Boise, 1986), 25.
17. U.S. Dept. of the Interior, Fish and Wildlife Service, "Upper Snake River Storage Optimization Study, Fish and Wildlife Problems and Needs" (1988), unpublished paper.

18. U.S. Dept. of Agriculture, Soil Conservation Service, *Snake River Basin Cooperative Study, Middle Snake Main Report* (Boise, 1982), 164.
19. Elwood Mead, *The Use of Water in Irrigation*, Bulletin 86 (Washington, D.C.: U.S. Dept. of Agriculture, Office of Experiment Stations, n.d.).
20. U.S. Dept. of the Interior, Geological Survey, *Water Use on the Snake River Plain* (Boise, 1988), 21, 35.
21. Idaho Dept. of Water Resources, diversion data, through 1987.
22. U.S. Dept. of the Interior, Geological Survey, *Water Use in the United States, 1980* (Washington, D.C., 1981).
23. U.S. Water Resources Council, *The Nation's Water Resources* (Washington, D.C., 1978).
24. Idaho Dept. of Water Resources, data printouts, through 1987.
25. *Irrigation Journal* (Van Nuys, Calif.), annual surveys, through 1987.
26. U.S. Dept. of Energy, *Geohydrologic Story of the Eastern Snake River Plain and the Idaho National Engineering Laboratory* (Washington, D.C., 1986), 22.
27. U.S. Dept. of Agriculture, Soil Conservation Service, *Upper Snake Main Report*, 6; and *Middle Snake Main Report*, 2.
28. Bio/West, Inc., "Feasibility Analysis of Water Conservation Measures Relative to the Jackson Lake Dam Safety Program" (Boise, 1983), unpublished report for the Bureau of Reclamation.
29. Idaho Dept. of Water Resources, *Reducing Irrigation Costs Through Energy Savings* (Boise, 1983), brochure.
30. Carlotta Collette, "Energy Efficient Irrigation," *Northwest Energy News* (Portland, Oreg.), Nov. 1984, 18–21.
31. Brent A. Claiborn, *Predicting Attainable Irrigation Efficiencies in the Upper Snake River Basin* (Moscow: University of Idaho, Water Resources Research Institute, 1975).
32. Snake River Technical Advisory Committee to Swan Falls Study, Committee of the Legislative Council, "Needed Water Resources Programs in the Snake River Basin" (Idaho, 1983), 13, unpublished paper.
33. U.S. Dept. of Agriculture, Soil Conservation Service, *Upper Snake Main Report*, 3.
34. U.S. Dept. of the Interior, Bureau of Reclamation, *Critical Water Problems Facing the Eleven Western States* (Washington, D.C., 1975).
35. Idaho Dept. of Water Resources, data printouts, through 1987.

Other Sources

Gottlieb, Robert. *A Life of Its Own.* San Diego: Harcourt Brace Jovanovich, 1988.
Harrison, David L., and Robert Wigington. "Water Rights: A Protection Tool for the West." *Nature Conservancy Magazine* (Arlington, Va.), Aug. 1987, 27.

Idaho Historical Society. *Idaho Yesterdays* (Boise). Spring 1986 (entire issue on the history of irrigation in Idaho).

Lindeborg, Karl H. *Economic Value of Water in Different Uses Within Agriculture.* Moscow: University of Idaho, Water Resources Research Institute, Aug. 1968.

Reed, Scott W. "The 99 Percent Solution and Other River Revolutions." *Northern Lights* (Missoula, Mont.), Nov. 1987, 20–22.

Interviews

Hal Anderson, technical services chief, Dept. of Water Resources, Boise, Idaho

Jim Ariola, Dept. of Water Resources, Boise, Idaho

Cherl Brower, Dept. of Health and Welfare, Boise, Idaho

Arvin Budge, U.S. Dept. of Agriculture, Washington, D.C.

Linda Burke, board member, Idaho Conservation League, Pocatello

Bob Burks, past president, Water Users Association, Wendell, Idaho

Ron Carlson, District 1 Water Master, Idaho Falls, Idaho

Ed Chaney, resource consultant, Eagle, Idaho

Sherl Chapman, executive director, Water Users Association, Boise, Idaho

Mike Creamer, attorney, Boise, Idaho

Jack Eakin, general manager, Twin Falls Canal Company, Twin Falls, Idaho

Jeff Fereday, attorney, Boise, Idaho

Pat Ford, journalist, Boise, Idaho

Ron Golos, Bureau of Reclamation, Boise, Idaho

Gene Gray, chair, Water Resource Board, Boise, Idaho

Jack Grover, Agricultural Stabilization and Conservation Service, Boise, Idaho

Reed Hansen, farmer and state legislator, Idaho Falls, Idaho

Keith Higginson, executive director, Dept. of Water Resources, Boise, Idaho

Huey Johnson, founder, Water Heritage Trust, Sausalito, Calif.

Lynne Krogh-Haupe, attorney, Dept. of Water Resources, Boise, Idaho

Tim McGravey, Barley Commission, Boise, Idaho

Ralph Mellon, Dept. of Water Resources, Boise, Idaho

Tony Morse, Dept. of Water Resources, Boise, Idaho

Ken Mulberry, farmer, Twin Falls, Idaho

Reed Oldham, Committee of Nine, Idaho Falls, Idaho

Scott Reed, attorney, Coeur d'Alene, Idaho

Rich Rigby, Bureau of Reclamation, Boise, Idaho

David Shaw, chief of adjudication, Dept. of Water Resources, Boise, Idaho

Perry Swisher, commissioner, Public Utilities Commission, Boise, Idaho

Thomas Trout, U.S. Department of Agriculture, Kimberly, Idaho

Stewart Udall, former secretary, Dept. of the Interior, Phoenix, Ariz.

Max Van Den Berg, director, Minidoka Project, Bureau of Reclamation, Burley, Idaho
Neil Wilton, Soil Conservation Service, Boise, Idaho

CHAPTER 5

Notes

1. Christopher J. Everts and David L. Carter, *Furrow Erosion and Topsoil Losses* (Moscow: Cooperative Extension Service and Agricultural Experiment Station, 1981).
2. David L. Carter, *Furrow Erosion Reduces Crop Yields* (Kimberly, Idaho: U.S. Dept. of Agriculture, n.d.).
3. Brad Knickerbocker, "Salt Where Crops Should Be," *Christian Science Monitor,* June 21, 1979, 12–13.
4. W. W. Frye and S. H. Phillips, "How to Grow Crops with Less Energy," *Yearbook of Agriculture* (U.S. Dept. of Agriculture) (1980).
5. U.S. Dept. of the Interior, Geological Survey, *Erosion and Sedimentation* (Washington, D.C., 1976), brochure.
6. Tim Palmer, *Endangered Rivers and the Conservation Movement* (Berkeley: University of California Press, 1986).
7. U.S. Dept. of the Interior, Fish and Wildlife Service, "Upper Snake River Storage Optimization Study, Fish and Wildlife Problems and Needs" (1988), unpublished paper.
8. Dan Kendall, "Congress to Debate Fungicide," *Idaho Statesman* (Boise), Dec. 12, 1989.
9. "Farm Official Says Growers Face Battle for Pesticides," *Idaho Statesman* (Boise), Dec. 7, 1989.
10. Steve Stuebner, "Report: Toxins, Dirt Foul Idaho Waters," *Idaho Statesman* (Boise), June 12, 1988.
11. Wilford R. Gardner, "Reflections on Water Management in Arid Regions," *Arid Lands Today and Tomorrow* (Boulder, Colo.: Westview Press, 1985).
12. U.S. Dept. of Energy, *Geohydrologic Story of the Eastern Snake River Plain and the Idaho National Engineering Laboratory* (Washington, D.C., 1986), 2.
13. Idaho Dept. of Health and Welfare and the Dept. of Water Resources, *Snake Plain Aquifer Technical Report* (Boise, 1985).
14. Idaho Dept. of Water Resources, data printouts, through 1987.
15. U.S. Dept. of the Interior, Geological Survey, *Water Use on the Snake River Plain* (Boise, 1988).
16. Idaho Dept. of Health and Welfare and the Dept. of Water Resources, *Snake Plain Aquifer.*

17. Fred Powledge, "The Poisoned Well," *Wilderness* (Washington, D.C.), Fall 1987, 40.

18. Snake River Technical Advisory Committee to Swan Fall Study, Committee of the Legislative Council, "Needed Water Resources Programs in the Snake River Basin" (Idaho, 1983), 21, unpublished paper.

19. Idaho Dept. of Health and Welfare and the Dept. of Water Resources, *Snake Plain Aquifer;* and U.S. Dept. of the Interior, Geological Survey, *Water Use on the Snake River Plain* (Boise, 1988), 36.

20. Idaho Dept. of Health and Welfare, *Idaho Water Quality Status Report and Nonpoint Source Assessment* (Boise, 1988).

21. Idaho Dept. of Health and Welfare and the Dept. of Water Resources, *Snake Plain Aquifer.*

22. Idaho Dept. of Health and Welfare, *Idaho Water Quality Status.*

23. Ibid.

24. U.S. Dept. of the Interior, Geological Survey, *Water Use on the Snake River Plain,* 37.

25. Idaho Dept. of Health and Welfare and the Dept. of Water Resources, *Snake Plain Aquifer.*

26. U.S. Dept. of Energy, *Geohydrologic Story,* 70.

27. Idaho Dept. of Health and Welfare, *Idaho Water Quality Status.*

28. Ibid.

29. Tom Harris, "Fed's Toxic Coverup Is Foiled by Newspaper," *High Country News* (Paonia, Colo.), Nov. 20, 1989, 9.

30. Idaho Water Resource Board, *State Water Plan* (Boise, 1986), 21.

31. Idaho Dept. of Health and Welfare and the Dept. of Water Resources, *Snake Plain Aquifer.*

32. Charles Little, "The Great American Aquifer," *Wilderness* (Washington, D.C.), Fall 1987, 43.

33. Katharine Collins, "Congressional Candidates Declare Support for Dams," *Casper Star Tribune* (Idaho), Oct. 25, 1988, A14.

34. U.S. Dept. of the Interior, Bureau of Reclamation, *Critical Water Problems Facing the Eleven Western States* (Washington, D.C., 1975).

35. U.S. Senate, letter from Governor Cecil Andrus to Representative John Dingell, *Congressional Record,* Dec. 18, 1987.

36. U.S. Dept. of the Interior, Fish and Wildlife Service, "Framework for Snake River Fish and Wildlife Studies" (1988), unpublished paper.

37. William Bailey and Roger Long, *The Economic Water Supply in Idaho* (Moscow: University of Idaho, Agricultural Experiment Station, 1975).

38. Snake River Technical Advisory Committee, "Needed Water Resources Programs," 38.

39. Richard W. Wahl and Frank H. Osterhoudt, "Voluntary Transfers of Water in the West," *National Water Summary* (Washington, D.C.: U.S. Dept. of the Interior, Geological Survey, 1985), 113–22.

40. Idaho Office of the Governor, "Framework for Final Resolution of Snake River Water Rights Controversy" (1984), 3, unpublished paper.

Other Sources

Concern, Inc. *Pesticides.* Washington, D.C., 1985. Booklet.
High Country News (Paonia, Colo.). Nov. 20, 1989, and Dec. 4, 1989. Entire issues on water quality.
U.S. Dept. of Agriculture, Soil Conservation Service. *Idaho's Soil and Water: Conditions and Trends.* Boise, 1984.
U.S. Dept. of Agriculture, Soil Conservation Service. *Soil Erosion by Water.* Washington, D.C., 1987.
U.S. Dept. of the Interior, Geological Survey. *United States Geological Survey, Circular 1002, Regional Aquifer System Analysis, Program of United States Geological Survey, Summary of Projects 1978–1984.* Boise, 1986.
Whittlesey, N., et al. *An Economic Study of the Potential for Water Markets in Idaho.* Moscow: University of Idaho, Idaho Water Research Institute, 1986.

Interviews

Rod Alt, Soil Conservation Service, Boise, Idaho
Rod Awe, Idaho Dept. of Agriculture, Boise, Idaho
Floyd Bailey, Soil Conservation Service, Boise, Idaho
Robert Barbo, Bureau of Reclamation, Boise, Idaho
Cherl Brower, Dept. of Health and Welfare, Boise, Idaho
Bob Burks, past president, Water Users Association, Wendell, Idaho
Gwen Burr, Dept. of Health and Welfare, Boise, Idaho
Ed Chaney, resource consultant, Eagle, Idaho
Sherl Chapman, executive director, Water Users Association, Boise, Idaho
Maggie Coon, Idaho Conservation League, Boise, Idaho
Jeff Fereday, attorney, Boise, Idaho
Bill Graham, Dept. of Water Resources, Boise, Idaho
Gene Gray, chair, Water Resource Board, Boise, Idaho
Reed Hansen, farmer and state legislator, Idaho Falls, Idaho
Keith Higginson, executive director, Dept. of Water Resources, Boise, Idaho
Dennis Hudson, U.S. Food and Drug Administration, Boise, Idaho
John Keys, regional director, Bureau of Reclamation, Boise, Idaho
Don Kramer, farmer and member, State Water Board, Boise, Idaho
Tim McGravey, Barley Commission, Boise, Idaho
JoAnn Mitters, Dept. of Health and Welfare, Boise, Idaho
Ken Mulberry, farmer, Twin Falls, Idaho
Gary Nelson, farmer, Hagerman, Idaho
Tom Nelson, attorney, Boise, Idaho

Sharon Norris, Soil Conservation Service, Boise, Idaho
Reed Oldham, Committee of Nine, Idaho Falls, Idaho
Bob Riley, Bureau of Reclamation, Boise, Idaho
Alan Robertson, Dept. of Water Resources, Boise, Idaho
Dick Rogers, Dept. of Health and Welfare, Boise, Idaho
Wally Scarburgh, Environmental Protection Agency, Boise, Idaho
Frank Sherman, Dept. of Water Resources, Boise, Idaho
Max Van Den Berg, director, Minidoka Project, Bureau of Reclamation, Burley, Idaho
Al Van Vooren, Dept. of Fish and Game, Boise, Idaho
Dick Whitehead, U.S. Geological Survey, Boise, Idaho
Richard Yankey, Soil Conservation Service, Twin Falls, Idaho

CHAPTER 6

Notes

1. Idaho Water Resource Board, *State Water Plan* (Boise, 1986), 35.
2. U.S. Dept. of Energy, Federal Energy Regulatory Commission, *The Twin Falls, Milner, Auger Falls, and Star Falls Hydroelectric Projects, Draft Environmental Impact Statement* (Washington D.C., 1987).
3. Hans Huth, *Nature and the American* (Lincoln: University of Nebraska Press, 1957), 173.
4. John Rosholt, "Irrigation and Politics," *Idaho Yesterdays* (Boise), Spring 1986, 21.
5. Idaho Dept. of Health and Welfare and the Dept. of Water Resources, *Snake Plain Aquifer Technical Report* (Boise, 1985).
6. U.S. Dept. of Energy, *Geohydrologic Story of the Eastern Snake River Plain and the Idaho National Engineering Laboratory* (Washington D.C., 1986), 8.
7. U.S. Dept. of the Interior, Geological Survey, *Water Use on the Snake River Plain* (Boise, 1988), 39.
8. U.S. Dept. of the Interior, Fish and Wildlife Service, "Upper Snake River Storage Optimization Study, Fish and Wildlife Problems and Needs" (1988), unpublished paper.
9. Mark Pratter, "Projects Spark Concern over Snake River Environment," *Times–News* (Twin Falls, Idaho), Nov. 30, 1986, 1.
10. Mark Higgins, "A Threat to the Snake River?" *Times–News* (Twin Falls, Idaho), June 29, 1987, 1.
11. R. Keith Higginson, "Instream Flow Needs and Competing Uses for Water" (Moscow: Idaho Water Resources Research Institute, 1976).
12. Idaho Dept. of Water Resources, *Draft State Water Plan* (Boise, 1976), 54.
13. Idaho Historical Society, *Three Island Crossing* (Boise, 1987), brochure.

14. Randy Stapilus, *Paradox Politics* (Boise: Ridenbaugh Press, 1988), 208.
15. U.S. Dept. of the Interior, Bureau of Outdoor Recreation, *Bruneau Wild and Scenic River, Idaho, Draft Environmental Impact Statement* (Seattle, 1975).
16. Stephen Stuebner, "Envirosafe Says Handling of Waste Improves," *Idaho Statesman* (Boise), June 19, 1988.
17. U.S. Dept. of the Interior, Bureau of Land Management, *Snake River Birds of Prey Area* (Boise, 1986), brochure.
18. John McCarthy, "Eyries in the Canyon," *High Country News* (Paonia, Colo.), May 16, 1980.
19. Pat Ford, "During the Boom, Idaho Succumbed to Good Sense," *High Country News* (Paonia, Colo.), Sept. 12, 1988, 19.
20. A. Kenneth Dunn, director, Idaho Dept. of Water Resources, letter to Idaho Water Resource Board, Jan. 1984.
21. Diane Jones, *Water, Energy, and Land* (Boise, Idaho Citizens Coalition, 1981).
22. Idaho Water Resource Board, *State Water Plan.*
23. Scott Reed, "The Other Uses for Water," *Idaho Yesterdays* (Boise), Spring 1986.
24. Idaho Office of the Governor, "Framework for Final Resolution of Snake River Water Rights Controversy" (1984), unpublished paper.
25. U.S. Dept. of the Interior, Bureau of Sport Fisheries and Wildlife, "Streambed Topography near Snake River Islands–Brownlee Reach" (Boise, 1975), unpublished paper.
26. Idaho Dept. of Fish and Game, "The Snake River Maintenance Flow Studies, 1975–1976" (1976), unpublished report.
27. U.S. House of Representatives, Committee on Energy and Commerce, 100th Congress, 1st Session, *Swan Falls Agreement Report* (Washington D.C., 1988).
28. Minutes, March 24, 1988, meeting on Swan Falls study, available from the Bureau of Indian Affairs, Portland, Oreg., area office.
29. U.S. Dept. of Energy, Federal Energy Regulatory Commission, "Joint Agreement Regarding Fish and Wildlife Studies" (Washington, D.C., 1988), unpublished paper.
30. U.S. Dept. of the Interior, Fish and Wildlife Service, "Upper Snake River Optimization Study," 7.

Other Sources

Greater Twin Falls Area Chamber of Commerce. *Snake River Canyon.* Twin Falls, ca. 1980. Brochure.
Gulick, Bill. *Snake River Country.* Caldwall, Idaho: Caxton, 1971.
"Thousand Springs," *Sun Valley Magazine* (Idaho), Winter 1987.

U.S. Dept. of the Interior, Bureau of Land Management. *Bruneau, Jarbidge River Guide.* Boise, 1988.

U.S. Dept. of the Interior, Bureau of Land Management. *Final Environmental Statement, Agricultural Development for Southwest Idaho.* Boise, 1980.

U.S. Dept. of the Interior, Bureau of Land Management. "River Segments Likely to Be Studied Under the Wild and Scenic Rivers Act." 1988. Unpublished paper.

"Where Trout Outnumber People 10,000 to 1." *Sunset,* May 1988.

Interviews

John Benedict, Bureau of Land Management, Boise, Idaho
Guy Bonnivier, Nature Conservancy, Ketchum, Idaho
Drich Bowler, Hagerman, Idaho
Bob Burks, past president and board member, Water Users Association, Wendell, Idaho
Sherl Chapman, executive director, Water Users Association, Boise, Idaho
Bill Chisholm, Buhl, Idaho
Jack Eakin, general manager, Twin Falls Canal Company, Twin Falls, Idaho
Pat Ford, journalist, Boise, Idaho
Roy Heberger, Fish and Wildlife Service, Boise, Idaho
Hugh Harper, wildlife biologist, Boise, Idaho
Keith Higginson, executive director, Dept. of Water Resources, Boise, Idaho
Jeff Jarvis, recreation planner, Bureau of Land Management, Shoshone, Idaho
Jill Joseph, Hagerman, Idaho
Rob Lesser, Boise, Idaho
Tom Nelson, attorney, Boise, Idaho
Reed Oldham, Committee of Nine, Idaho Falls, Idaho
John Peavey, state senator, Carey, Idaho
Wally Scarburgh, U.S. Environmental Protection Agency, Boise, Idaho
Larry Taylor, Idaho Power Company, Boise
Ron Watters, outdoor program director, Idaho State University, Pocatello
Duane Wilson, manager, Clear Springs Hatchery, Buhl, Idaho
Al Van Vooren, Dept. of Fish and Game, Boise, Idaho

CHAPTER 7

Notes

1. U.S. Dept. of Agriculture, Soil Conservation Service, *Snake River Basin Cooperative Study, Middle Snake Main Report* (Boise, 1982), 110.

2. Idaho Dept. of Health and Welfare, *Idaho Water Quality Status Report and Nonpoint Source Assessment* (Boise, 1988), 44.
3. U.S. Dept. of the Interior, Bureau of Reclamation, *Owyhee Project* (Boise, 1983), brochure.
4. Stephen Stuebner, "Coalition Seeks to Protect Payette Rivers," *Idaho Statesman* (Boise), April 28, 1988, C1.
5. Signe Sather-Blair, "Western Riparian Wetland Losses and Degradation: Status and Trends" (U.S. Dept. of the Interior, Fish and Wildlife Service, 1988), 22, unpublished report.
6. Johnny Carrey, Cort Conley, and Ace Barton, *Snake River of Hells Canyon* (Cambridge, Idaho: Backeddy Books, 1979).
7. Ibid., 113.
8. "Pacific Northwest Electric Generating Projects," *Northwest Energy News* (Portland, Oreg.), Aug. 1986, 13.
9. "Court Says Federal Agency Must Reconsider Habitat Needs of Cranes," *The Leader* (Washington, D.C.) (newsletter of the National Wildlife Federation), July 1989.
10. Pat Ford, "During the Boom, Idaho Succumbed to Good Sense," *High Country News* (Paonia, Colo.), Sept. 12, 1988, 19.
11. Northwest Power Planning Council, *Northwest Conservation and Electric Power Plan* (Portland, Oreg., 1986), 6–1.
12. Sather-Blair, "Western Riparian Wetland," 36.
13. Ibid., 36.
14. F. Dale Robertson, "Remarks Made by Co-Hosts," *American Rivers* (Washington, D.C.), Jan. 1989, 10.
15. Stan Allen, "Protected Areas in Idaho" (Boise: Northwest Power Planning Council, Oct. 1987), unpublished report.
16. Idaho Water Users Association, "Testimony of the Idaho Water Users Association, Inc., Before the Northwest Power Planning Council" (June 3, 1988), unpublished paper.
17. Idaho House of Representatives, Resolution no. 54, March 1988.
18. Scott W. Reed, "The Public Trust Doctrine in Idaho," *Environmental Law* (Northwestern School of Law of Lewis and Clark College, Portland, Oreg.) 19 (1989):655.
19. Diane Jones, *Water Energy, and Land* (Boise: Idaho Citizens Coalition, 1981), 36.
20. Pope Barrow, John D. Echeverria, and Richard Roos-Collins, *Rivers at Risk: The Concerned Citizens' Guide to Hydropower* (Washington, D.C.: Island Press, 1989).

Other Sources

Crawford, Tim. "Protecting Henry's Fork from Hydro." *Idaho Conservation League News* (Boise), Oct. 1986.

Curtis, Ruth L. "Conservation Comes Home," *Northwest Energy News* (Portland, Oreg.), Dec. 1986.

Idaho Power Company. *A Land of Opportunity.* Boise, ca. 1987. Brochure.

Idaho Power Company, Frederick J. Cochrane, and George C. Young. *Hydro Era: The Story of Idaho Power Company.* Boise, 1978.

"Itinerant Sturgeon." *Northwest Energy News* (Portland, Oreg.), Dec. 1986.

Jenning, Steve. "The Potato Billionaire." *Northwest Magazine* (Portland, Oreg.), Oct. 28, 1985.

Mahar, Dulcy. "It Still Makes Sense." *Northwest Energy News* (Portland, Oreg.), May 1985.

McClane, A. J. *McClane's Field Guide to Freshwater Fishes of North America.* New York: Henry Holt and Co., 1965.

Ocrowley, Janet. "Hydro Project Threatens Snake's Star Falls." *Idaho Citizen* (Boise), June 1987.

Stuebner, Stephen. "Report: Toxins, Dirt Foul Idaho Waters." *Idaho Statesman* (Boise), June 12, 1988.

U.S. Dept. of the Interior, Bureau of Land Management. *Fish and Wildlife 2000.* Washington, D.C., ca. 1986.

U.S. Dept. of the Interior, Bureau of Land Management. *Owyhee River Boating Guide.* Boise, 1988.

U.S. Dept. of the Interior, Fish and Wildlife Service. *Deer Flat National Wildlife Refuge.* Boise, 1986. Brochure.

U.S. Dept. of the Interior, Heritage, Conservation, and Recreation Service. *Owyhee Wild and Scenic River Study.* Seattle, 1978.

Interviews

Stan Allen, Dept. of Fish and Game, Boise, Idaho

Jim Ash, Fish and Wildlife Service, Boise, Idaho

Bert Bowler, Dept. of Fish and Game, Lewiston, Idaho

Mark Briscoe, Idaho Power Company, Hells Canyon Dam

Gwen Burr, Dept. of Health and Welfare, Boise, Idaho

Kevin Coyle, American Rivers Council, Washington, D.C.

Frank Craighead, wildlife biologist, Moose, Wyo.

John Fazio, Northwest Power Planning Council, Boise, Idaho

Pat Ford, journalist, Boise, Idaho

James Goller, member, Northwest Power Planning Council, Boise, Idaho

Hugh Harper, wildlife biologist, Boise, Idaho

Beth Heinrich, Northwest Power Planning Council, Boise, Idaho

Keith Higginson, executive director, Dept. of Water Resources, Boise, Idaho

Martin Litton, river outfitter, Lewiston, Idaho

Bob Lohn, Northwest Power Planning Council, Portland, Oreg.

Liz Merril, staff member, Idaho Conservation League, Boise, Idaho

Notes, Other Sources, and Interviews

Freda Miller, Halfway, Oreg.
Marty Montgomery, Northwest Power Planning Council, Boise, Idaho
Scott Montgomery, Friends of the Payette, Boise, Idaho
Karen Nelson, Northwest Power Planning Council, Boise, Idaho
Kent Olsen, director, American Rivers, Washington, D.C.
William Platts, riparian consultant, Boise, Idaho
Gary Richardson, Public Utilities Commission, Boise, Idaho
Jim Ruff, hydrologist, Northwest Power Planning Council, Portland, Oreg.
Frank Sherman, Dept. of Water Resources, Boise, Idaho
Pat Sowers, Halfway, Oreg.
Tony Sowers, Halfway, Oreg.
Gary Spackman, Dept. of Water Resources, Boise, Idaho
Stephen Stuebner, journalist, *The Idaho Statesman*, Boise, Idaho
Perry Swisher, member, Public Utilities Commission, Boise, Idaho
Larry Taylor, Idaho Power Company, Boise, Idaho
Al Van Vooren, Dept. of Fish and Game, Boise, Idaho
Will Whelen, Idaho Conservation League, Boise, Idaho
Wendy Wilson, director, Idaho Rivers Project, Boise, Idaho

CHAPTER 8

Notes

1. William Ashworth, *Hells Canyon* (New York: Hawthorn Books, 1977), 66.
2. Idaho Dept. of Water Resources, *Draft State Water Plan* (Boise, 1976), pt. 2, 7.
3. John Rosholt, "Irrigation and Politics," *Idaho Yesterdays* (Boise), Spring 1986, 22.
4. Idaho Water Resource Board, *State Water Plan* (Boise, 1986), 35.
5. U.S. Dept. of Agriculture, Forest Service, *Hells Canyon National Recreation Area, Environmental Impact Statement* (Lewiston, Idaho, 1987).
6. John Crowell, letter to Max Peterson, U.S. Dept. of Agriculture, Forest Service, June 13, 1983.
7. U.S. Dept. of Agriculture, Forest Service, *Hells Canyon*, 46.
8. "Archaeologists to Excavate 'City' Sites in Hells Canyon," *Idaho Statesman* (Boise), May 3, 1988.
9. Don Moser, *The Snake River Country* (New York: Time–Life, 1974).
10. Ashworth, *Hells Canyon*, 157.
11. U.S. Dept. of Agriculture, Forest Service, *Hells Canyon*, 5.
12. Walter Hickel, *Who Owns America?* (New York: Coronet, 1972), 140.
13. Ashworth, *Hells Canyon*, 194.

Other Sources

Carrey, Johnny, Cort Conley, and Ace Barton. *Snake River of Hells Canyon.* Cambridge, Idaho: Backeddy Books, 1979.

Collins, Robert O., and Roderick Nash. *The Big Drops.* San Francisco: Sierra Club Books, 1978.

Garren, John. *Idaho River Tours.* Beaverton, Oreg.: Touchstone Press, 1980.

Marine, Gene. *America the Raped.* New York: Avon, 1969.

National Geographic Society. *America's Majestic Canyons.* Washington, D.C., 1979.

Norton, Boyd. *Snake Wilderness.* San Francisco: Sierra Club Books, 1972.

Palmer, Tim. *Endangered Rivers and the Conservation Movement.* Berkeley: University of California Press, 1986.

Peirce, Neal. *The Mountain States of America.* New York: Norton, 1972.

U.S. Dept. of Agriculture, Forest Service, *Rim to Rim, a Visitor's Guide to Hells Canyon National Recreation Area.* Lewiston, Idaho, n.d.

U.S. Dept. of Agriculture, Forest Service. *The Wild and Scenic Snake River.* Lewiston, Idaho, 1985.

U.S. Dept. of the Interior, National Park Service. *Snake Wild and Scenic River Study.* Seattle, 1979.

Williams, G. P., and M. G. Wolman. "Effects of Dams and Reservoirs on Surface-Water Hydrology." *National Water Summary.* Washington, D.C.: U.S. Geological Survey, 1985.

Interviews

Stewart Allen, recreation specialist, University of Idaho, Moscow
John Barker, river outfitter, Lewiston, Idaho
Myrna Beamer, jet boat outfitter, Lewiston, Idaho
Bruce Bowler, attorney, Boise, Idaho
Scott Calhoun, Hells Canyon National Recreation Area, Oreg.
Curtis Chang, manager, Great River Journeys, Lewiston, Idaho
Frank Craighead, wildlife biologist, Moose, Wyo.
Jackie Foresman, Snake River Preservation Council, Lewiston, Idaho
Pete Gross, river guide, Lewiston, Idaho
Jim Grothe, president, Northwest Powerboaters Association, Lewiston, Idaho
Hugh Harper, wildlife biologist, Boise, Idaho
Floyd Harvey, insurance salesman, Lewiston, Idaho
Lonnie Hutson, river guide, Lewiston, Idaho
Luna Leopold, hydrologist, University of California, Berkeley
Don Litton, river guide, Lewiston, Idaho
Martin Litton, Great River Journeys, Lewiston, Idaho
Laurel Rubin, river conservationist, Minam, Oreg.

Art Seamans, assistant area ranger, Hells Canyon National Recreation Area, Oreg.
Violet Shirley, Forest Service, Kirkwood Bar, Idaho
Larry Taylor, Idaho Power Company, Boise

CHAPTER 9

Notes

1. Boyd Norton, *Snake Wilderness* (San Francisco: Sierra Club Books, 1972).
2. Bernard DeVoto, *The Course of Empire* (Lincoln: University of Nebraska Press, 1952).
3. U.S. Army Corps of Engineers, *Lower Snake River Fish and Wildlife Compensation Plan* (Walla Walla, Wash., 1983).
4. Signe Sather-Blair, "Western Riparian Wetland Losses and Degradation: Status and Trends" (U.S. Dept. of the Interior, Fish and Wildlife Service, 1988), unpublished report.
5. Northwest Power Planning Council, *Columbia River Basin Fish and Wildlife Program* (Portland, Oreg., 1987).
6. Don Magers, "Voice of the Northwest," *Northwest Energy News* (Portland, Oreg.), Dec. 1986.
7. "Snake River Coho Extinct," *Idaho Clean Water* (Boise), Fall 1987.
8. Northwest Power Planning Council, *Columbia River Basin* (Portland, Oreg.), 38.
9. Carlotta Collette, "A Dilemma in Common," *Northwest Energy News* (Portland, Oreg.), March 1985.
10. Northwest Power Planning Council, *Columbia River Basin*, 41.
11. Bonneville Power Administration, *Backgrounder, the World's Largest Fish Story: The Columbia River's Salmon* (July 1987), 13.
12. "Fish Bypass Facilities Get Push from Panel," *Idaho Statesman* (Boise), June 8, 1988.
13. Paula Walker, "What to Do When the River Runs Dry," *Northwest Energy News* (Portland, Oreg.), Aug. 1987.
14. Ed Chaney, *Cogenerating Columbia River Basin Anadromous Fish and Hydroelectric Energy*, American Society of Civil Engineers, Coastal Zone (1987), international symposium.
15. Cecil Andrus, "Swan Falls Legislation," July 24, 1987, unpublished paper.
16. Northwest Power Planning Council, *Columbia River Basin*, 5.
17. U.S. Army Corps of Engineers, *Fish Passage 1987* (Walla Walla, Wash., 1988), table 93.
18. David G. Rice, *Marmes Rockshelter Archaeological Site* (Pullman: Washington State University, Laboratory of Anthropology, 1969).

Other Sources

Columbia/Snake River Marketing Group, the Columbia/Snake River System. Portland, Oreg., n.d. Brochure.

Interviews

Dale Aldridge, director, Port of Lewiston, Idaho
Teri Barila, Army Corps of Engineers, Walla Walla, Wash.
John Barker, outfitter, Lewiston, Idaho
Ted Bjornn, assistant leader, Fish and Wildlife Research Unit, University of Idaho, Moscow
Bert Bowler, fisheries biologist, Dept. of Fish and Game, Lewiston, Idaho
Ed Chaney, resource consultant, Eagle, Idaho
Dug Dugger, public affairs director, Army Corps of Engineers, Walla Walla, Wash.
Howard Funke, attorney, Shoshone and Bannock tribes, Fort Hall, Idaho
Garth Griffin, Army Corps of Engineers, Lower Granite Dam, Wash.
Roy Heberger, Fish and Wildlife Service, Boise, Idaho
Keith Higginson, executive director, Dept. of Water Resources, Boise, Idaho
David Hurson, Army Corps of Engineers, Walla Walla, Wash.
John Leier, Army Corps of Engineers, Walla Walla, Wash.
John Maxson, Army Corps of Engineers, Walla Walla, Wash.
Joe Murar, Army Corps of Engineers, Walla Walla, Wash.
Mike Passmore, biologist, Army Corps of Engineers, Walla Walla, Wash.
Dexter Pitman, Dept. of Fish and Game, Boise, Idaho
James Royce, colonel, Army Corps of Engineers, Walla Walla, Wash.

CHAPTER 10

Notes

1. Margaret Sanborn, *The Grand Tetons* (New York: C. P. Putnam and Sons, 1978).
2. "By a Dam Site," *Time*, June 19, 1944.
3. Montana Magazine, *Greater Yellowstone* (Helena, 1984).
4. Tim Palmer, *Endangered Rivers and the Conservation Movement* (Berkeley: University of California Press, 1986).
5. U.S. Dept. of the Interior, Bureau of Reclamation. *Jackson Lake Dam Modification* (Boise, ca. 1986), brochure.
6. Bio/West, Inc., "Feasibility Analysis of Water Conservation Measures Relative to the Jackson Lake Dam Safety Program" (Boise, 1983), unpublished report for the Bureau of Reclamation.

7. Robert W. Righter, *Crucible for Conservation* (Niwot, Co.: Colorado Associated University Presses, 1982), 11.

8. Notes in water rights file, Grand Teton National Park, "November 26, 1988: Meeting with Clifford Hansen and Concerned Parties."

9. Righter, *Crucible for Conservation*, 114.

10. Dennis Brownridge, "A Top Park Service Official Goes Out Shooting," *High Country News* (Paonia, Colo.), June 22, 1987.

11. U.S. Dept. of the Interior, National Park Service, *Resource Management Plan* (Moose, Wyo., 1986), 208.

12. Clynn Phillips, *Jackson Hole Fishery Resources, Economic Implications of Management Alternatives* (Jackson, Wyo., Jackson Hole Alliance for Responsible Planning, 1987), E8.

13. Joseph Piccoli, "Fish Numbers Plummet: Stream Flows Are Blamed," *Jackson Hole Guide*, Feb. 22, 1989, A9.

14. U.S. Dept. of Agriculture, Forest Service, *Snake River, Wyoming, a Potential Wild and Scenic River, Final Statement and Report* (Washington, D.C., 1979), appendix.

Other Sources

Clark, Tim W. *Ecology of Jackson Hole, Wyoming, a Primer.* Jackson, Wyo.: Clark, 1981.

Fryxell, Fritiof. *The Tetons, Interpretations of a Mountain Landscape.* Berkeley: University of California Press, 1938.

Huser, Verne, and Buzz Belknap. *Snake River Guide.* Boulder City, Nev.: Westwater Books, 1972.

Jones, Chris. *Climbing in America.* Berkeley: University of California Press, 1976.

McPhee, John. *Rising from the Plains.* New York: Farrar Straus Giroux, 1986.

Price, Larry. *Mountains and Man.* Berkeley: University of California Press, 1981.

Runte, Alfred. *National Parks: The American Experience.* Lincoln: University of Nebraska Press, 1979.

Sprague, Marshall. *The Mountain States.* New York: Time–Life, 1967.

Interviews

Dick Barker, river outfitter, Moose, Wyo.

Al Bath, biologist, Greater Yellowstone Ecosystem Bald Eagle Research Project

Russ Bickler, forestry consultant, Jackson, Wyo.

Len Carlman, Jackson Hole Alliance for Responsible Planning, Jackson, Wyo.

Ed Christian, Grand Teton National Park, Moose, Wyo.

Melissa Connor, archaeologist, National Park Service, Lincoln, Nebr.
Frank Craighead, wildlife biologist, Moose, Wyo.
Jon Erickson, Wyoming Game and Fish Dept., Jackson, Wyo.
Glen Exum, climber, Jackson Hole, Wyo.
Marshall Gingery, assistant superintendent, Grand Teton National Park, Moose, Wyo.
Robin Gregory, Grand Teton National Park, Moose, Wyo.
Clifford Hansen, rancher, former U.S. senator, Jackson Hole, Wyo.
Pete Hayden, biologist, Grand Teton National Park, Moose, Wyo.
Ann Humphrey, Teton Science School, Kelly, Wyo.
Verne Huser, river guide, Albuquerque, N. Mex.
Ed Ingold, Trout Unlimited, Jackson, Wyo.
John Keys, regional director, Bureau of Reclamation, Boise, Idaho
Luna Leopold, hydrologist, University of California, Berkeley
David Love, geologist, Jackson, Wyo.
Anna Moscicki, city councilmember, Jackson, Wyo.
Eric Olsen, hydrologist, Teton Science School, Kelly, Wyo.
Phil Shephard, Teton Science School, Kelly, Wyo.
Patrick Smith, chief ranger–naturalist, Grand Teton National Park, Moose, Wyo.
Robert Smith, geophysicist, University of Utah, Salt Lake City
Roger Smith, teacher, Teton Science School, Kelly, Wyo.
Jack Stark, superintendent, Grand Teton National Park, Moose, Wyo.
Kaz Thea, Teton Science School, Kelly, Wyo.
John Turner, commercial raft operator and state senator, Jackson Hole, Wyo.
Dusty Zaunbrecher, resource consultant, Jackson, Wyo.

CHAPTER 11

Notes

1. U.S. Dept. of Agriculture, Forest Service, *Snake River, Wyoming, a Potential Wild and Scenic River, Final Statement and Report* (Jackson, Wyo., 1979), 19.
2. Clynn Phillips, *Jackson Hole Fishery Resources, Economic Implications of Management Alternatives* (Jackson, Wyo.: Jackson Hole Alliance for Responsible Planning, 1987), E14.
3. "Will the Real Mayor Please Stand Up," *Jackson Hole Guide*, July 6, 1989, A4.
4. Jackson Hole Alliance for Responsible Planning, "Recommended Program Plan for Snake River Activities" (1989), 1, unpublished report.
5. U.S. Dept. of Agriculture, Forest Service, *Snake River, Wyoming*, 46.

6. J. D. Love and John C. Reed, Jr., *Creation of the Teton Landscape* (Moose, Wyo.: Grand Teton Natural History Association, 1971), 44.
7. Angus M. Thuermer, Jr., "Simpson Will Work to Keep County Safe from Snake, INEL," *Jackson Hole News*, Dec. 21, 1988.
8. U.S. Army Corps of Engineers, *Jackson Hole, Wyoming, Flood Protection Project* (Walla Walla, Wash., 1989), 15.
9. U.S. Dept. of the Interior, Fish and Wildlife Service, "Draft Fish and Wildlife Coordination Act Report for the Jackson Hole Snake River Flood Protection/Levee Maintenance Project" (1989), unpublished report.
10. County assessor's records, 1988.
11. Jackson Hole Alliance for Responsible Planning, *Recommended Program Plan*, 6.
12. Leigh Ortenburger, "The Hayden Survey Expedition of 1872," *Naturalist* (Minneapolis, Minn.), Spring 1976.
13. Orrin H. Bonney and Lorraine Bonney, *Battle Drums and Geysers* (Chicago: Swallow Press, 1970).
14. U.S. Dept. of Agriculture, Forest Service, *Snake River, Wyoming*, 122.

Other Sources

Melnykovych, Andrew. "Wallop Needs to Heed Voters' Message," *Casper Star Tribune* (Idaho), Nov. 21, 1988.
Murie, Margaret, and Olaus Murie. *Wapiti Wilderness*. New York: Knopf, 1966.
Saylor, David J. *Jackson Hole, Wyoming*. Norman: University of Oklahoma Press, 1970.
Teton County Planning Office. *Teton County Water Quality Management Program for Teton County 208 Planning Agency*. Jackson, Wyo., 1978.
U.S. Army Corps of Engineers. *Jackson Hole Flood Control Project Letter Report*. Walla Walla, Wash., 1988.
U.S. Dept. of Agriculture, Forest Service. "1987 Snake River Management Plan." 1987. Unpublished report.

Interviews

John Amodio, director, Jackson Hole Land Trust, Jackson, Wyo.
Norm Ando, Bridger–Teton National Forest, Jackson, Wyo.
Don Barney, Public Works Dept., Teton County, Wyo.
John Bradley, director, County Planning Commission, Teton County, Wyo.
Jim Caplan, planner, Bridger–Teton National Forest, Jackson, Wyo.
Len Carlman, director, Jackson Hole Alliance for Responsible Planning, Jackson, Wyo.
Jon Erickson, biologist, Wyoming Game and Fish Dept., Jackson, Wyo.

Frank Ewing, river outfitter, Jackson, Wyo.
Alan Galbraith, hydrologist, Bridger–Teton National Forest, Jackson, Wyo.
Bob Gifford, Army Corps of Engineers, Walla Walla, Wash.
Floyd Gordon, biologist, Bridger–Teton National Forest, Jackson, Wyo.
Earl Hardeman, rancher, Jackson Hole, Wyo.
Pete Hayden, biologist, Grand Teton National Park, Moose, Wyo.
Clifford Hansen, rancher and former U.S. senator, Jackson Hole, Wyo.
Julie Holding, Jackson Hole Land Trust, Jackson, Wyo.
Luna Leopold, hydrologist, University of California, Berkeley
David Love, geologist, Jackson, Wyo.
Adair Mali, Jackson Hole Alliance for Responsible Planning, Jackson, Wyo.
Breck O'Neil, river outfitter, Jackson, Wyo.
Leslie Peterson, commissioner, Teton County, Jackson, Wyo.
Bill Resor, rancher, Jackson, Wyo.
James Royce, colonel, Army Corps of Engineers, Walla Walla, Wash.
Mary Shouf, Teton County Planning staff, Jackson, Wyo.
Rick Sievers, river guide, Jackson, Wyo.
Susan Simpson, museum curator, Jackson, Wyo.
Brian Stout, supervisor, Bridger–Teton National Forest, Jackson, Wyo.
John Turner, dude ranch owner, Jackson Hole, Wyo.
Mike Whitfield, biologist, Greater Yellowstone Coalition, Bozeman, Mont.
Jim Wood, Army Corps of Engineers, Walla Walla, Wash.
Suzanne Young, director, Chamber of Commerce, Jackson, Wyo.

CHAPTER 12

Notes

1. Todd Wilkinson, "GYE Report Says More Protection Needed to Save Embattled Bruin," *Greater Yellowstone Report*, Winter 1989, 7.
2. Chris Servheen, presentation for the Teton Science School, Kelly, Wyo., 1989.
3. Frank Craighead, *Track of the Grizzly* (San Francisco: Sierra Club Books, 1979), 230.
4. Wilderness Society, *An Unraveling Tapestry* (Washington, D.C., 1987), booklet.
5. William D. Newmark, "Legal and Biotic Boundaries of Western North American National Parks: A Problem of Congruence," *Biological Conservation* 33, 1988, 197–208.
6. U.S. Dept. of the Interior, Fish and Wildlife Service, "Swan Falls Negotiations" (1988), unpublished paper.

Other Sources

Clark, Tim W., and Ann H. Harvey. *Management of the Greater Yellowstone Ecosystem, an Annotated Bibliography.* Jackson, Wyo.: Northern Rockies Co-operative, 1988.

Interviews

Renee Askins, The Wolf Fund, New Haven, Conn.
John Baglien, district ranger, Bridger–Teton National Forest, Jackson, Wyo.
Len Carlman, director, Jackson Hole Alliance for Responsible Planning, Jackson, Wyo.
Ernie Day, conservationist, Boise, Idaho
Pat Ford, journalist, Boise, Idaho
Ann Harvey, biologist, Jackson, Wyo.
Les Inafuku, Yellowstone National Park, Flagg Ranch, Wyo.
Paul Lawrence, Jackson Hole, Wyo.
Jerry Mernan, Yellowstone National Park, Flagg Ranch, Wyo.
Mardy Murie, Moose, Wyo.
Leslie Petersen, commissioner, Teton County, Jackson, Wyo.
Chris Servheen, Interagency Grizzly Bear Committee, Missoula, Mont.
John Turner, dude ranch owner and state senator, Jackson Hole, Wyo.
Louisa Wilcox, Greater Yellowstone Coalition, Bozeman, Mont.

Acknowledgments

While my pursuit of the Snake River story was a profoundly individual endeavor, hundreds of people were helpful; many are listed under interviews. Barbara Dean provided the fine counsel and support that I think every writer wishes he had from his editor, and the full Island Press staff were excellent working partners.

Helping me to not endure but enthusiastically enjoy two winters at the Snake River headwaters while I wrote the book, the Teton Science School in Wyoming provided me a log cabin, a wood pile, and the resources of the school in return for occasional instructional programs and a reasonable fee. My thanks to Jack Shea, the director, and to the school's superb staff for hospitality, information, and, most of all, companionship, and especially to Phil Shephard, Ann Humphrey, Mary Ashworth, and Roger Smith.

The R.K. Mellon Foundation provided funding for me to survive while I worked on the book; the support of George Taber and the foundation members is much appreciated, as is the role of American Rivers and Friends of the River. Patagonia, Inc., provided generous assistance when I had to buy a new van for use in this and future projects. It should be understood, however, that the concept for the book, its themes, and its focus were not on the agenda of any organization or person except the author.

While criticism in this and other regions of the West is heaped upon government workers at every level, I found dozens of state and federal employees to be knowledgeable, honest, and hardworking. I found widespread concern, curiosity, and a willingness to help, especially at the middle and lower levels of the bureaucracies.

In response to my many questions, spokesmen for irrigation were candid and forthright, which was essential.

For wading through most or all of the draft manuscript and offering many suggestions, I want to thank Hugh Harper and Pat Ford; also Jerry Meral, who has reviewed nearly all of my books with sharp insight and editorial skill. Nancy Jacques read the copy and provided much talent with the map, photo selection, and design. Ronnie James helped with word processing and offered some well-deserved editorial chastisement. Mark Anderman printed the photos.

Thanks to Mad River Canoe for outstanding equipment and to Great River Journeys. Also to library staffs in Jackson, Idaho Falls, and Boise; at the University of Idaho, Idaho State University, and Boise State University; and at various agency libraries.

Chapters and sections of chapters were reviewed by about forty people—all experts in their fields—who offered scarce time and valuable knowledge on virtually every aspect of the book.

Index

Acre foot, defined, 5
Agriculture, 63–66, 90–91, 186
  See also Irrigation, Snake River
    plain
Alpine Canyon, 261–267
Alsek River, 233
Alt, Rod, 130
American Falls Dam, 14, 29, 41, 50,
    55–61, 66, 67–68
American Rivers, 72, 193, 195, 264
Anadromous fish, see Salmon
Anderson, Hal, 104
Andrus, Cecil, Governor, 73, 75, 90,
    93, 98, 116, 128, 157, 165, 195,
    212, 226
Appenay, Arnold, 42–43
Archaeology, 184, 208, 227, 228,
    234
Army Corps of Engineers, 53, 59,
    63, 194, 206, 218–227, 253–260
Arrowrock Dam, 54
Asotin, 192, 215

Bakes, J., Justice, 96
Ballard, David, Governor, 41, 46
Barker, Dick, 242, 246
Barker, John, 206, 218
Barney, Don, 254–257
Bechler River, 28, 72
Bio/West, 105, 235–236
Birds, 11, 14, 17–19, 28, 31, 40, 51,
    157, 187–188, 241
Birds of Prey Natural Area, 157

Bjornn, Ted, 222, 227
Blackfoot, 14, 29, 37–38, 141
Bliss Dam, 155, 184
Boating, 237
  see also Canoeing, Rafting
Boise River, 54, 78, 154, 187, 189
Bonneville County Planning Com-
    mission, 17–18
Bonneville Dam, 221, 224
Bonneville flood, 184
Bonneville Power Administration,
    194, 223–226
Bonnivier, Guy, 148
Bowler, Bert, 224
Bowler, Bruce, 211–213
Bradley, John, 251, 254–256,
    259–260
Bray, Gail, 6
Bridger–Teton Wilderness, 270–274,
    278
Brisbin, James, 7
Briscoe, Mark, 190
Brower, Cheryl, 15, 124–125
Brownlee Dam, 183, 188–190, 197,
    221, 225
Bruneau Project, 92
Bruneau River, 156, 189
Bureau of Land Management, 11,
    39, 94, 143–145, 152
Bureau of Reclamation, 19–23,
    28–29, 53, 58–82, 127–129,
    205, 225, 234–236, 244–248
  see also names of dams, Irrigation

313

Burg, Amos, 189
Burke, Linda, 90
Burks, Bob, 20, 60, 106, 109, 119, 225, 132, 144, 150

Calderas, 27, 33, 231
Caldron Linn, 143–145
Canals, 26–27, 31, 52, 105
    see also Diversions
Canoeing, 9–12, 25–27, 30–32, 38–40, 183–188, 232, 241–243, 261–267
Canyons, 201, 262
    see also specific names
Carey Act, 54, 64, 92
Carlman, Len, 237, 262–270, 281
Carlson, Ron, 25, 57, 96, 100
Carter, David, 113
Carter, Jimmy, President, 73–75
Central Valley, Ca., 13, 33, 63, 73, 114, 130
Cfs, defined, xi
Chaney, Ed, 100, 132, 136, 224–226
Chang, Curtis, 206
Chapman, Howard, 240
Chapman, Sherl, 25, 46–47, 75, 107–109, 126, 130–132, 164, 225
Cheney, Richard, 81, 256
Chief Joseph, 210
Chisholm, Bill, 150–151
Church, Frank, 212–213
C.J. Strike Dam, 156
Clarkston, 217
Clearwater River, 72, 217–218, 222, 225
Climbing, 237
Colorado River, 13, 49, 63, 72, 85, 115, 141, 205
Colter Bay, 232
Columbia Basin Project, 92
Columbia Plateau, 33
Columbia River, 4–5, 23, 73, 183, 194, 221–224, 228–230

Committee of Nine, 20–23, 52, 62, 69, 75–76, 80, 119, 130, 244, 266, 280
Conley, Jerry, 153
Conner, Melissa, 234
Corliss, Earl, 79, 81
Cottonwoods, 12–16, 27, 30, 185–187, 243, 246–247, 252
Craighead, Frank, 189, 205, 234, 244, 274
Crowe, Frank, 235
Crowell, John, 207

Dalles Dam, 223
Dams, 6, 53–56, 72–73
    costs, 29, 58–62, 66–70, 219, 223–226
    safety, 29–30, 55, 61–63, 72, 79, 235–237
    sites, proposed, 37, 51, 78–81, 145, 152, 189, 192–193, 210–211, 215, 236, 265–266
    See also names of dams, Hydro-electric dams
Day, Ernie, 280
Deakin, Jack, 58
Deer Flat National Wildlife Refuge, 162, 184
Degrading riverbed, 185, 205, 215, 246
Delaware River, 205
Desert Lands Entry Act, 54, 64, 92, 157
DeVoto, Bernard, 9
Dingell, John, Congressman, 128, 194, 162
Diversions, 26–27, 31, 54, 141–146, 186–188, 193, 221
    see Canals, Instream flow
Doane, Gustavus, 234, 262
Douglas, William O., Justice, 212
Dworshak Dam, 218, 225

Eagles, 10, 16, 19, 67, 242–245, 252, 265
Eakin, Jack, 110
Elk, 40, 237, 271
Elk Creek Falls, 195
Elk Ranch Dam, 239
Emma Matilda Lake, 237
Endangered species, 81, 148, 221, 227, 248, 252
  see also Eagles, Grizzly bears
Energy savings, 107, 191–192
Enterprise, 197
Environmental Protection Agency, 150, 260
Erickson, Jon, 244–245, 252, 257
Erosion, 63, 84–85, 94, 113–114, 220
Evans, Brock, 211
Evans, Dan, Governor, 213
Evans, John, Governor, 161–162, 190, 195
Ewing, Frank, 264

Fawsett, Al, 146
Federal Energy Regulatory Commission, 99, 144–145, 162, 165, 191–196, 215
Federal Power Commission, 189, 210–212
Fereday, Jeff, 98, 132
Fish, 23, 38–45, 50, 160–164, 186, 209, 243, 252
  see also Salmon, Trout
Fish and wildlife mitigation, 191–194, 219–226
Fish and Wildlife Service, 13–16, 20, 67, 70, 115, 150, 153, 162, 183, 194, 223, 234, 248, 256, 258, 277
Fish Creek, 254
Fish farms, 149–150
Fishing, 20, 27, 152, 243–244
  see also Trout
Flagg Ranch, 232
Flat Creek, 239

Flood zone, 258–259
Flow, volume, xii, 5, 10, 26, 27, 68, 187, 204–205, 229
Ford, Pat, 90, 98, 159, 165, 195, 280
Forest Service, 5, 18, 193, 206–207, 264–266
Fort Hall Bottoms, 39–40, 45, 66
Frémont, John, 155
Fritz, Ned, 273
Fryxell, Fritiof, 238
Funke, Howard, 42–52, 57, 163, 222

Gale, Ruth, 28, 62
Galloway Dam, 80, 226
Gardner, Wilford, 118
Genesis, 89
Geological Survey, 10, 29, 70, 79, 108, 115, 118, 122
Geology, 30, 33, 184, 201, 233–235, 251, 254
Gingery, Marshall, 237–238, 247
Goller, James, 196
Gordon, Floyd, 265
Grand Canyon, 189, 201–202, 205, 246
Grand Teton National Park, 13, 233–248, 234, 237–240, 249, 264, 271
Grand Valley, 9
Grand View, 156–157
Grande Ronde River, 197, 211
Gray, Gene, 21, 98, 118, 136
Grazing, cattle, 91, 203, 208, 221, 238, 252–253
Greater Yellowstone Coalition, 275–276
Great River Journeys, 202–203, 206, 211
Greys River, 267
Griffith, Jack, 41, 50
Grizzly bears, 209, 232, 274–275
Gros Ventre River, 233, 238, 250
Grothe, Jim, 207, 209, 215

Groundwater, 84, 118–126,
    147–149, 152, 281

Hagerman, 116, 125, 184
Hagerman reach, 152–154
Halfway, Or., 197
Hansen, Clifford, 239, 245, 253,
    256–257
Hansen, Reed, 60, 65, 81, 87, 98,
    125, 137
Hardeman, Earl, 251–253
Harper, Hugh, 157, 199–200,
    205–210, 215
Harvey, Floyd, 211–214
Hatcheries, 222–223, 252
Hayden expedition, 272
Hayden, Pete, 70, 232, 236, 239,
    246, 252, 257
Hays Ranch, 17–18
Heberger, Roy, 165, 223
Heinrich, Beth, 194–195
Heise, 10, 26, 33
Hells Canyon, 184, 189, 199–216
Hells Canyon Dam, 188–190,
    204–205
Hells Canyon Preservation Council,
    209, 212
Henry's Fork, 10, 27–29, 154, 195,
    231, 243, 275
Henry's Fork Foundation, 27–28
Henry's Lake, 54, 58, 69
Hickel, Walter, 212
Higginson, Keith, 92, 98, 106, 108,
    119, 123, 142, 154, 164–165,
    194–196, 225
High Country News, 136
High Mountain Sheep Dam,
    210–213
Hill, Mark, 21
Hoback River, 261
Hodel, Donald, 237
Homedale, 184, 186
Hoover Dam, 187, 235
Hoyt, Marv, 25

Hudson's Bay Company, 6
Hunt expedition, 143, 262
Huser, Verne, 241
Hutson, Lonnie, 203, 206
Hydroelectric dams, 31–32, 36,
    50–51, 99, 144, 152–155, 219,
    265–266, 280
Hydroelectric power, 159–162,
    188–197, 204, 210–215
Hydrology, 11, 20–22, 41, 69, 185,
    205, 246–253

Ice Harbor Dam, 219, 223, 228
Idaho, 34–35, 71, 151, 276
    see also specific place names
Idaho Conservation League, 90
Idaho Department of Fish and
    Game, 19–20, 23, 68, 97–98,
    153, 163, 187, 190, 196, 211,
    221, 224
Idaho Department of Water Re-
    sources, 50, 57, 63, 79, 92, 98,
    101–102, 108, 116–117,
    120–121, 124, 126, 128, 136,
    150, 153, 155, 160, 163, 186,
    193, 195
Idaho Falls, 29, 31–32, 36
Idaho Falls dams, 31–32
Idaho House of Representatives, 195
Idaho National Engineering Labora-
    tory, 122, 124
Idaho Power Company, 53, 61, 130,
    144–145, 153, 156, 158–163,
    190–191, 225, 276
Idaho Power Company in Hells Ca-
    nyon, 188–192, 206
Idaho Rivers Planning and Protec-
    tion Act, 154, 188
Idaho State Water Plan, 21, 154, 159
Idaho Water Resource Board, 71, 79,
    93, 96–98, 136, 196, 205
Idaho Water Resources Research In-
    stitute, 50, 107

Idaho Water Users Association, 20, 25, 46, 75, 107, 124–126, 137, 162, 193, 195
Idaho Wildlife Federation, 162, 211
Imnaha River, 197, 210–211
Instream flow, 20–24, 28, 38, 44–47, 51, 68–69, 75, 77, 86, 88, 93, 96–102, 141–144, 160–165, 205, 224–226, 244–247
Irrigation, 21–22, 34, 41, 46–47, 53–57, 83–139, 159, 185, 238–239, 245
  see also Agriculture, Diversions
Island Park, 33
Island Park Dam, 28, 55, 61–62, 68, 77, 80

Jackson, 249–251, 259
Jackson Dam, 55–62, 66–69, 72, 82, 105, 120, 141, 232, 234–236, 240, 242–245, 274
Jackson, Henry, 92
Jackson Hole, 14, 233–234, 237–240, 244, 249–261, 266, 271
Jackson Hole Alliance, 237, 244, 250–252, 259–260, 270
Jackson Hole Land Trust, 251–252, 259–260
Jackson Hole National Scenic Area, 251
Jarvis, Jeff, 152–153
Jenny Lake, 237
Jet boats, 203, 206–207
John D. Rockefeller, Jr. Parkway, 232
Jordan, Len, Senator, 208

Keys, John, 19, 57, 68, 72, 76, 79–80, 137–138, 236
King Hill, 33
Kings River, 201
Knievel, "Evel", 144, 146
Kootenay River, 194
Kramer, Don, 118

Lamm, Richard, Governor, 58
Land development, 17–18, 94, 250–251, 257–260, 273
Lawrence, Paul, 273
Leeks Marina, 234
Leigh Lake, 237
Leopold, Luna, 70, 246, 253, 258–259
Lesser, Rob, 142–144
Levee, Jackson Hole, 249, 252–260
Levees, 27, 59
Lewis and Clark, 43, 217–218, 228
Lewis River, 231
Lewiston, 206, 217–218
Little Goose Dam, 219, 223–224, 228
Little Salmon River, 23
Litton, Martin, 189, 202, 209, 211
Lochsa River, 217
Lostine River, 197
Lost River, 147
Love, David, 233, 235, 254
Lower Granite Dam, 216–228
Lower Monumental Dam, 219, 223, 227–228
Lower Salmon Falls Dam, 152
Lynn Crandall Dam, 11, 19, 80, 137

Malheur River, 189
Marmes Man, 227–228
Marsing, 186
McCall, Tom, Governor, 92, 213
McClure, James, Senator, 80, 213, 216
McNary Dam, 23, 224, 229
Mead, Elwood, 101
Mickelson, "Mick", 27
Miles, Harold, 162
Milk River, 15
Miller, Freda, 189
Miller, George, Congressman, 64, 70, 73, 141–143, 195

Milner Dam, 36, 38, 51–52, 54, 78, 89, 111, 141–146, 155, 163–164, 225, 245, 276, 280
Miners inch, defined, 84
Minidoka Dam, 34, 51, 55, 67
Minidoka Project, 55–56, 61, 66, 82, 91–94, 130, 236
Minimum streamflow, *see* Instream flow
Mississippi River, 13
Missouri River, 13, 15, 185
Mormons, 54
Mulberry, Ken, 83–87
Mullaney, Matt, 159
Murie, Mardy, 280
Murtaugh, 143

National Marine Fisheries Service, 163, 225
National Park Service, 232, 236–240, 246–253, 274–275
National Recreation Area, 213
Natural Resources Defense Council, 75
Nature Conservancy, The, 28, 148
Navigation channels, 206, 218–220, 229
Nelson, Gary, 133–135
Nelson, Morlan, 157
Neuberger, Richard, 202
Newmark, William, 276
Nez Perce Dam, 208, 211
Niagara Falls, 146
North Platte River, 78
Northwest Power Planning Council, 54, 67, 155, 163, 194–196, 222–227, 248, 277

Ohio River, 13
Oldham, Reed, 52, 58, 60, 65, 69, 88–89, 100, 119, 126, 141, 265
O'Neil, Breck, 265
Oregon, 186
 see also Hells Canyon
Oregon Trail, 155
Owyhee Dam, 68, 187

Owyhee River, 186–189, 197
Oxbow Bend, 236, 240
Oxbow Dam, 189–190

Pacific Creek, 269
Packwood, Bob, 212–213
Palisades Dam, 9, 14, 20–24, 55, 58–60, 66–68, 72, 77, 104, 111, 120, 126, 205, 245, 266
Pasco, 218, 229
Passmore, Mike, 219
Payette River, 115, 154, 165, 187–189, 193, 195
Peavey, John, 137, 158–161, 165
Pesticides, 94, 122
Peterson, Leslie, 276
Pioneer power plant, 158–159
Pittsburgh Landing, 206–208
Platte River, 191
Platts, William, 13, 40, 98, 137, 196, 185
Pollution, 23, 37, 50, 62, 71, 84, 115–126, 149–150, 153, 186
Pope, James, Senator, 55
Population, 7, 35, 217
Potatoes, 65, 90–91, 117
 see also Agriculture
Priest River, 154
Public Trust Doctrine, 24, 245

Quarries, 232–233

Rafting, commercial, 143, 152, 202, 242–243, 263–265
Randolph, John, 19, 27
Reagan administration, 74, 266
Reclamation Reform Act, 127
Reed, Scott, 25, 76, 99, 136, 161
Resor, Stanley, 253
Righter, Robert, 235
Riley, Bob, 36, 74, 77–78, 129, 225
Rio Grande River, 141
Riparian habitat, 12–22, 27–30, 39–40, 66–69, 152, 156, 164, 185, 187, 205, 215, 219, 234, 246, 252, 256, 273

Roberts, 29–32
Robertson, Dale, 193
Rock Creek, 147
Rockefeller, John D., Jr., 238
Rockwood, Dale, 22
Rocky Mountains, 233
Rogers, Dick, 124
Roosevelt, Franklin, President, 238
Royce, James, 223, 226, 253,
    255–256, 258

Sacramento River, 235
Salmon, steelhead, 44–46, 49–50,
    147, 158, 163, 189–195, 215,
    218, 220–227
Salmon Falls Creek, 189
Salmon River, 69, 73, 153, 165, 193,
    195, 205, 211, 214, 220–225
Salt River, 15, 267
San Joaquin River, 75
Savannah River, 14
Sax, Joseph, 25
Saylor, John, 213
Schwarz, Dick, 23–24
Seamans, Art, 207–208
Selway River, 217
Servheen, Chris, 274
Shasta Dam, 235
Shaw, David, 101, 108
Shellenberger, Joe, 273
Shelley, 37
Sherman, Frank, 124
Shirley, Violet, 208
Shoshone and Bannock tribes, 34,
    40–47, 61, 71, 132, 138,
    162–163, 222, 226–227, 248
Shoshone Falls, 146–147, 190, 277
Shoshone Lake, 231
Shoshone River, 270
Siltation *see* Erosion
Silver Creek, 243
Simplot, J.R., 157, 188
Simpson, Alan, Senator, 255, 266
Smith, Patrick, 236, 242
Smith, Roger, 240

Snake River:
    naming of, 43, 217, 262
    plain, 30–52, 120–121
    see also Agriculture, Irrigation
    source, 173–174, 178, 281
    statistics, 4, 5, 8
Snake River Canyon National Park,
    146
Snohomish River, 153
Soil Conservation Service, 63, 94,
    99, 105–106, 110, 113–117,
    129–130, 147
South Fork, 9–27
South Fork Coalition, 17
South Platte River, 15
Sprinklers, 85, 104, 106, 115
Stanislaus River, 72
Stapilus, Randy, 22
Stark, Jack, 232, 236, 239, 242
Stegner, Wallace, 54, 113
Storer, Claude, 22
Stout, Brian, 266
Sturgeon, 153, 163, 183–184
Subsidies, 60–65, 93–94
    see also Dams, Water
Surplus crops, 63 64, 93–94, 134
Swan Falls, 128, 231
Swan Falls agreement, 158–166, 276
Swan Falls Dam, 157–158, 183, 189
Swans, 28–29, 62, 75, 132, 252
Swan Valley, 11, 19
Swisher, Perry, 88
Symms, Steve, Senator, 117, 213

Tahoe, Lake, 18, 260
Targhee National Forest, 28
Taylor, Larry, 161, 191–192, 206
Tennessee River, 14, 53
Teton County, 254–259
Teton Dam, 29–30, 61, 73, 77–80,
    135, 137
Tetons, 31, 233
Teton Science School, 240, 270, 275
Thousand Springs, 79, 120, 124,
    147–150, 195

Three Island Crossing, 155–156
Tourism, 244, 251, 264
Tributaries, 5–6
Trout, 10, 19–23, 27, 78, 243–244
Trout, Thomas, 106, 114, 123
Trout Unlimited, 25, 72, 75
Turner, John, 243, 256
Twin Falls, 145, 147, 277
Twin Falls Canal Company, 54, 58, 83, 144–145
Twiss, Bob, 259
Two Ocean Lake, 237

Udall, Stewart, 88, 115, 136
Upper Salmon Falls Dam, 149
U.S. v. Oregon, 221
U.S. Water Resources Council, 21, 73, 103

Van Den Berg, Max, 52, 56, 58, 68, 77, 127
Van Vooren, Al, 14, 143, 153, 193

Walcott, Lake, 51
Wallop, Malcolm, Senator, 81, 125, 266, 270
Wallowa Mountains, 197
Wallowa River, 197
Water Bank, 131, 141, 144–145
Water:
  budget, 224–226
  conservation, 85–86, 103–115, 126–134, 164, 197, 236
  contracts, 75–76
  costs, 21, 58–62, 66, 84, 102, 115, 129–134
    see also Dams
  export, 78–79, 92–93
  marketing, 44, 48, 132–133
  quality *see* Pollution
  rights, 22–25, 28, 43–49, 57–58, 83, 86–87, 94–102, 107–109, 138, 144, 159–160, 244–245

  rights adjudication, 101–102, 108–109, 162, 166
  storage *see* Dams, Dams by name
  use, 100–103, 107–108
Water Resources Development Act, 220, 255
Waterton River, 15
Watters, Ron, 50, 143
Watt, James, 240, 276
Weiser, 33
Weiser River, 81, 188–189
Wetlands, 14, 16, 27, 41, 232, 260
Whitewater, 142–143, 188–189, 199, 203–204, 261–267
Whitfield, Mike, 265
Whitman, Narcissa, 155
Wilcox, Louisa, 276
Wild and scenic rivers systems, 92, 154–156, 186, 188, 197–199, 213–217, 258, 266, 271
Wilderness, 11–13, 202, 213, 270–272
Wildlife, 16–19, 30, 33, 160–163, 219, 241, 243, 246, 252, 270, 272–276
Wildlife mitigation, 59, 67, 76
Wiley Dam, 152
Wilson, 234
Wilton, Neil, 106
Winters Doctrine, 44–45
Wister, Owen, 235
Wolves, 243
Wyoming Compact, 245
Wyoming delegation, 238, 255–261, 275
Wyoming Game and Fish Department, 239, 244, 252, 257

Yellowstone ecosystem, 16, 265, 272–276
Yellowstone National Park, 27–28, 33, 231–232, 237, 248, 270–278
Yellowstone River, 164, 228, 275

ALSO AVAILABLE FROM ISLAND PRESS

Ancient Forests of the Pacific Northwest
By Elliott A. Norse

Balancing on the Brink of Extinction: The Endangered Species Act and Lessons for the Future
Edited by Kathryn A. Kohm

Better Trout Habitat: A Guide to Stream Restoration and Management
By Christopher J. Hunter

Beyond 40 Percent: Record-Setting Recycling and Composting Programs
The Institute for Local Self-Reliance

The Challenge of Global Warming
Edited by Dean Edwin Abrahamson

Coastal Alert: Ecosystems, Energy, and Offshore Oil Drilling
By Dwight Holing

The Complete Guide to Environmental Careers
The CEIP Fund

Economics of Protected Areas
By John A. Dixon and Paul B. Sherman

Environmental Agenda for the Future
Edited by Robert Cahn

Environmental Disputes: Community Involvement in Conflict Resolution
By James E. Crowfoot and Julia M. Wondolleck

Fighting Toxics: A Manual for Protecting Your Family, Community, and Workplace
Edited by Gary Cohen and John O'Connor

Forests and Forestry in China: Changing Patterns of Resource Development
By S. D. Richardson

The Global Citizen
By Donella Meadows

Hazardous Waste from Small Quantity Generators
By Seymour I. Schwartz and Wendy B. Pratt

Holistic Resource Management Workbook
By Allan Savory

321

In Praise of Nature
Edited and with essays by Stephanie Mills

The Living Ocean: Understanding and Protecting Marine Biodiversity
By Boyce Thorne-Miller and John G. Catena

Natural Resources for the 21st Century
Edited by R. Neil Sampson and Dwight Hair

The New York Environment Book
By Eric A. Goldstein and Mark A. Izeman

Overtapped Oasis: Reform or Revolution for Western Water
By Marc Reisner and Sarah Bates

Plastics: America's Packaging Dilemma
By Nancy Wolf and Ellen Feldman

The Poisoned Well: New Strategies for Groundwater Protection
Edited by Eric Jorgensen

Race to Save the Tropics: Ecology and Economics for a Sustainable Future
Edited by Robert Goodland

Recycling and Incineration: Evaluating the Choices
By Richard A. Denison and John Ruston

Reforming The Forest Service
By Randal O'Toole

The Rising Tide: Global Warming and World Sea Levels
By Lynne T. Edgerton

Saving the Tropical Forests
By Judith Gradwohl and Russell Greenberg

The Sierra Nevada: A Mountain Journey
By Tim Palmer

Trees, Why Do You Wait?
By Richard Critchfield

War on Waste: Can America Win Its Battle With Garbage?
By Louis Blumberg and Robert Gottlieb

Western Water Made Simple
From *High Country News*

Wetland Creation and Restoration: The Status of the Science
Edited by Mary E. Kentula and Jon A. Kusler

Wildlife and Habitats in Managed Landscapes
Edited by Jon E. Rodiek and Eric G. Bolen

For a complete catalog of Island Press publications, please write: Island Press, Box 7, Covelo, CA 95428, or call: 1-800-828-1302.